coverups & copouts

ISBN 1-86958-643-3

© Text 1998 Tom Lewis
The moral rights of the author have been asserted

© 1998 Hodder Moa Beckett Publishers Ltd

Published in 1998 by Hodder Moa Beckett Publishers Limited
[a member of the Hodder Headline Group]
4 Whetu Place, Mairangi Bay, Auckland, New Zealand

Designed, produced and typeset by Hodder Moa Beckett Publishers Ltd
Printed by Australian Print Group

To Ian for your birthday
June 13 '98
Mum 'n' Dad.

coverups
& copouts

TOM LEWIS

Hodder Moa Beckett

DEDICATION

To the late John Kennedy, former editor of
the *New Zealand Tablet*, and the late Christine Stevenson.
Their support and encouragement to write this book kept me going.

ACKNOWLEDGEMENTS

I would like to thank the thousands of people who
demonstrated and signed petitions for a commission
of enquiry into the Dunedin Sex Ring Scandal of 1984

People from all over New Zealand who wrote to me
and my family offering support

Michael Steel, Alistair Morrison, John Kennedy, Bruce Ansley,
Pat Booth, George Burke, Chris Anderson, Jock Anderson,
Selwyn Byers, Michael Holloway, Judith Brown, Paul Stevenson,
Roly Stedman, Keith Morrow, Walter Nelson, Michael Walton

My wife and family

Contents

	Introduction	**7**
1	**Death of a Monarch**	**9**
2	**Beating the Blues**	**17**
3	**Police Training**	**23**
4	**Life as a Rookie**	**27**
5	**The Officer Class**	**31**
6	**Playing Cops and Robbers**	**37**
7	**Criminal Investigation Branch**	**43**
8	**The Legal System and Legal Profession**	**59**
9	**New Zealand's Ned Kelly**	**67**
10	**Lewis on the Run and on Holiday**	**91**
11	**Protecting the Prince and Teddy**	**115**
12	**Nursemaiding the VIPs**	**123**
13	**Casualties of War**	**141**
14	**Whatever happened to 'Jorgy'?**	**177**
15	**Paedophiles, Prostitutes, Police and Payoffs**	**183**
16	**The Aftermath**	**243**
17	**Getting the Police that the Public Deserve?**	**247**
18	**Leadership**	**257**
19	**The Final Curtain**	**267**
20	**Shades of Misleading Cases**	**277**

About the Author

Tom Lewis was born in Dunedin and educated at St Patrick's Convent School, St Edmund's Christian Boys School and Christian Brothers High School.

His police career spanned almost twenty years, seventeen of which were spent in the Criminal Investigation Branch. Much of his CIB career was spent in the Drug and Criminal Intelligence squads. He was officer in charge of both squads at various times during the seventies and eighties. He also worked as an undercover agent and operator.

He resigned from the New Zealand Police in 1986.

In 1987 he joined the Westpac Banking Corporation in Perth, Western Australia.

Since 1987 he has lived in Perth, London and Sydney and currently resides in Burleigh Heads on Queensland's Gold Coast. He lives there with his wife Teresa, daughter Tania and granddaughter Maria. His two sons, Tony and Christopher, live in Auckland and Christchurch respectively.

Introduction

*C*overups and Copouts is a book that takes a look at our corrupt society – a society that has turned a blind eye to crooked politicians, entrepreneurs, business leaders, public officials (including the judiciary), local body councillors and police officers.

Of course, not all of the above are corrupt – far from it. The problem is that corruption is flourishing because it is not being flushed out and those involved are not being brought to justice.

Its insidious effects were best illustrated across the Tasman at the recent New South Wales Royal Commission into police corruption, headed by Justice Wood. Corruption in the police was found to be widespread and young recruits were inducted into the corrupt system as soon as possible, some on their first day on the job.

No doubt an in-depth inquiry with wide terms of reference would also expose serious corruption among our elected representatives whether they be federal, state or local body.

The syndrome which has allowed corruption to flourish is based on crushing those who dare to attempt to expose it. Those who dared to speak out have suffered the consequences. Nowhere is this more apparent than in the police services of Australia and New Zealand.

Whistleblowers or, as they are known in the police culture, 'dogs', are subjected to harrassment, false allegations and sometimes trumped up criminal charges. Even Police Commissioner Peter Ryan, the Englishman brought in to clean up the NSW Police Service, expressed his fears to the NSW Police Board. Prior to his appointment, Ryan spoke of his very real concerns if he got the top job. If he took tough decisions to fight ingrained corruption he also feared more sinister attacks upon himself, such as the use of planted evidence and threats to personal safety. Already, he and his wife have been subjected to scurrilous rumour regarding their marriage and private life.

If this can happen to the service's most senior police officer, what chance does the rank and file whistleblower have?

Speaking from my own experience of corruption, after having studied other attempts to expose it, I can confirm that the dice are loaded very heavily against the whistleblower.

Various bureaucratic institutions have been set up in Australia to deal with corruption. Not one of them, however, has protected the whistleblower. Most have seen their careers ruined and few have found any avenue of redress. Little wonder, then, that corruption has flourished.

The New Zealand public have a 'holier than thou' attitude to Australia when it comes to policing, and while there may have been some justification for that in the past, it is certainly not the case now.

At least the Australians have ordered commissions to look into their various police services. Some of them can now move on.

New Zealand has steadfastly refused to do so, apart from the Compton inquiry earlier this century when a police commissioner was using police constables to work for him personally. Instead, they have just talked about it: "Isn't it awful, isn't that dreadful, isn't this wicked . . ." That seems to be the way of New Zealanders and their media.

Does the whole common structure need to be reviewed? Many experts would say at least one tier of that structure should be removed.

Police I have spoken to believe that a massive restructuring of the New Zealand Police Service is long overdue, with the main reform aim being to have less police bureaucracy.

In New Zealand, senior police officers are not used to public scrutiny and, in fact, resent it. To be fair to them, however, neither are politicians, the judiciary, the legal profession or public servants.

As the New Zealand police have made an 'art form' out of writing off complaints over the years the Police Complaints Authority is a toothless tiger.

It is hoped this book will cause the public to think more about the corruption and coverups in our society and then, hopefully, do something about it when they encounter it.

Surely it's time for some professionalism at the top? Not just in the police, but across the board.

While this book is often critical, it does offer some solutions based on twenty years' experience in the police and a further twelve years studying the Australasian legal systems and police departments around the world

Tom Lewis   January, 1998

1

Death of a Monarch

Dunedin was once described by comedian Billy Connolly as the destination of immigrant Scots who were looking for a dreary, dismal Scotland in the Pacific.

On 14 October 1981, it was far from dreary and dismal. It was mid-spring and Dunedin in spring is one of the most beautiful cities in the world. With its mix of Edwardian and Victorian architecture, the spring shrubs and flowers in full bloom and its unique position at the head of the Otago harbour, the city looked an absolute picture from the air.

This was the sight that greeted Queen Elizabeth, the Duke of Edinburgh and their royal entourage as their aircraft circled low over the city before landing at Momona Airport. The royal party were looking forward to a reasonably relaxed day as their schedule was not particularly taxing with only a lunch and the opening of a science wing at the Otago Museum programmed. In between they would walk among the citizens of Dunedin in the city centre, the Octagon, and again later at the Museum Reserve.

As they left the plane, they could see thousands of well-wishers crowding around the barriers in and around the terminal building. After being introduced to local dignitaries, the Queen and the Duke walked over to the crowd and went through the ritual of hand shaking and exchanging greetings. After a few minutes, they got into the VIP vehicle that would take them, under police escort, to Dunedin city.

Along the 30-kilometre route, they waved to the thousands of schoolchildren lining the motorway and suburban streets. As they neared the city they noticed that the streets had been decorated with flower boxes, plants and banners. The sun was shining, the crowds vocal and happy as they welcomed their Queen to this Edinburgh of the South Pacific.

The Queen and Duke were scheduled to attend a prize-giving ceremony and lunch at the Savoy, one of Dunedin's oldest restaurants. Before that, they were to walk among the people for approximately 200 metres, through the Octagon and then south for 50 metres along Princes Street just before entering the Savoy building.

Thousands thronged the Octagon that lunch hour. All were eager to get at least a glimpse of the Queen, perhaps even a word and a handshake. They pushed forward from behind the barriers that separated them from the roadway, which had been closed to traffic where the Queen and her entourage were slowly walking.

The Queen and the Duke actually looked as though they were enjoying their 'meet the people walk' as it had been described in their royal tour itinerary. The Duke, in his customary position a few metres to the rear of the Queen, stopped and chatted to children and the elderly. He was dressed in a grey lounge suit and the Queen was attracting favourable comment about her matching light green coat and hat.

The mood was festive. Flags were waving, adults and children alike were cheering and clapping. The elderly and the disabled had been moved to the front of the crowd and the royal couple stopped regularly on their walk to talk to them.

It was a great occasion for the people of Dunedin, a city of monarchists. After the ugly scenes a few months earlier when there had been anarchy in the streets over the controversial Springbok rugby team's visit, when pro-tour factions fought with anti-tour demonstrators, this royal visit was proving to be a means of uniting the city once again.

As the royal party reached the southernmost end of the Octagon, above the cheering and clapping the crack of a firearm was heard.

Time was frozen. The Queen appeared to stumble slightly, then she plunged forward as though tripping, and fell head first to the pavement. A red stain could be seen spreading rapidly across the back of her green hat as she lay there prostrate.

There were a few seconds of deathly silence then pandemonium. Women and children started screaming. Bodyguards, the Duke of

Edinburgh and police rushed to her assistance.

Many police were standing transfixed. Then the spell was broken when a man yelled, "Some bastard has shot the Queen!"

Absolute confusion now as the police are suddenly galvanised into action as they try to control the crowd. Many are pushing forward to get a better view of the fallen monarch while others are screaming and attempting to get out of the area fearing another shot will be fired. Some of the politicians accompanying the royal party on the walk are screaming at police. The tall figure of Mayor Skeggs can be seen gesticulating, his hands and arms going in every direction.

In the distance, an ambulance siren can be heard as it races towards the scene. Some plainclothes police are seen hurriedly escorting a man carrying a small leather bag – a doctor from a nearby medical centre. Uniform police are running hither and thither trying to clear a path for the now rapidly approaching ambulance.

Twenty metres away, a tall, slightly built, red-haired youth quietly makes his way out of the Mission building near the Octagon cinema onto Upper Stuart Street. He is carrying a large canvas bag, similar to those used by cricketers. He unlocks a ten-speed bicycle at the intersection of Moray Place and Upper Stuart Street before cycling north on Moray Place.

Christopher John Lewis is 17 years old, a seventh-form schoolboy and he has just assassinated the Queen of England and the Commonwealth.

Although outwardly cool his mind is in turmoil. He cannot believe how easy it was. Even the cops standing to the left some 10 metres in front of him had not looked around when he fired. They had seemed mesmerised by what was taking place in front of them. It was unreal, just too easy. He had been prepared to die to change history but unbelievably he had been able to assassinate her and just walk away.

He went over the events in his mind as he cycled through the Otago University campus. It had been the perfect position for the perfect shot all right. Nobody was looking up and obviously the cops had no one looking down, no one on top of buildings. It was just unbelievable.

To think he had in those two seconds changed the history of not only the monarchy but the British Commonwealth, the world. He had put

New Zealand to the forefront of world news. Now he would rank with the greatest assassins of all time. His name would be mentioned in the same breath as Lee Harvey Oswald and all the other assassins throughout the centuries. He would rank right up with the best because he had got away with it.

. As he had thought, the large green hat the Queen was wearing presented the perfect target. He had aimed at the centre of her hat and he had watched her stumble before falling face down on the pavement. It would be a miracle, he thought, if she survived a bullet to the head.

He was now getting close to his flat on the university campus. His flatmates should be still at lectures so he would have time to hide the rifle and bag with his cache of other weapons in the garden.

He was right. There was no one home. Lovingly and meticulously, he removed the rifle from the bag, placing it in a sheet of plastic. Before burying it in the ground, he allowed himself a smile of satisfaction. Christopher John Lewis smiled from the mouth only. His eyes were the dull, shuttered eyes of the psychopath.

After a light lunch on the verandah, he dressed in his school uniform and prepared to return to school. Although outwardly calm, he was still excited. This was the greatest high in his life. Not just excitement but pride in what he, Christopher Lewis, had achieved with one bullet. His place in history was assured, for he was the man who had assassinated the Queen!

There was only one problem – for that to happen he would have to be caught. He had expected to be caught but he had not only been too smart for them he may have been too smart to get the recognition he craved.

He turned on the radio in time to catch the 1.30 p.m. news. There was only one item. The assassination. He had indeed succeeded. The news that the Queen was dead had just been confirmed by Prime Minister Muldoon, who vowed that no stone would be left unturned as police began their hunt for the terrorists that had committed this horrific crime.

Christopher Lewis was suddenly annoyed. The police were barking up the wrong tree if they were looking for a terrorist group. This was his moment of glory and his alone. He had done it without any assistance whatsoever.

This is, of course, a fictional account but it came within seconds of becoming reality on that October day. Christopher John Lewis was only seconds from assassinating the Queen as she walked in the Octagon. From his vantage point in the Mission building arcade, he had the opportunity for an extremely simple shot at the Queen. She was scarcely 25 metres away and easily targeted by her large green hat.

He had just removed the rifle from the bag and was preparing to take aim when two uniform police officers, unaware of the bloodshed they were about to prevent, strolled a few metres up the hill in order to obtain a better vantage point. They strolled right into Christopher John Lewis's line of fire.

This caused him to abort that attempt. In those two seconds, two police officers changed history! The Queen had been spared, for the moment.

Frustrated that his attempt on the Queen's life had been thwarted when he was so close to achieving his objective, Lewis rode his bicycle to the Museum Reserve to implement Plan B. He went to a nearby building which overlooked the reserve where she was to once again walk among the people and, from a window high up in that building, he prepared to make his second attempt on the monarch's life.

This attempt has been well documented and it is now accepted that, despite police denials, a shot was aimed at the Queen and the bullet went somewhere near the royal party. What we do not know, thanks to the police cover-up, is just how close he came to succeeding at the Museum Reserve. The rifle was not ballistically tested nor was the ammunition. The spent cartridge cases were not even searched for.

Despite an attempt by police to deflect press and public attention from the Octagon incident onto the attempt at the museum, it is now accepted that if Lewis had succeeded in firing a shot from his position in the Mission building arcade in the Octagon then it is almost certain the Queen would have perished.

While it is horrendous that this could have happened – and almost did – it is equally horrendous that the cover-up in 1981 allowed Lewis to go on to commit other brutal crimes, including without a doubt the murder of Tania Furlan.

This book will show how the police cover-up in 1981 became enmeshed in other cover-ups over the ensuing years until the present day and for the first time establish a link between the cover-up of the assassination attempt on the Queen and the Dunedin sex ring inquiry of 1984.

The New Zealand police would like to have the nation believe that corruption is something that happens in other countries but in recent years their record is starting to match the well-documented corruption and dishonesty of their Australian counterparts.

In recent timess, we have seen New Zealand coppers before the courts ranging from Wanganui Police Chief Alec Waugh being charged with travel expense fraud to a detective who claimed he had been the victim a satanic attack and finally admitting that he had inflicted the injuries on himself and burnt his house down as part of an insurance fraud!

Then between late 1996 and early 1997, three Lower Hutt police were found to be illegally in possession of CIB documents. Another policeman is facing charges for possessing illegal steroids.

Two police officers were disciplined for allowing a 'friendly' publican to get off drink-drive charges if he made a charitable donation.

A senior officer, suspected of drink-drive offences at a Wellington checkpoint at Christmas, was let off without being charged. This despite the fact he showed signs of being under the influence and failed two tests. The subsequent inquiry did not result in serious charges being laid.

A number of police officers in the Gisborne district were stood down from duty while an inquiry was carried out into allegations that they had been supplying drugs.

A Northland constable was charged in court with assaulting his de facto wife.

A Christchurch police officer was committed for trial charged with making a fraudulent insurance claim in relation to the burglary of his flat.

A Westport constable was due to go to trial on an assault charge laid last November.

A senior Tauranga police officer was facing disciplinary action over his role in leading a 30-strong team policing unit that broke up a party at Mt Maunganui on New Year's Eve.

This is just a selection of the alleged offences New Zealand's 'guardians' have been involved in recently. Imagine what a Royal Commission, along the lines of the NSW Royal Commission into the police, would uncover.

Letting the police investigate their own has clearly not succeeded. The 'Caesar investigating Caesar policy' always ensures the truth does not emerge.

Many who have been in authority in police organisations have tended to adopt dismissive and, in some instances, vindictive approaches to anybody who has dared stand up for what they believed to be right.

For their efforts, those who have spoken up have been discredited, together with their families. Their careers have been ruined, their lives made a misery. In some police organisations, trumped-up charges have even been made.

Australia has, over the past decade, exposed areas of corruption in the police, public servants, and politicians at the highest level. New Zealand, however, has shown a marked reluctance to order inquiries into allegations of corruption and the like.

I have spent ten years investigating and studying corruption after being the victim of what was regarded by many people as a major cover-up by the New Zealand police and the Labour government of the time regarding the Dunedin children's sex ring scandal.

I have also exposed the attempt by police to mislead the public and cover up the attempted assassination of the Queen by Christopher John Lewis during her 1981 Royal Tour of New Zealand.

This book sets out the details of these deceits and proposes long-term strategies to inhibit corruption in the future.

2

Beating the Blues

Almost five o'clock on a cold Dunedin morning. Princess Street, the city's main street, is deserted except for a city council street-sweeping machine as it trundles along pushing the night's garbage ahead of it.

Three dark figures materialise from the shadows of a building. They are dressed in heavy greatcoats to keep out the bitter winds which whistle through the streets. As they make their way down Lower Stuart Street, their banter carries several blocks.

These are not intoxicated university students returning to halls of residence; they are, in fact, the local constabulary about to finish another night's duty.

The three beat constables line up inside the police station together with their colleagues who have been either on watch-house duty or car patrol.

"Anything to report?" the night station sergeant asks as he sways before the parading constables, his speech slurred, his tie undone and his tunic unbuttoned. He too has had a hard night, his liquor having been supplied by one of the motor patrols.

There was usually little to report. Dunedin, a university city, had a relatively well-behaved population in the mid-sixties, and the city died at night, especially after midnight.

Even the keenest of the hotelier's after-hours traders called a halt around the witching hour. One or two would ply their trade after midnight but even they closed at about two o'clock.

From the time the night shift started at 9 p.m. until midnight, the patrols would have enough work to keep them occupied. After midnight, radio calls were few and far between and the old saying, "The devil finds work for idle hands" certainly applied. Boredom was possibly the main cause of the excessive drinking by the police.

The only report that the sergeant would be likely to receive would concern those publicans who had not met their obligations during the night. They would be singled out for special attention for the remainder of the week. After all, if they were not willing to play the game that beat constables and sergeants had been playing for years, they would have to face the consequences.

The publicans of the mid-sixties were usually owner-operators. They were hard-working, hard-drinking characters and the majority of them were very pro-police. They provided the police with information about the movements and activities of criminals and many a criminal arriving in the city marvelled at just how quickly the police became aware of their presence.

The fact that Dunedin had, over the years, enjoyed a crime clearance rate which was the envy of the rest of the country was due in no small measure to the unique relationship between the publicans and the police.

Virtually every publican in town used to attend the annual police ball and most made a substantial contribution of alcoholic drinks.

In return, the publicans expected preferential treatment and they certainly got it. Many a sergeant recently transferred to Dunedin on licensing duties tried to close down the after-hours trading in the city but all failed.

For the beat constable, a simple phone call to any one of the hotels on his beat would result in the back door being left open for him.

Over a drink or two (or three) with the publican, he would discuss the movements of the licensing squad and negotiate the night's 'takeaways' to be picked up later by a patrol. He might also sit down to a sumptuous meal, with the old City Hotel a favourite among the beat cops for supper.

However, the beat constable knew enough never to 'overwork' any particular hotel. They were patronised fairly and equally.

Whatever takeaways were left after suppertime 'happy hour' would be divided among the shift and transferred to private cars. Alternatively, the proceeds could be consumed at an early morning police party. These were usually rowdy affairs and were attended by nurses from the night shift at the nearby public hospital.

All the publicans considered they were getting a good deal. After all, they were virtually immune from prosecution and the police did other favours like turning a blind eye to illegal gaming on licensed premises, often a very lucrative source of extra income.

The police also did favours like arriving on closing time to help the publican get rid of unwanted guests, collecting debts and sorting out matters like dud cheques that had been passed.

The only real problem was the 'breaking in' of a new sergeant. Once I accompanied a sergeant, new to the city, on hotel visits. After a routine visit to a hotel in Dunedin's infamous Rattray Street, we were about to leave when the publican came out of the bottle store adjacent with a bottle of whisky and a dozen bottles of imported beer and said, "Give this to Bob and the boys on the shift." Bob was the night station sergeant and was the officer in charge of the city during the night shift.

I could see the new sergeant was non-plussed so I mentioned something about it being Bob's birthday and that he had purchased the liquor earlier in the day and had asked me to pick it up for him so he could shout for the boys. The publican, known as Larry the Trout, caught on quickly and started nodding in agreement.

We took the liquor back to Bob, and I left him with the new sergeant to sort things out. He obviously did, because the new recruit certainly entered into the spirit of things during future hotel visits.

Looking back now I ask myself was this corruption? If corruption is defined as being influenced by or using bribery or graft then it certainly was. 'Favours for the boys' in Dunedin were widespread, institutionalised and endemic. These 'favours' sometimes involved police receiving free liquour and meals in return for information regarding licensing squads' movements.

Since studying corruption in Australia, the UK and the USA, I have found similarities between what was occurring in Dunedin and what occurred in other places, particularly in New South Wales and Queensland. Most of the corrupt officers identified in NSW and Queensland stated that they started by taking liquor and free meals.

As one example, NSW Detective Senior Constable Duncan Demo told the police royal commission in Sydney in July 1996 that on his first day on the job he was taken to the back room of the Barrel brothel where all the prostitutes were sitting around naked.

He and his 'buddy' (another police officer assigned to show him the ropes) drank beer with them for a couple of hours. He accepted an offer to 'feel' one of the girls and things just went from there. He accepted that was the way of things.

As a beat patrol officer he accepted his first payment of cash from a detective sergeant for turning a blind eye to corrupt activity. It was $50.

Royal Commissioner Justice Wood described the situation in the NSW police force as follows: "I am absolutely satisfied that young, decent police officers get corrupted by other persons in minor ways which extend gradually to payments of money.

"The situation is, once they are compromised, they are hooked and can do nothing about it in future. It is an occasion for extreme sorrow."

The Fitzgerald inquiry in Queensland exposed similar trends and there is no doubt whatsoever in most people's minds that corruption exists in other Australian states, particularly in Victoria and Western Australia.

Where does this leave New Zealand?

The recently retired Commissioner of Police Dick McDonald, commonly known as 'Teflon Dick' because of his reluctance to speak out on anything during his term in office, broke his silence just before his retirement: "To the best of my knowledge there is no corruption in the New Zealand police."

The last commissioner to make that statement was Tony Lauer, Commissioner for Police for New South Wales. He had said the same thing time and time again as mounting evidence clearly showed that his police force was out of control, taking cash, liquor, free meals, and good times whenever they wanted, in exchange for turning a blind eye to crime.

There have been many concerns expressed about the New Zealand police during the past fifteen years. Although there is no real evidence of widespread corruption, there has been evidence of cover-ups.

Because of the cover-ups and the police culture, the lack of investigative journalists, and because it is a small country where the media are often heavily influenced by the government, the New Zealand police have not come under the scrutiny they should have, given the public's concerns.

New Zealanders cannot keep believing it cannot happen in their country.

All the fears of conspiracy, corruption and human venality have been expressed too often for comfort.

3

Police Training

The New Zealand Police Training School was situated approximately thirty kilometres north of Wellington at Trentham.

To say that the conditions at this former military camp were less than ideal would be an understatement. The food was terrible! At breakfast, little black balls were dumped onto plates and, according to the serving staff, these were eggs that had been cooked the night before and left in the refrigerator until morning. The porridge moved with weevils and most recruits dined on bread and jam three times a day.

The camp administration seemed preoccupied with keeping the 94 males out of the sleeping quarters of the six females. Elaborate security measures were put in place and we were warned that any fraternisation during our three-month training course would result in dismissal.

Our hut commander was an ex-London 'Bobby' who, because of his previous rank, had access to the army sergeant's mess. He ran a sly-grog operation as well as the camp's only crown and anchor board. He was an enterprising chap who probably did well in the New Zealand police.

We were confined to camp every night, except Saturday, but were allowed into Upper Hutt city on Friday nights. The Provincial Hotel there was the scene of some very serious drinking by police recruits after classes on a Friday. Although many of the trainee constables were under-age, they considered the risk worth it.

On many a Friday night, the local Upper Hutt police were called to the hotel to sort out disturbances involving overworked (and over-lubricated) police recruits.

Another highlight of our Friday night excursions into Upper Hutt was the visit to the Greasy Spoon restaurant for a decent meal. Steak, eggs, onions and chips were shovelled down deprived throats. It was food, glorious food – at least once a week anyway.

With stomachs rebelling against the vast quantities of food and beer, and the unaccustomed process of food digestion, we would travel back to Trentham camp courtesy of the New Zealand Railways electric unit.

On one occasion, a group of recruits missed the last unit back to Trentham but they noticed one parked at the Upper Hutt Railway Station, which by this time was deserted.

The four well-oiled policemen managed to open a door and squeeze into the driver's compartment. The control handle was found and the unit shot down the line towards Trentham with four less-than-capable trainee cops at the controls.

There was absolute panic at train control in Wellington with their electronic control board showing an unscheduled train rocketing toward the city from Upper Hutt!

The train was later found abandoned just past Trentham. An extensive inquiry was allegedly held but the perpetrators were never found. It remained another of the great mysteries of the New Zealand Police Training School.

Every police recruit who graduated from Trentham could tell amusing and sometimes amazing stories about their time there. However, we were there to work, and we did.

Despite the mental and physical grind, most recruits enjoyed Trentham.

This was due in no small part to the excellent instructors, including the commandant, Chief Superintendent Ted Hotham, who was popular and a fine administrator. He had been a successful sportsman in his day and those of us who were active in sport received every encouragement.

The course achieved its objectives in that by and large it did prepare us for our police careers. What was never addressed nor, in fact, even mentioned was corruption.

This course was one of two courses which were run at the Police Training School. The other was the Police Cadet Course, a nineteen-month training course for young men straight from school.

Recruiting police straight out of school was an absolute disaster as these young men had no experience of life other than school and the Police Training School.

After approximately twenty years, the system was scrapped. However, its legacy still lingers as a number of former cadets have now made it to some of the top positions in the New Zealand police. One, Dick McDonald, recently retired as Commissioner. Based on correspondence I read in New Zealand newspapers just before his retirement, I had to conclude that his time in office did little to enhance the image of the New Zealand police.

Similar systems have been tried in various states in Australia with a similar outcome.

One of the big problems in recruiting police is that people underestimate the job. They throw twenty-year-olds in without realising it is without a doubt one of the hardest jobs in the world. The job demands an enormously broad range of skills, but at twenty years of age a person has neither the strong education in behavioural sciences nor the necessary life experience to get by.

In the United Kingdom, the USA and Canada, the entry age to the police has been raised. The British are hiring police aged from 24 and some are being employed in their 30s and 40s. Personally, I believe the ideal age for recruitment should be within the age range of 24 to 40.

Two other factors would improve recruitment. First, more female officers would help to counteract the male macho problem of police culture.

Second, better-educated police would be less insular in their outlook. The young, basically uneducated officer is likely to be more impressed by a station full of corrupt older police than a university graduate would be.

More civilian involvement in recruitment and training and closer links with universities would help break down the closed-shop, military-style education the police currently receive.

Such moves might help improve public perceptions of the police, and counter the view of police recruitment offered in this letter to the editor published in a Sydney newspaper in July 1996:

For years I have laboured under the impression that the prime requisite for being accepted into membership of the NSW police force was to be reasonably large in stature and somewhat smaller in IQ. Imagine my chagrin in reading part of a job description by Kate McClymont (Sydney Morning Herald, 4 July) where innocent young detective constables have naked prostitutes sitting on their knees while consuming copious quantities of alcohol (and presumably palming tax-free $100 notes).

This must surely be a job created in heaven, and obviously it takes a clever person to get a job such as this. In fact, police service takes on a whole new meaning!

Why, I ask, cannot these job fringe benefits be available to other members of the community?

4

Life as a Rookie

After leaving the Police Training School, I was posted to Dunedin. Before beginning duties in the uniform branch, I was singled out for undercover gaming and licensing duties. It was a distasteful job and I did not enjoy it.

These were the days of 6 o'clock closing and some suburban hotels had been flouting the licensing laws by having lodgers 'cover' after-hours drinkers. A lodger was permitted to have three 'guests' so long as he, or she, paid for the guests' drinks.

I would book into the hotel as a lodger and cover the after-hours patrons who would pose as my guests in the event of a police raid. When the licensing police arrived, I identified those who had been paying for their own drinks thereby committing a breach of what were ridiculous licensing laws.

I was certainly not popular with the publican or his patrons. After one particular police raid, I returned to the room I had booked to find my overnight bag and clothing had been thrown from the window, two storeys up. They were draped over trolley bus wires seven metres above the road. I considered myself lucky not to be out there with them!

Other 'serious' crimes I was instructed to detect were the sale of tote tickets, liquor raffles and race 'picks'. These activities went on in every hotel in Dunedin, and they were not difficult to detect. Prosecutions for what seemed to me to be relatively harmless pursuits appeared hard to justify.

I later learned that, with the 'warning system' that was operating in Dunedin, this was one of the few ways the licensing squad could get a 'catch'.

After a few weeks, I began duty in the uniform branch in Dunedin. The Dunedin Central Police Station was a century-old building steeped in history. Executions had been regularly carried out in the enclosed yard during the days of the Central Otago gold rush.

During the two years I spent there I was fortunate to work under the supervision of some of the best NCOs (sergeants and senior sergeants) in the New Zealand police. The products of the cadet system were just starting to be promoted and I was fortunate that my early years in the police were influenced by the NCOs from the old school.

This was particularly so when I relieved at suburban stations. The sergeants there accepted that they were responsible for their 'patch', their suburb. They did not shrink from responsibility for their staff nor the crime in their area. These men actually resented any attempt at interference on their patch from Dunedin Central Police Headquarters. Their only real contact with Central was their weekly meeting with the District Commander.

The majority of police were employed in the field, as front-line police officers. Compare that with today when it has been estimated that as few as 5 per cent work in the key response areas of policing such as drugs, crime against person, theft or road safety.

In the mid-sixties, paperwork was kept to a minimum. The sergeant in charge would check his paper work at the beginning of a shift and at the end – usually about an hour a shift.

Compare this with the present situation where these people are desk bound attempting to deal with the mountains of paperwork which emanate from the bureaucrats at Police Headquarters.

Much of this paper work could be eliminated and the remainder attended to by civilians. This would put the trained police officer back where he should be – on the streets.

The tragedy of the present situation is that young police officers today are being denied the opportunity of receiving on-the-job training from their sergeants and other experienced officers.

The value of such training was brought home to me early in my career. I was walking the beat with the sergeant in charge of the

North Dunedin police station when a barman from a nearby hotel ran towards us. He was covered in blood and his clothes were torn. I recognised him as the barman from the Captain Cook Hotel, a well-known student watering hole.

He told us that a large-scale brawl was in progress in the public bar of the hotel between bikies and students.

I was about to break into a run, eager to get to the action, when the sergeant grabbed my arm and said, "You run to a fire and walk to a fight."

As we walked toward the hotel he told me it was pointless running without a plan of action. By forcing yourself to walk, you had time to think before getting there. He added that it also gave the brawlers time to tire each other out.

Outside, we were greeted by a bloodied and bedraggled manager. The noise from the bar was deafening, glass breaking, screaming and yelling.

I was panicking just standing there watching the chaos inside but I was jolted back to reality when the sergeant said to the manager, "Where's the switch board?"

He was led to the passageway and he began pulling the appropriate fuses out, plunging the bar and hotel into darkness. The effect was immediate, almost complete silence. The sergeant then opened the door, shone his torch around and called out, "Police! You have two minutes to clear the area before we start making arrests."

It was a shame-faced lot that started filing out of the bar into the light. As they shuffled past, the manager pointed out the ringleaders and we arrested them without any problems.

Over the next eighteen months, before joining the CIB, I marvelled at the ability of that particular sergeant, and particularly his coolness in dangerous situations and his ability to defuse potential flash points.

He often emphasised that our job was to prevent, detect and solve crime but he repeatedly made the point that prevention could only be achieved by a strong police presence on the streets.

As a consequence, we always allocated at least four hours of our shift to walking the beat, and we always had at least one constable on foot in our suburb at any given time. His belief was that police on the beat gave the public a greater sense of security.

New York police have clamped down on the so-called minor offences such as urinating in a public place, drinking or smoking pot in the street, soliciting, disorderly or offensive behaviour, obscene language, fighting, graffiti and so on, and for the first time in years the streets are becoming safe again. Not only that but the murder rate has dropped 40 per cent. One of the main factors in this turnaround has been putting police back on the streets and making precinct commanders responsible for the plan and carrying it out.

Perhaps it's time for the Australian and New Zealand police to take note of a simple solution to the gradual degeneration of police departments all over the world: get back to basics.

5

The Officer Class

At the risk of being accused of living in the past, I have to say that the commissioned officers in the police today come a poor second to their predecessors of 25 years ago.

I have spoken to serving police officers in NSW, Victoria, Western Australia and Queensland and most believe that many of the commissioned officers regard themselves as being above police regulations and in some cases above the law.

My own experiences tend to confirm this and it would seem that once someone becomes a commissioned officer (inspector through to commissioner), an even stronger brotherhood is found to exist than among the lower ranks. It was described by former New Zealand Commissioner of Police Ken Thompson as an 'esprit de corps' when he was interviewed by John Kennedy, editor of the *New Zealand Tablet*, in 1985.

Thompson was attempting to explain away a number of indecent assaults on females carried out by a high-ranking District Commander, a Chief Superintendent. Instead of charging this man in the courts, Thompson arranged for him to be given the opportunity to resign on medical grounds. This individual suddenly discovered a heart problem. It was quite ironic that he was well known throughout New Zealand as a marathon runner. The heart problem quickly disappeared once he received his superannuation cheque!

When I was posted to Dunedin the District Commander was Chief Superintendent Gideon Tait. He was a blunt but honest man who called a spade a spade and was later cast out of the police hierarchy for that reason.

Tait was a fitness fanatic, a non-drinker and non-smoker who stuck rigidly to a low-fat, high-calorie diet. He was also a very religious man, and completely incorruptible.

Tait had allegedly been sent to Dunedin to stop the after-hours liquor trading and he honestly believed he was winning the battle. He was encouraged in this belief by his sergeants, who zealously waged war against a select group of publicans.

These unfortunates had curried disfavour by not supplying liquor in sufficient quantities or quality. Despite his naiveness, Tait mixed well with all ranks and he certainly appreciated the pressures young policemen faced in the job although his constant warnings about the dangers of liquor and loose women largely fell on deaf ears.

If there was an officer class in those days I certainly was unaware of it. The middle management just did not exist and apart from Tait the district had only two other commissioned officers, a Superintendent and an Inspector. They were also highly regarded and mixed well with all ranks.

Compare this with today where in Dunedin the numbers of commissioned officers employed had, by 1990, more than trebled. This has been a consistent trend in various cities throughout New Zealand and Australia. It certainly has not contributed to increased efficiency, however, because as the bureaucracy has grown so have the salaries of the various commissioners and the commissioned officers who have attached themselves to the gravy train.

The rank and file police, particularly those in the front line, have little respect for the commissioned officers of today. By and large, these officers are seen as out of touch, and some are seen as more interested in promoting their own cause than the welfare of the men under them.

In calling into question the calibre of commissioned officers in the various police forces one should examine the performances of the men at the top over the past ten to fifteen years, the Commissioners of Police.

To a large degree their performances have illuminated, with

brilliant intensity, many breathtaking instances of total incompetence, dishonesty and, at best, deliberate bureaucratic stonewalling.

Whether they were from Queensland, NSW, Victoria, the Northern Territory, New Zealand or the Australian Federal Police, they have all, at various times, demonstrated that they were well versed in the insular nature of the police culture.

Without exception, the response to serious allegations has been, "This too shall pass," "Let's all keep our heads down and hope the flak doesn't hit anyone," "Sit tight, hold the line and life will return to normal." Examples include former disgraced Queensland Police Commissioner Terence Lewis, at present serving fourteen years' jail for corruption. He maintains even to this day that he is innocent and there was little corruption in his police force.

In NSW, recently retired Police Commissioner Tony Lauer strongly resisted calls for a royal commission of inquiry into the NSW police, stating that there was no evidence of widespread corruption despite strong evidence that his police force was an out-of-control organisation riddled with corruption..

Even when a royal commission was announced, Lauer insisted that there was no need for such an inquiry. During the inquiry, as the tentacles of corruption reached the highest ranks, even into his office, Lauer insisted he was right and everyone else was wrong.

It raises the question that if Lauer was honest how could he not know or even suspect the corruption going on all around him. How on earth could he be so out of touch?

The Victorian police are well overdue for a royal commission. Their propensity to shoot first and ask questions afterwards has resulted in a number of deaths which could have been avoided. Subsequent inquiries have been cover-ups.

Brian Bull, a former Commissioner of Police in Western Australia, was given fast track promotion by the Labour government of disgraced premier Brian Burke. Bull made it to Commissioner from the rank of sergeant, jumping about eight ranks and hundreds of other police senior to him and more highly qualified.

It was obvious to everyone but the police that a royal

commission should have been held into the Mickelberg case, the burglary of the Perth Mint.

Bull managed to stand firm in the true traditions of the police culture and resist the calls for a royal commission or even an independent inquiry. He was so paranoid that he ordered police surveillance to be carried out on his deputy.

Although Bull has now retired the problems in the WA police continue.

Ken Thompson, the New Zealand Commissioner of Police, earned notoriety with his handling or mishandling of the children's sex ring scandal which rocked Dunedin and New Zealand in 1984 and 1985.

Thompson was allegedly involved in other cover-ups involving a number of his senior commissioned officers. These were serious matters and those responsible should have faced trial.

Thompson also stood firm but the pressure eventually got to him and he suffered a heart attack.

All of this poses the obvious question, what can be done about the lack of a competent officer class in our police forces?

Even after a brief look at the careers of some of the men leading our various police forces in recent years one has to ask, how did they get through the system? Is there a system in place to ensure the top man gets the top job? I think not.

There have been Commissioners of Police in recent years who were mentally unstable. One in particular became so withdrawn and depressed he locked himself in his office at Police Headquarters all day. Important documents requiring his signature were slipped under the door of his office. He ran his department in this manner until his retirement. The blue line stood firm throughout. No one would dare speak up and risk being branded a whistleblower.

Another, a born-again Christian, spent much of his time on his knees praying. Anyone entering the Commissioner's office would be invited to join him in prayer.

I can personally recall an officer in charge of a city police station hiding in a locked toilet while the station was being attacked by hundreds of violent, drunken new year revellers attempting to rescue friends arrested earlier in the evening. This person left his badly out-numbered subordinates to it. Some were badly injured and they only just managed to hold on.

His reward? Promotion!

How do we solve the problems at the top? Perhaps the police forces of Australasia need a modern 'officer class'. Fewer commissioned officers certainly but a more elite officer. A commissioned officer better educated under a system that trains the whole man or woman in not only the appropriate police and academic skills but also teaches responsibility, courtesy, consideration for others and to put duty before self.

The graduate high-fliers in the police of the future should not only receive training in leadership but financial control and other management skills before they reach the rank of superintendent.

It is a fact that the commissioned officers of police in Australasia would not hold down a job in management in the real world. Out there you cannot juggle the figures.

The crime returns we are handed by the police are, as a general rule, false. The clearance rate quoted would not stand up to scrutiny.

It is time a system was put in place which will ensure they do not turn in on themselves but display a genuine openness to the rest of society.

One of the problems with all police officers is that they are unable to recognise the perverse culture that surrounds them. Could this be because they have spent their entire lives surrounded by it . . . like a fish in water?

Finally there is a good argument to be made for a Commissioner of Police appointed from outside the police service. The main difficulty would be finding people suitably qualified who understand the police culture.

One possibility is High Court Judges or District Court Judges. Personally I favour the latter. High Court Judges, by virtue of their position, are sometimes divorced from reality. A District Court Judge is dealing with police and criminals on a day-to-day basis and they are usually younger, which is an important consideration.

A three-to-five year contract would ensure a change of management style on a regular basis.

The operational policing would remain in the control of a career police officer with the rank of Assistant Commissioner.

This proposal would ensure that the man or woman at the top was not compromised by brother officers.

6

Playing Cops and Robbers

From beat cop to patrol car driver was the next step in my police career. The junior man on the beat was assigned to a more experienced constable and together they would patrol a designated part of the city or suburbs.

Back in the mid-sixties, most of the constables I drove on night patrol were very experienced men, often in their late forties or early fifties.

Compare this with the present situation where two 'rookies' are the norm in a patrolcar. This situation is not restricted to police in patrol cars, it is everywhere in the police service where inexperienced, often very immature young people try to do a job which may require them to play several roles in one day.

The normal duties of protecting people and property, responding to crime by investigation and the apprehension of offenders are only part of the duties of a police officer. During an eight-hour shift, young police officers can find themselves in a variety of delicate situations.

I can recollect starting one shift with a fatal motor accident in which a runaway truck had hit a small car killing all three occupants, a baby of eight months and the parents.

After taking the bodies to the morgue and stripping and cleaning them in preparation for identification and a post mortem, the next-of-kin had to be advised.

This is a task every police officer dreads but on this particular occasion it was worse because two families were involved and someone from those families had to come back to the morgue and attempt to identify the mangled remains of the three victims.

Around 8 a.m. it was time for a quick breakfast. After the events of the morning, a cup of tea was about all the stomach could handle.

At 8.30 a.m. we attended a domestic dispute. A well-known businessman had assaulted his wife after she had returned from a bridge evening at 4 a.m.

She wanted him charged with assault and I was more than eager to oblige but my more experienced partner took me aside and advised me against it. He told me that most women in this situation later had a change of heart and would want to withdraw the charges and then the police became the meat in the sandwich, drawing criticism for acting hastily.

He sat down with the wife and by acting as mediator managed to reconcile the couple after giving the husband an official caution.

The next assignment was a shop-lifting complaint from a large supermarket. This resulted in the arrest of a 75-year-old man for the theft of a tin of sardines and a small torch.

As soon as arrest procedures were carried out, it was back to the morgue to attend the post mortems of the road accident victims.

Post mortems I dreaded, particularly when a baby was involved. The pathologist was Dr Eric D' Ath, commonly known as Dr Death. He was, of course, very interested in his work and he expected the police officers who had to witness the post mortem to be just as interested.

The post mortem started, as usual, with the removal of the skull cap.

The sound of the small electric handsaw screaming as it cut through flesh and bone sickened me but worse was to follow as D' Ath lifted off the top of the skull and took out the brain. He would bring the brain over and we would make notes in our notebook as he explained the cause of death if it related to the brain.

After examining the brain, he would turn to the body, taking a scalpel and slicing down from the throat to the pubic area. The flesh would be peeled back and the fat and muscle cut through to get at the various body organs.

Once again, the heart and various parts of the body were brought to us for examination. After watching three postmortems, one of which was carried out on a baby, lunch was out of the question.

While returning to the station we were directed to a cliff-top on the Otago peninsula where a man was threatening to jump into the sea 30 metres below. We spent the next three hours on the cliff trying to talk the man out of jumping. On several occasions I thought he was about to return to safety but each time he would return to the edge of the cliff. My partner almost lost his life trying to get close to him.

Although at that stage we did not even know his name, let alone what religion he was, someone back at police operations decided to send a minister of religion to negotiate with him. This was done without consultation with us and it proved to be disastrous. When he saw the car with the minister pull up, without any warning he jumped off the cliff into the sea below. Because of the treacherous currents along that particular stretch of coastline his body was never recovered.

By this time it was 4 p.m. in the afternoon and we had worked eleven hours without a break. We had started the day with death and destruction and in between we had been required to witness the post mortems of the victims. By day's end, my partner and I were physically and emotionally drained.

His advice to me was, "Let's drown our sorrows." That was exactly what we did and some three or four hours later we emerged from an inner city bar the worse for wear. It was a scenario that was repeated many times during my police career.

At times the death, destruction and human tragedy a police officer witnesses in the course of a shift just has to be blocked out before he can face his wife and children at home. Alcohol was, and still is, the favoured method of blocking out the horror of sudden and violent death.

While on the subject of suicide, I could never comprehend why people had to kill themselves in a manner which caused the maximum shock and grief to those left behind. I refer to the shotgun in the mouth scenario or in fact the placing of any firearm in the mouth or aiming at any other part of the anatomy. For the person finding the body, the horror of finding a loved one splattered all over the wall or floor can trigger trauma from which they never recover.

Hanging was another favoured method of suicide. Again the effect on the person locating the body is traumatic. Jumping from cliffs or highrise buildings also ensured a badly mangled body.

As a police officer, I was always grateful to those people who decided to go with dignity. They usually got themselves comfortable, wrote a farewell letter explaining why they were ending their lives and then either took an overdose of pills, turned the gas oven on, or retired to their car and connected a hose to the exhaust, locked the garage and started the motor. No mess, no fuss. The effect on those left behind is at least minimised.

There is no doubt that for many police officers the constant exposure to sudden, violent death causes trauma and stress. I never came to grips with it and I am sure many young, and not so young police officers today have the same problem.

Recovering bodies from the sea, lakes or rivers where they may have been for weeks was also a horrible experience. Even later in my career as an experienced detective sergeant, attending a homicide where a woman had thrown her young baby into the open fire left me shattered.

Recovering the charred remains from the fire was something I will never forget.

Every police officer can no doubt tell horror stories which relate to sudden and violent deaths, and it is an accepted part of the job. The problem is it is only one aspect of the job. Imagine a young constable having attended a 'hanging' suicide. He or she would have to cut the deceased down, carry out morgue procedures (i.e., strip the body), arrange identification and then notify and console the next-of-kin. Attendance at the post mortem would also probably be necessary. After all of this, it would be back to normal duty, perhaps attending a domestic dispute or a pub brawl or any one of the many duties which befall a police officer during a shift. The effect of the trauma of the previous few hours, the suicide or whatever, may be still with that police officer.

Later in my career, as a supervising detective sergeant, I became aware that behavioural changes could certainly occur among some individuals when they were exposed to sudden and violent death. With the limited resources at my disposal, I did try to keep them out of the front line for the rest of the shift.

As in any job you learn to take the good with the bad and I certainly experienced good times during my two years in the uniform branch.

When I speak to police today they state they were initially attracted to a police career because of the variety of the work. That was as true in the sixties as it is today. Country relieving, court escort duty, prisoner escort (taking a prisoner to a maximum security prison in another city), inquiry office relieving, search and rescue, incident patrol. These were just some of the duties I was involved in during those two years as a uniform branch constable.

Variety, excitement and mateship more than made up for the unpleasant duties.

7

Criminal Investigation Branch

I n late 1969, I began work in the Criminal Investigation Branch (CIB). Initially I was relieving detectives who were away at special training courses and I started on bicycle theft inquiries, generally regarded as the lowest position in the CIB structure.

My first day saw me in the office of the Chief Detective, James Arthur Marshall, known to all and sundry as 'Chief'. He was an impressive man with his mane of steely grey hair, his solid build and blue eyes which seemed to stare right through you.

I was aware of his reputation as a 'hard man' as my colleagues in the uniform branch had warned me about the 'Chief'. He was disliked among the uniform branch for a number of reasons, the main one being he headed all internal inquiries, dealing with the serious complaints made against staff in the uniform branch or the CIB.

If you committed a breach of police regulations or any criminal offence you could expect no mercy. He was also something of a snob and was perceived to regard the uniform branch as the poor relation of the police service. There was no doubt that despite his unpopularity in some quarters he was respected by virtually everybody who came into contact with him.

The period I spent with Marshall that first day lasted no more than an hour but at the end of that time I knew exactly what was expected of me in 'his' CIB. I also knew where I stood as far as he was concerned – right at the bottom of the pecking order.

Jim Marshall was an extremely competent man and he had ability well above his rank of Detective Senior Sergeant. Although he was responsible for the day-to-day running of the CIB office, he was answerable to the head of the CIB, a commissioned officer.

When I began duty in the CIB, Detective Chief Inspector Bill Hollinshead was its overall head. He was rarely seen and during my time under him he was on an out-of-town inquiry which was shrouded in secrecy. It was later revealed that he was investigating a senior magistrate for perjury, whom he later arrested. Hollinshead was then transferred to Police Headquarters in Wellington.

He was replaced by a younger man, Emmet Mitten, an excellent policeman and a man with vision who many predicted would become Commissioner in due course. Mitten was not the 'hands-off' leader Hollinshead appeared to be but by and large he left Marshall to run the CIB office.

It was rumoured that Marshall was very well off and did not even need his police salary. He owned a substantial home in Dunedin's most salubrious suburb, Maori Hill, and also owned a number of student flats and houses. His cousin was Sir John Marshall, the New Zealand Prime Minister.

Perhaps his leadership qualities were inherited but he certainly had to be respected as a strong leader, a man of character. He always provided a sense of direction in times of turmoil, and he was certainly able to exercise authority. He demonstrated an ability to delegate but considered the buck stopped with him, and he could work with his subordinates effectively because he made everyone aware of what he expected of them.

I did find myself at odds with Jim Marshall a few times, particularly in the early stages of my career in the CIB. He was a stickler for tradition and believed the wearing of a felt hat was an essential part of a detective's equipment. Maybe it was a result of the ribbing I got from my uniform branch colleagues before transferring about going to join the 'felt hat' brigade, but for whatever reason I thought it absurd to have to wear a hat just to become a detective, so I refused. I was, of course, out of order because most of the other young detectives on trial had complied.

Eventually, however, Marshall accepted my argument and I did not buy the hat. He then turned his attention to my sporting commitments warning me on a number of occasions that if he ever decided sport was interfering with my work then I would be put back to the uniform branch. I accepted this because he was giving me a warning and I knew only too well that he would carry out his threat. I respected him for that.

Many years later when I had become the head of the drug squad, I learned that Jim Marshall, the 'hard man', was also a very compassionate and caring person. I was the guest speaker at a Lions Club function held in a building owned by the Orphans Club of Dunedin.

The person who introduced me spoke for ten minutes about the charitable work and the money that had been raised by Jim Marshall for the orphans of the city over many years.

A police constable on 'trial' in the CIB spent six months attempting to prove he was suitable to qualify for the rank of detective constable. The usual criteria was the number of 'catches' made during the six-month period. Appropriately, Marshall placed emphasis on the quality of the 'catches'. A constable on 'trial' could nominate over a hundred 'catches' for the six months even if a considerable number might relate to minor offences such as shoplifting or interfering with a motor vehicle. Alternatively, another constable might have fewer 'catches' but serious ones such as burglary, rape, armed robbery and so on.

These types of offences usually meant Supreme (now High) Court trials before a judge and jury and required considerable work in preparing the file for the crown prosecutor. As a result, quality 'catches' were rated more highly.

In the late sixties, charges such as idle and disorderly, insufficient means of support, frequenting with felonious intent, loitering with intent, and consorting with known criminals, were regularly laid and Jim Marshall believed, and rightly so, that police should, and must use the powers given to them. His motto was 'use them or lose them'. He was acutely aware of the civil libertarians who maintained such laws were draconian, open to abuse and therefore should be repealed.

Every working day without fail, Marshall would leave the office at 12 noon. He would walk from the CIB office to the Octagon, the town centre, where he would catch a bus to his home. After lunch, he would walk the three miles back to the CIB office through the town and past the grassed area of the Octagon where various undesirables seemed to congregate.

Once back in the office at 1.15 p.m., he would summon the young aspiring detectives to his office and list the criminals and suspects he had seen during his walk. He would always finish with the remark, "Boys, there are so many crims in the Octagon they are hanging off the trees. Bring them all in and find out what they are about."

A couple of car loads of keen young policemen would roar up to the Octagon and round up all the criminals and suspects and bring them down to the office. They would be interviewed and, of course, many confessed to crimes they had committed.

Those who did not had to prove that they were not idle and disorderly, had lawful means of support (a hard one this if you were unemployed), or that they were not guilty of the other offences previously mentioned. It was a method Marshall used to test the interviewing techniques of his aspiring detectives. The police officers really had nothing on these people so to elicit from them details of crimes they had committed was no mean feat.

He also believed in the value of informants and this was often an ideal opportunity to cultivate an informant. With his approval, we were encouraged to 'trade' but only for minor offences such as idle and disorderly. We were also encouraged to help people who were not criminals but who, for whatever reason, were down on their luck.

If they had no fixed abode they were transported by us to the Salvation Army Home in the city or if they were out of work taken to the Labour Department offices where temporary employment could be arranged.

Jim Marshall was not just a man for the times. He was, in fact, very adaptable and his methods, based on common sense, are still relevant today.

After serving my six months' CIB trial, I applied for my detective constable rank. I listed my "catches", which averaged out at around five arrests a week, and included two serious charges which resulted in Supreme Court trials.

One was the Rendezvous Milk Bar case which created a considerable amount of publicity in Dunedin due to the alleged seduction of young boys at the rear of the milk bar by former beauty queen Barbara Anne Dickson.

The explicit nature of the evidence ensured a full court gallery each day of the trial. It was alleged that Dickson had employed a thirteen-year-old girl at the milkbar after school, who introduced her fourteen-year-old boyfriend to Dickson.

Dickson took a fancy to the young man and seduced him in her bedroom at the rear of the shop. She then offered to show her thirteen-year-old employee 'how to do it'. The offer was accepted and Dickson gave a demonstration with the girl's boyfriend before assisting in the seduction of her young employee.

Dickson's reputation as a seducer of boys resulted in her milkbar becoming a regular haunt for youths after school and of an evening. A number of young girls also frequented the milkbar and this set the scene for the offences that were to follow.

I had been investigating a theft and while interviewing a suspect I did the usual thing and asked him what else he had been up to. His answer absolutely rocked me. The youth gave a blow-by-blow description of a sex orgy in which he had participated some days earlier at the Rendezvous Milk Bar.

After further inquiries, I interviewed over a dozen youths and young girls all who admitted being involved in these nefarious activities at the rear of the Rendezvous Milk Bar.

Barbara Dickson emerged as a young woman who obviously had a voracious sexual appetite. She seduced boys as young as twelve years old and openly ridiculed any of them who did not perform up to expectations. The twelve-year-old had his penis likened to a spring carrot due to its lack of size. She was also very proud of her breasts, telling the youths and girls that they were 38-inch D cup.

While this no doubt made the young girls feel inferior and had the youths lusting after her, Dickson was more than happy to share the youths and to actively assist the girls to have sex.

When I interviewed Dickson, she openly admitted seducing the boys but she was more reticent when it came to admitting her role in the sexual initiation of the girls. Dickson told me she did not believe she had done anything wrong as the boys wanted sex but didn't know how to do it and she had merely assisted them. "All perfectly natural," she said.

Dickson was charged with aiding and abetting unlawful sexual intercourse, in relation to her arranging and demonstrating to the young girls how to have sex. We were unable to charge her in relation to the seduction of the boys as there was not an appropriate charge, nor was there a complaint!

Dickson elected trial by jury and the case was before Justice Trevor Henry in the Dunedin Supreme Court. The trial received huge publicity with the national newspaper *Truth* devoting front-page coverage. The local news media also highlighted the case.

A close friend of mine, Patrick Finnigan, defended Dickson and although she was convicted he managed to keep her out of prison. No mean feat considering the publicity and the shock, horror reaction of conservative Dunedinites.

One of the amusing aspects of the trial was the attendance each day of a half-dozen of the Dunedin blue-rinse set. These middle-aged matrons would arrive together, with their knitting, and proceed to be disgusted and shocked, tut-tutting at regular intervals while knitting. It was standing room only in the gallery as the public flocked to see the former beauty queen and to hear the evidence of the youngsters she had seduced.

I felt sorry for Dickson when I saw the witnesses. Some of the boys, resplendent in school uniform, looked like choirboys, pictures of innocence, while the girls gave the impression butter would not melt in their mouths. Some of the witnesses were so small they could not even be seen when they were in the witness box.

Dickson was only twenty-four years old and she was an attractive woman. In her evidence she maintained she had been initiated into sex by a relative in a similar way. She stated that she had always appreciated having been shown how to have sex properly and how to enjoy it. To her way of thinking she had done nothing wrong.

After her term of probation was completed, Barbara Dickson left Dunedin. Her reputation was such that she would have had to endure rumour and innuendo for the rest of her life had she chosen to remain.

My application for detective constable rank was declined by Jim Marshall on the grounds that I had been absent for a month of the CIB trial representing the New Zealand police at athletics and rugby. I argued with him that such representation was regarded by the department as being 'on duty'. His argument was I had not completed a full six-month CIB trial and until I did he would not approve my rank. Although I was far from impressed I had no choice but to wait another month. At the end of that time, I became a detective constable, with the appropriate pay increase.

Marshall summoned me to his office and handed the memorandum to me, congratulating me as he did so. He said, "You have two years to go before attending the CIB course and becoming a detective. Don't let sport delay that." I accepted his warning and sport was put on the backburner for the next two years.

Those two years were spent on various CIB squads such as Break (Burglary), Car (unlawful taking, theft ex-car), Theft, and Fraud. I also spent a short period working with the drug squad and I did undercover work.

Once again I consider myself fortunate that in my early days as a detective I had the benefit of working with experienced detective sergeants and detective senior sergeants. The products of the ill-conceived cadet system had not at that time reached senior ranks.

One of the first things I did learn in the CIB was that it was war. When dealing with the criminal element one learned that they did not play by the Marquess of Queensberry rules and a good detective soon realised there was no such thing as a level playing field when it came to dealing with hardened criminals and their lawyers.

I clearly recollect an old detective sergeant telling me, "Never give a sucker an even break. They'll die in your arms."

I also remember on a major inquiry being told by the officer in charge just before interviewing a suspect, "I can't tell you exactly how this bastard should be bricked in, but I expect you to do it." It was a pretty clear message that the end justified the means.

Planting of evidence was not widespread although it did occur, as Arthur Allan Thomas will confirm. Verballing, however, did occur although it was usually more subtle than that engaged in by Australian police. It was more of a case of rearranging the words used and perhaps leaving out a word or two here and there. The suspects were usually of low intelligence and their memories, often befuddled by substance abuse or whatever, just could not cope with long interviews. It was therefore a simple matter to take a verbal statement made by a suspect and by slight alterations change the context.

The use of force to obtain a confession was widespread and the secret was to leave no evidence such as bruises or lacerations. Phone books were very handy in this regard.

The threat of force was also effective. Many a suspect capitulated when taken to a small interview room by two burly detectives. Often it merely took the preliminary action of taking off a watch, or the rolling-up of shirt sleeves before the suspect would talk.

One of the worst beatings I ever saw inflicted on a suspect was by a senior commissioned officer. The suspect had been brought in for questioning over having in his possession a quantity of explosives and detonators. He had been carrying the gelignite, detonators, batteries and other paraphernalia in a carton while travelling on a bus. The officer had obviously visualised the carnage and destruction in the inner city if this carton had gone off. Accordingly, he dealt out his own form of summary justice.

Corruption in the form of receiving money for favours was not widespread. It certainly did exist as I found out when I was working undercover in the drug scene in Auckland. I had arranged with a drug dealer to make a buy from him at Auckland airport but I was warned by the head of the Auckland drug squad that the officer in charge of the CIB at the airport was suspected of working in with the Mr Asia syndicate, the very drug ring I had infiltrated.

I could not change the venue without raising suspicion so I had to keep my appointment knowing that my cover could be blown by this person. It was a nerve-racking time for me, especially the meeting after the airport rendezvous as I did not know whether I had been seen by him and exposed. Had that happened I would have been lucky to survive.

The Auckland surveillance squad had assured me I had nothing to worry about as they would have me under surveillance at all times. I later found out that they had lost me as soon as I got into the drug dealer's car. Fortunately for me, he did not try a cash rip-off.

While working with the Dunedin drug squad early in my CIB career, I became concerned with the close relationship that appeared to have developed between an Asian drug dealer and the officer in charge of the drug squad.

From a reliable informant I learned that the head of the drug squad and one of his detectives were making frequent trips to a well-known ski resort where they were regularly entertained on the Asian's boat not to mention being feted in restaurants and hotels.

It was also alleged that he and the other detective were supplied with women. I made some inquiries and learned that despite numerous trips to the resort they had not made one arrest.

It was a difficult situation as I was only a junior detective constable and the allegations had come through an informant, not always the most reliable source of information. I passed the information on to Jim Marshall and suggested he could interview my informant. This was not the norm because in those days the identity of an informant was never divulged to anyone.

Marshall accepted the offer. He later told me that there had been insufficient evidence to prove corruption but there had been enough to warrant a review of the drug squad. He told me the officer in charge would be transferring.

Another incident that illustrated possible corruption was an undercover operation to expose gaming and illegal bookmaking offences. The operation was timed to coincide with a certain detective taking a month's leave. It was alleged that he would have alerted the suspects.

In 1980, I investigated a detective sergeant who was allegedly passing information to criminals about police surveillance operations. We were able to establish that he had passed on information but we were unable to find any evidence of financial gain. The officer concerned was not dismissed and the reason we were given was because he was an alcoholic.

After two and a half years of CIB training, I was told that I would be attending the CIB qualifying course at the Police Training School at Trentham. This was the culmination of training and failure at the qualifying course meant an instant return to the uniform branch and the end of a CIB career.

A few weeks before I was due to fly to Wellington for my qualifying course, I was on CIB night patrol. At approximately 4.30 a.m. I was advised by police operations that they had received an emergency call from my wife who was hysterical. She had reported a man armed with a knife attempting to get into the house and threatening to kill her.

I ordered my driver to head to my home at top speed. We were there in ten minutes and I met a dog handler who told me the offender had disappeared. When I rushed into the house I found my wife and three young children huddled in a corner.

My wife was in a state of shock. Although she was trying to speak, the words would not come out. My son told me a man with a knife had tried to get in but the safety chain had stopped him. He said the man was swearing and slashing at the chain with his knife. Although the children were in a state of shock, they had not been as badly affected as my wife. To this day, she still suffers from the effects of that experience and she periodically has vivid nightmares in which she relives that night of horror.

The dog handler ran a successful track and the offender, a man I had recently arrested, was apprehended later that day. That was some consolation but I was left with a family absolutely shattered as a result of the experience.

Worse was to follow as I was contacted by Jim Marshall who told me that I was expected to resume duty that night. Poor old Jim copped the anger and emotion that had been building up inside me and I told him in no uncertain terms where to go.

After a further two weeks, it was obvious to me that my wife was in no condition to be left alone while I went off to a detective qualifying course for nine weeks. I asked Marshall if my attendance at the course could be postponed.

He told me that would not be possible and if I did not go I would have to go back to the uniform branch. He advised me to think it over. I was convinced that I had no choice and I was set to resign from the CIB, but my wife, knowing what it meant to me, insisted that she would be all right and that relatives and friends would rally around. Reluctantly I agreed.

It turned out to be the biggest mistake I ever made as the relatives and friends assisted for a time but then left my wife to her own devices. She became sick and almost suffered a nervous breakdown, forcing me to go back from the course each weekend at my own expense until I finally arranged for her to come to stay in Wellington.

It was an extremely difficult period with the pressure of having to pass the course and my wife's sickness weighing heavily on me.

I will always be grateful to the course co-ordinator, Detective Sergeant Tom Watkins, for his support and assistance.

It was a situation that would not happen today and it should not have happened then. The police department of the time demonstrated scant regard for the welfare of its staff by insisting I leave my wife and family for a prolonged period after the trauma they had experienced, due entirely to the fact that they were the family of a police officer.

One incident that occurred at the end of the course classically illustrates the police culture of protecting their own even when a serious offence was committed.

A group of us were rushing to the airport to catch the last flight out of Wellington to return home when it became apparent that we might not get to the airport in time. The mini-bus was driven by one of the instructors, a detective sergeant. He was asked by a detective constable to stop at the nearest telephone box so he could ring the airport to discover whether the flight was on schedule. After making his phone call he announced, "No need to hurry boys, they are not on schedule any more."

A few seconds later, I heard laughter from the back of the minibus. I then got a tap on the shoulder and I was told that he had made an anonymous call stating there was a bomb on board the plane.

Quite frankly I did not believe what I had been told but as we approached the perimeter of the airport I noticed a plane being towed away from the terminal building to the end of the runway. Once inside the terminal the chaos was apparent and the bomb scare was confirmed. The plane was delayed for over an hour. Bags were removed, the plane was checked thoroughly and we all adjourned to the bar.

I looked at the perpetrator. He didn't appear to have a worry in the world, sitting there sipping his beer.

This was a classic illustration of how the police culture works. Here was a man, a police officer, who had just committed a serious criminal offence, sitting there safe in the knowledge that the 'brotherhood' would not speak up. Not one of us spoke up or even discussed it again.

In the early seventies I became known as the man with the photographic memory because I recognised an escapee from Pentridge prison in Victoria, who had been on the run for seven years.

I had recently been transferred to the Break Squad office where his 'Wanted' poster hung above my desk. I was strolling to work one afternoon when I saw a man resembling the escapee. I followed him and when he entered a restaurant I walked up behind where he was seated and said, "Hello, Colin." He immediately turned in acknowledgement but his smile froze as he realised he had been sprung.

The arrest received maximum publicity and the escapee later admitted to hundreds of criminal offences, all committed during his seven years on the run in New Zealand.

I arrested my first murderer shortly after my detective's

qualifying course and it was a most unpleasant inquiry.

A young couple, aged 17 and 18 years respectively, had a young son aged 15 months. These were the days before the Domestic Purposes Benefit and a young man fathering a child out of wedlock was required by law to support that child until it was sixteen.

These two young people were immature and ill equipped to be parents. The young man had returned to his family home leaving the mother and his young son on their own. He still visited them, although he was later to admit it was more for his own sexual gratification than to see his son.

The young mother pleaded with him to come back so they could all be together. He agreed on the condition she kill their son. He said, "He's like a millstone around my neck. I'm going to be paying for the kid for years." Finally after intense pressure the mother agreed but she looked to her partner for guidance as to how the murder should be carried out.

He told her of a television programme he had watched where a woman had drowned almost instantly after being dragged along the bottom of the bath quickly by the ankles, which caused water to fill her lungs instantly.

After killing the child in this manner she was told to pretend that she had left it alone in the bath for a short period while taking a phone call. The death would then appear accidental.

The killing was carried out as planned. The uniform branch attended the death and treated it as an accident. This was understandable as they were confronted by a distraught mother who gave her version of events in between sobs and hysterical screaming.

One of the constables decided that the file should go to the CIB before going to the coroner and the acting chief detective, Dave Warner, assigned the investigation to me. Detective Constable Jim Millar, now the officer in charge of the Dunedin police district, assisted me.

Our suspicions were aroused when we read the file. As family men, we found it hard to believe that any mother would leave a young child in a bath unattended for a lengthy period.

Background checks on the two parents revealed that McKewen,

the father of the child, was a heavy drinker and associated with criminals and undesirables. Robson, the mother, had become pregnant at sixteen and although more intelligent than McKewen was very much under his influence.

Our inquiries started with their associates and it was there we got our breakthrough. The criminal class are not, as a rule, very loyal to each other and among McKewen's friends we found a few who were willing to talk. Even though they were criminals, they drew the line at murdering babies and they repeated what McKewen had told them, "Sharon had drowned the kid."

As a result of these interviews we were able to establish that McKewen regarded the child as a liability and although Robson was alleged to have murdered the child it was thought that he was the instigator.

Detective Constable Millar and I went to McKewen's home at Mosgiel. After a preliminary chat he agreed to accompany us to the CIB office for questioning. At the same time Detective Barbara Kelk was interviewing Robson.

After lengthy interviews both confessed and they were jointly charged with the murder of their son. McKewen described in detail in his signed statement how he had masterminded the murder as a result of watching a television programme. The programme showed a woman murdered in the bath after her husband violently grabbed her ankles and pulled her underwater from one end of the bath to the other causing almost immediate loss of consciousness and drowning.

Robson admitted that she had carried out McKewen's instructions and when the baby lost consciousness she left it lying under the water to ensure it drowned.

At the subsequent High Court murder trial, both defence counsel attacked the way the admissions had been obtained and the length of the interviews. It was claimed that both McKewen and Robson had been intimidated and the interviewers had worn them down and eventually they had agreed to anything. They attempted to have the admissions made by Robson and McKewen thrown out.

They were unsuccessful and both Robson and McKewen were

convicted of their son's murder and sentenced to life imprisonment.

McKewen's lawyer immediately appealed to the Court of Appeal against his client's conviction, which was unsuccessful. Undeterred, he appealed to the Privy Council in London. This appeal was also rejected.

The McKewen family were simple working-class people and they could not accept that their son could be found guilty of murder when he was not present when the crime was committed. They sent death threats to the officer in charge of the case and to me. Rather than have them arrested and charged we asked the head of the CIB to warn them.

It was apparent that much of this unpleasantness could have been avoided if their son's lawyer had explained the law to them and how it applied to their son. Unfortunately his Privy Council trip only gave them false hope.

8

The Legal System and the Legal Profession

Many people mistakenly think that as the police appear to be the largest part of the criminal justice system the rise in crime and the fear of crime, which affects so many of us, is a problem for the police alone to solve.

It is not that simple. The justice system in Australia and New Zealand tends to resemble an iceberg. The police service is that part above the surface, very visible and subject to the criticism and fears of society. Yet the part that exerts at least as much, if not more influence – the legal system, the rules of evidence and the legal profession – lies beneath the water line.

There they shelter from the criticism and fears of society. They are very quick to criticise the police knowing full well that the police, a disciplined organisation, are not permitted to respond.

The public depend upon our system of justice to support them and many people consider it is letting them down. Public confidence is decreasing rapidly because it is now seemingly incapable of handling the job it should be doing. Symptomatic of this failure are the well-publicised miscarriages of justice, where the Court of Appeal or High Court releases people because their convictions were 'unsafe' or unsatisfactory.

The system we have inherited has many good points but it tends to serve the needs of its rules and rituals rather than the public, and the people – victims, witnesses, defendants and jurors – who are caught up in it. Many people believe it needs a clear vision for the future and this it certainly does not have.

In simple terms, an ideal justice system requires two essential and clear fundamentals:

- The innocent must be acquitted and the guilty convicted.
- The search for truth must be paramount.

Yet, believe it or not, getting to the truth is not even part of our present system. Instead it is a game. It is an adversarial combat, a contest between lawyers, usually doing their very best for their clients, be they prosecution or defence, to obtain a conviction or an acquittal but NOT to discover the truth. Discovering the truth may result from this combat but equally it may not.

What, then, does the average citizen expect from the criminal justice system? They will tell you that they expect a trial to result in a cold analysis of all the evidence available and the reaching of an objective conclusion based on that: "This is what happened, and so-and so did or did not commit this crime." The reality is, of course, far removed from this.

One classic example of the system failing people arises from 'plea bargaining'. A guilty plea from a defendant at the start of a trial does save a huge amount of court time, money and work. In return, a judge may, and usually does, impose a reduced, suspended, or non-custodial sentence.

Plea bargaining has been around in Australia and New Zealand for a long time and I admit that it has advantages and can meet some clients' needs. It is, however, fraught with danger. The biggest danger is that in Australasia it is becoming standard practice.

The practice has been indulged in by corrupt police and corrupt lawyers who have received favours from criminals for 'arranging' a light sentence and evidence of this is emerging from the NSW Royal Commission.

Another major problem with the legal system is that it tends to forget the victim or victims. They see offenders going unpunished or inadequately punished and next time they may be reluctant to report a crime or offence. Also they may, as many have, decide to take the law into their own hands.

The other people who are often badly treated under our present system are witnesses. They often wait for hours in a corridor outside a courtroom face to face with defendants and their supporters, feeling rather intimidated.

Inside the court itself it is the norm for their evidence and honesty to be challenged. The gladiatorial system demands it!

To the best of my knowledge the criminal justice system has never addressed such issues. Those who work in the system – not just police but magistrates, judges, lawyers and others – acknowledge the problems but they are part of the system, a system very resistant to change. What is agreed, however, is that the present system lacks a clear sense of direction.

Would an inquisitorial justice system provide a viable alternative? This could mean everyone would be working together to establish the truth. Perhaps then the question of innocence or guilt would follow naturally.

What would such a system be like?

First, we need proper guidelines for both the disclosure of prosecution material to the defence and – this will cause an outcry from lawyers – the key elements of the defence case to the prosecution.

The current rules, together with the right of silence, allow an accused's lawyers to produce, at the last moment, 'ambush defences', which cannot then be challenged or tested. This often results in an acquittal when subsequent investigation shows the defence facts to be, at best, dubious. This causes frustration and anger among victims and police.

In the NSW Royal Commission, it has been stated that some police officers resort to 'verballing' and planting evidence out of sheer frustration with the legal system. While this type of behaviour can never be condoned, it has to be acknowledged that police, particularly CIB officers investigating horrific crimes, are often placed under intense pressure by the public, the media and their own hierarchy to make early arrests.

In order to make that arrest they have been known to fabricate evidence, justifying such conduct by asserting that they are just levelling out the playing field.

Likewise, victims can be tempted to resort to criminal acts in order to exact retribution on an accused who, they believe, has beaten the system. I have seen respectable people who were victims of crime so frustrated after seeing a guilty person escape justice due to a technicality that they have resorted to 'bush justice', the hiring of a thug to exact retribution. It is becoming widespread in both Australia and New Zealand.

Another problem is delays. Delays are endemic in the justice system and something needs to be done urgently to rectify the problem. Much of it is due to the public service mentality which permeates the justice system.

Such delays give defendants extra advantages. Witnesses' memories fade, the victims' sense of grievance dissipates and it becomes even more difficult to keep the prosecution case intact.

Late guilty pleas – after all the witnesses and the accompanying evidence have been unnecessarily assembled at court – cause additional and unnecessary costs. They also cause disruption and resentment which could have been avoided.

In the search for the truth, the pre-trial review or conference has saved time and resolved some problems. There, the admissibility of evidence and the use of statements, rather than calling witnesses, have succeeded in reducing apprehension about trials and reduced trial times, which has resulted in reduced court costs.

Certain lawyers, many of whom are benefiting from legal aid, are of course keen to milk the system by creating delays, not using the pre-trial review or conference in the manner intended and taking every avenue of appeal open to their client even when that person is obviously guilty.

I remember a relatively unknown lawyer milking the system in the 1970s. He orchestrated a free trip to London - all expenses paid - courtesy of the tax payer, via the legal aid system.

The other obstacle in our search for truth is often the legal profession.

Let me quote playwright Jean Giraudoux, who wrote in 1935,

"There is no better way of exercising the imagination than the study of law. No poet ever interpreted nature as freely as a lawyer interprets the truth."

Some years later Giraudoux was even more direct: "You are a lawyer. It's your duty to lie, conceal and distort everything and slander everybody."

In the 18th century, Benjamin Franklin displayed cynicism about lawyers with the comment, "God does work wonders now and then . . . Behold a lawyer, an honest man."

Despite their training, high incomes, the elaborate trappings of their profession (wigs, gowns and so on), lawyers, and the legal profession in general, are seen by the public to be lacking in credibility and compassion. They now tend to be rated in the context of dodgy used car salesman, insurance agents or even brothel owners.

This has been brought about by the exorbitant fees charged by lawyers for providing services and advice which are often found to be flawed.

A year or two ago, during a morning gym session, I spoke to a well-known Sydney property developer who told me he was taking one of his lawyers out for lunch that day. He went on to tell me that the lawyer in question had been engaged by his firm over a development approval and had represented them in court the previous day.

The property developer was delighted because the lawyer had actually read the file before court and was fully conversant with its contents.

Here was a man, a multi-millionaire, who employed QCs to act for his firm on a regular basis, for exorbitant fees of course, telling me he was delighted to find one who had actually read the file before the hearing.

He told me the majority turned up to court without being even remotely conversant with the file. They would ad-lib their way through the proceedings, relying, as he put it, on 'bullshit' to get them through. Often the bullshit was not enough and it was the client who was the loser.

The public have been slow to wake up to the fact that the vast majority of lawyers are dollar driven. Many are totally incompetent and many are plainly dishonest.

Perhaps the following story best illustrates the public perception of lawyers: a medical research laboratory began replacing white rats with lawyers and when asked why offered three reasons – there are more lawyers than rats, sometimes researchers become fond of rats . . . and there are some things even a rat won't do.

With all the widespread publicity and discussion of the need for an independent authority to investigate police perhaps it is also time to discuss the need for an independent body to investigate the ever-increasing number of complaints against the legal profession, with dishonesty being the most prevalent.

Those who have been forced to turn to law societies in either Australia or New Zealand with their complaints will acknowledge that such bodies should not be investigating their own members.

In Australia, the Lionel Murphy case should have given the public an insight into how easy it is to corrupt the legal system. Lionel Murphy was a High Court judge and a former Attorney-General in the Whitlam government. Police had obtained evidence from secret tapes which indicated that he had attempted to pervert the course of justice.

As a consequence of this and an attempt by Murphy to influence Clarrie Briese, the Chief Magistrate, in a case involving a friend of Murphy, he was charged.

In 1985, he was found guilty of attempting to pervert the course of justice and sentenced to eighteen months' imprisonment. He appealed and was granted a retrial, at which he was subsequently acquitted. Within weeks, Murphy was under investigation again, this time facing further inquiries from a parliamentary committee asked to examine fourteen allegations that were partly derived from the police tapes.

Murphy ducked and dived in every direction in an attempt to wreck the inquiry, including questioning its legitimacy. He refused to appear before either of the senate inquiries, submitting instead written statements which invoked, among other things, judicial independence.

Although he gave evidence in his first trial he exercised his right to make an unsworn statement at his second trial thereby avoiding cross-examination. He was aware the prosecution had new information that they intended to put to him, and this action effectively negated that.

Then came his greatest act of arrogance and defiance. Diagnosed with terminal cancer, he insisted on his right to return to the High Court bench, this despite protests from all and sundry, including the Chief Justice, Sir Harry Gibbs, that he should not sit while under investigation on such serious matters.

Lionel Murphy died while the controversy raged around him. His Labour mates in the Hawke government quickly moved to wind up the commission of inquiry and they passed legislation to prevent any public access to the material for 30 years.

All of this did nothing to allay public concern. Here was Lionel Murphy, the man who had been paraded by the ruling Labour Party as the next Chief Justice of the High Court, the highest role in the highest court in the land, having the findings made by a commission of inquiry into his activities hidden from public scrutiny for 30 years.

Those of us who have worked in the justice system have long been aware that all is not well there. Many judges and magistrates, like Lionel Murphy, give the impression that they believe they are above the law. The public, rightly or wrongly, believe they are an arrogant lot who like to surround themselves with an aura of mystique. It appears that they are accountable only to their peers – another example of Caesar investigating Caesar.

This, of course, is nothing new. Even twenty years ago, when judges and magistrates were often crusty, unsympathetic types who had fought their way across North Africa into Italy and the Normandy beaches or through the jungles of South-East Asia, the judiciary actively protected their own.

I can clearly remember a magistrate in Christchurch who was allowed to continue to sit on the bench despite the fact that he got himself hopelessly drunk every lunchtime.

In the mid-seventies, I had to fly to Christchurch with a number of other police officers and civilian witnesses to give evidence in a defended hearing. I was advised by the court orderly and deputy registrar that the magistrate could not continue after lunch on the first day because he was intoxicated. Because the hearing had been set down for two days, it was decided to adjourn the matter for a fortnight. We duly flew back to Christchurch a fortnight later only to have the matter adjourned again due to the magistrate's intoxication after another long lunch.

As officer in charge of the case, I felt I had to lodge a complaint with my superiors as the civilian witnesses were starting to ask questions.

I was told that nothing could be done as magistrates and judges were virtually above the law. Only the Governor-General could dismiss them and that had to be on the recommendation of the Minister of Justice. I was told it would only happen if it was a serious matter, a criminal offence.

My witnesses and I continued to fly to Christchurch at the taxpayers' expense until the prosecution evidence had been completed. It remained a 'mornings only' hearing with the magistrate concerned continuing to write himself off every lunch time. The hearing, which should have been concluded in two days, dragged on for over a month due to the interrupted sessions. The additional cost to the taxpayer was enormous.

I spoke with a Justice department official about it and he reiterated that nothing could be done because magistrates and judges were a law unto themselves.

I was so incensed that I decided to advise the newspaper *Truth* about the fiasco that was occurring daily in Christchurch. They carried out their own investigations and ran a story which exposed the magistrate concerned.

This forced the judiciary's hand. They removed the offending magistrate from criminal and civil matters and then created a position for him to hear liquor and licensing applications!

9

New Zealand's Ned Kelly

It was spring, early October 1981. The sun was shining, and tranquillity reigned in the leafy suburb of Andersons Bay, an upper-middle-class area in Dunedin.

At around 10.30 on that balmy morning, the suburb was just coming alive with locals shopping or enjoying a walk in the sunshine.

It was a typical midweek working day for the two female employees of the Andersons Bay Post Office, which incorporated a savings bank branch, pensions pay-out counter as well as its primary function of a post office. Their four or five customers included two young girls from the local Catholic primary school who were banking the school students' weekly savings.

The tranquillity was shattered a few minutes after 10.30 that morning when the door of the post office was thrust open and three armed men in military uniforms burst in. Staff and customers recoiled in horror as the leader of the group screamed, "This is a fucking holdup! Lie face down on the floor!"

As they hurried to obey, he screamed, "Faster or I'll shoot you!", firing a shot which narrowly missed a terrified customer diving for the floor.

Staff and customers could hear the robbers rifling the tills and the safe. When one of the customers lifted her head slightly, the leader of the robbers screamed he was going to shoot her. He was talked out of it by his two co-offenders, who said, "We've got the money. Let's get the hell out of here."

Reluctantly he agreed, yelling a warning to customers and staff that anybody who came to the door would be shot. The robbers left as quickly as they had arrived, leaving staff and customers numb with shock. They did not know that they had witnessed the first of many hold-ups and serious crimes to be carried out by Christopher John Lewis, who would become New Zealand's, if not Australasia's, worst criminal.

His first armed hold-up had been carried out with military precision. One could have been forgiven for thinking that this was the work of three professional criminals. In fact, the robbery was committed by three 17-year-old youths during the mid-morning recess at the nearby high school two of them attended.

During that twenty-minute recess, they, along with Lewis, had biked from the school grounds to an old garage where they had previously hidden firearms and paramilitary uniforms, the proceeds of earlier gunshop burglaries.

After donning the uniforms and arming themselves, they cycled around the corner to the post office and carried out the armed robbery.

After the robbery, they returned to the garage where they changed out of the paramilitary uniforms. They then hid the uniforms, firearms and cash from the robbery in the ceiling of the garage.

The three youths then cycled back to school stopping en route to assist police push their patrol car, which had run off the road racing to the robbery scene, back onto the road.

On returning to the classroom, two of the youths sat an examination. They passed that examination with marks that put them among the top five students in the class.

Christopher John Lewis, the undisputed leader of the gang, was not happy. He had timed the robbery and escape with a stop watch. He was most concerned that the operation had gone two minutes over his estimated time schedule.

He relented somewhat when his co-offenders pointed out that the time taken to assist the police would have accounted for the additional two minutes.

This was the same Christopher John Lewis who later became the subject of a political and police cover-up after he attempted to assassinate the Queen during the 1981 Royal Tour of New Zealand.

In order to protect their reputation, and that of the government of the day, the New Zealand police embarked on a campaign to deliberately play the incident down.

The fact that their lack of security and planning almost cost the monarch her life was reason enough to organise a cover-up. The reasons given to those directly involved was that if it came out that security was as slack as it had been all future royal tours of New Zealand would be in jeopardy and the New Zealand police would be ridiculed. To quote the words used: "Fleet Street will have a ball."

A deal was struck with Christopher Lewis and from that day on he had to be kept away from the media at all costs.

Despite the fact that he was regularly committing serious crimes such as armed robbery, the press and public were kept in the dark about Lewis's propensity for crime and violence – this despite evidence and his own admission that he had planned and attempted murders in the past.

In 1996, when CHOGM (the Commonwealth Heads of Government Meeting) was held in New Zealand, Lewis was given a paid holiday courtesy of the police. The fact that he was allegedly involved in bank robberies and had, in fact, been named as a suspect was obviously not a consideration.

In November 1996, on a talkback programme, during which the author was a guest speaker, one of Lewis's intended murder victims warned the police that unless they stopped misleading the public about this man, and acknowledged he was a menace to society and put him away, someone would lose their life.

Some nine months later his warning turned out to be tragically prophetic when the battered body of expatriate Australian Tania Furlan was found in her Howick home. Her eight-week-old baby had been abducted after her mother had been murdered and was later found abandoned and unharmed in a churchyard in another Auckland suburb.

Three months later the offender was arrested but in another

bizarre turn of events his name was suppressed for some weeks. When that suppression was finally lifted by Justice Robertson in the Auckland High Court, it was revealed that Christopher John Lewis had been charged with the murder of Tania Furlan and the abduction of her baby.

A number of people believe Lewis could well be classified as the New Zealand equivalent of Australia's Ned Kelly. In fact his crimes, arsons, armed robberies, abduction, murders and attempted murders make Kelly seem almost angelic.

One may well ask why any law enforcement body would adopt such an accommodating attitude to arguably the most dangerous man in Australasia.

To find the answers we have to retrace our steps to Dunedin. And as we retrace our steps it should be kept in mind that of the many crimes Lewis has committed the public will be aware of only those he has been charged with. He learned early in his criminal career that co-offenders talk and if he did the big jobs alone the chances of being caught would be considerably reduced. Lewis only ever acknowledged to interviewing police what he knew they knew. Nothing more unless there was a deal. How many unsolved murders Lewis committed in New Zealand is impossible to know because he had no particular modus operandi. In other words, his criminal offending did not follow a pattern for although he planned meticulously he still remained completely unpredictable.

Food for thought as we trace part of the remarkable criminal career of this man.

In October 1981, I was the officer in charge of the CIS (Criminal Intelligence Section) in Dunedin. The main duties of this section were to organise and run covert operations such as undercover police, surveillance squads, close liaison with the SIS (Security Intelligence Service), and collating all information coming into the section and the dispersal of it to the appropriate squads.

During my time there I also carried out a number of internal inquiries. These related to allegations of serious misconduct by police or civilian staff.

On Friday, 10 October, I was told of an armed robbery at a small suburban post office. The initial reports indicated that three armed men, dressed in paramilitary uniforms, had burst into the post office terrorising the two female tellers and customers before escaping with $10,000 in cash. It was also reported that a shot had been fired which had narrowly missed two young women who were held hostage for a time.

The offenders had not been seen arriving or leaving the post office by passersby and had disappeared without trace so we had to interview the officers who had attended the crime scene in order to assess the way the robbery had been carried out and thereby compile a suspect list for the inquiry team.

We also had to have our surveillance squad ready to move into position should observations be required on any suspects identified.

The main object in a major operation or inquiry is to keep calm and to follow the guidelines learnt at detective training courses. Unfortunately, the head of the Dunedin CIB at that time was an officer who had no formal CIB training whatsoever. He had not even attended a CIB course let alone carried out the probationary two and a half years on-the-job training required of all aspiring detectives before attending the detectives qualifying course.

This man was not known for being a lateral thinker. He would go off on tangents and listen to very junior officers who would try to impress him by giving him names off the top of their heads as suspects. He should have told them to refer all suspects to the CIS where the information could be collated. Instead he became obsessed with the theory that the offenders' sawn-off shotguns and paramilitary gear meant they were members of either the local Maori gang or motorcycle gang. Valuable time was lost in the early days of the inquiry as staff, acting under his direct orders, raided Maori and bikie gang headquarters.

As a result of these raids, evidence of other crimes was found and this resulted in staff being sidetracked from the major inquiry to process prisoners for lesser charges such as burglary, theft and drugs.

Unfortunately, our 'leader' did not remember that one must always keep an open mind during a major investigation. It is counter-productive to get locked into one line of inquiry or one suspect or group of suspects. The incoming evidence has to be constantly examined and read carefully. Suspects have to be eliminated, which means their alibis have to be painstakingly checked by interviewing witnesses who could possibly verify their story, and material evidence has to be tested.

If a serious crime is not solved in the first 24 hours or if you do not have at least some promising leads then the hard slog of suspect elimination can take months, even years.

Fortunately, our leader lost interest in the robbery after giving the initial press conferences and with the royal entourage about to arrive in Dunedin for the 1981 tour his attention was diverted.

I also had to switch my attention to the royal tour as the CIS had a big role to play in advising the Operational Commander and the Commissioner of Police of real and potential extremists, dissidents and radicals.

On 14 October 1981, my squad and I were in close proximity to the royal party and their bodyguards. We had a 'meet the people' walk scheduled for around 11 a.m. in the Octagon.

During this, I was walking with one of my staff about four metres behind the Queen and Duke while ahead were the normal dignitaries, parliamentarians, local mayor, the Commissioner of Police and the royal bodyguards. It was a sunny day and the crowd were in good spirits, as were the royals.

The royal party then attended a civic luncheon before going to the Museum Reserve on the Otago University campus for another walk-about.

Our intelligence had warned us that a group of local IRA supporters were intending to demonstrate. I knew some of these people and I did not consider them a serious threat.

They did, however, surprise. As the royal couple walked through the reserve, the Queen shook hands and spoke with well-wishers while the Duke went in the opposite direction.

Whenever this occurs it does create problems for security but we split our forces and I ended up close behind the Duke. I saw an attractive girl in a rather revealing dress pushing forward against the rope barrier trying to shake the Duke's hand. He was keen to oblige, however, and as he shook her hand a miniature coffin was thrust into his arms.

One of his bodyguards grabbed the coffin, gave it to me and pushed the Duke away obviously fearing that it could be an explosive device. I vividly remember the shocked and confused look on his face.

We quickly removed the small coffin which had on it the name of an IRA loyalist who had apparently starved himself to death in H Block in an Irish prison.

Perhaps because of that diversion I did not hear anything that sounded like a gunshot although later that afternoon two other detectives mentioned to me that they had heard a gunshot.

At that time I thought they were probably just imagining it as earlier in the day we had had a security scare when a person in a southern suburb which was on the Queen's route was apprehended for firing at birds with a .22 rifle. This incident had caused some panic and everyone was edgy as a result.

After the royal visit it was back to the Andersons Bay Post Office robbery. Our esteemed leader decided to cut back the inquiry team. He asked me if I would take charge of the suspects squad. I argued with him that as the officer in charge of the CIS I should not be used on operational matters.

He persisted, stating that because I had been overseeing the elimination of suspects through the CIS office I knew the file better than any of the other NCOs (detective sergeants and sergeants). He assured me I would not have to interview the suspects or carry the arrest file, thereby ensuring I would not have to give evidence in any court proceedings.

Somewhat reluctantly I agreed, even though it was contrary to CIS guidelines. Of course, I was still expected to run the CIS office and now I was being given additional duties.

The person assigned to take over the file and prepare it for court was a detective senior sergeant who was known as 'tired old John'. Even our leader had no faith in him whatsoever when it came to solving a serious crime.

My first job was to reread the file. After I became fully acquainted with the inquiry once again, I sat down to formulate a plan of attack.

I remembered the advice of my old mentor, Jim Marshall: "If you are drawing a blank with your inquiry after a couple of weeks, go back to the source." As we had little else to go on, it seemed like a good idea.

I had been allocated two junior detectives, Tony Harrod and Murray Galland. Harrod had worked under my supervision on the Break (burglary) squad when he was a trainee detective and I knew he was a dedicated police officer. Galland was the junior of the two and although I had not worked with him I had heard good reports about him.

So this was my 'suspects' squad.

When we discussed the robbery, I found both detectives receptive to the idea of going back to the scene to see whether such things as area inquiries and the interview of witnesses had been done satisfactorily.

Success came more quickly than expected. The next day we carried out area inquiries, a painstaking task involving going to neighbouring properties to ask owners whether they had seen anything suspicious before, during or after the robbery.

As Harrod drove through Andersons Bay, he noticed a youth wearing an army flak jacket similar to those described by witnesses to the robbery. The youth gave his name as Paul — and he acknowledged that he lived nearby and attended the local high school, Bayfield High School. He told Harrod that his father was a Samoan preacher.

As they talked, the detective noticed that Paul was perspiring freely and he was shaking so he decided to take Paul back to the CIB office for further questioning.

After putting Paul in an interview room, Harrod came to my office and told me about his suspicions. When I accompanied him back to the interview room and was introduced to Paul I noticed he avoided eye contact. He sat with his head lowered, staring at the floor.

He was reasonably composed as we went through a few basic questions such as his address and class at school but as soon as I began to question him about his whereabouts on the morning of 10 October he became agitated. He said, indicating Harrod, "I have told him that I was at school." He then shouted, "and I can prove that."

I grabbed him by the shoulders and said, "But can you prove to me you were at school all day, Paul?"

He yelled back, "Yes."

At this point I yelled back at him, "But, Paul, you will have to prove to me and Mr Harrod that you never left the school grounds because we both believe you were one of the three who robbed the Andersons Bay Post Office that morning."

I pushed his head back so that he had to look at me and I could see the fear and guilt in his eyes. Although he continued to deny his involvement I knew we had one of the robbers.

After another fifteen minutes of questioning, Paul broke down and admitted he had been one of the three. A short time later he named Christopher John Lewis and Geoff — as his co-offenders.

I got their addresses from him and after a briefing I sent Detective Galland to get Geoff. Detective Harrod, who had been present during most of my interview with Paul, was sent to Lewis's address.

By now it was late afternoon so I decided to take Paul to his home so I could have a search carried out for material evidence linking him and the others to the robbery. He had already told me his share of the money was hidden in bush at the rear of his parents' property.

Paul was the eldest in a family of six children and his parents were decent, law-abiding people. Both were deeply religious and were shocked when they learned of his involvement in the robbery. As a parent, I felt for them.

We searched the bush for the money from the robbery but with darkness descending we couldn't find it. It was found the next day.

I asked Paul's father to accompany us back to the CIB where Paul was to be interviewed at length. At the CIB office I decided to interview him myself because I had established a rapport with him and to brief another detective would take up valuable time.

I was aware of the importance of having a full confession from him before the interviews of Lewis and Geoff had progressed too far. It would give us a base from which to question them.

The tale Paul told me absolutely amazed me.

At that time I had been a police officer for some fifteen years and a detective for over twelve years but I had never heard anything to compare with Paul's confession.

He began by acknowledging that Lewis was the leader of the group and he in turn received his orders from a person known to him only as the 'Snowman'. He stated that the group commanded by Lewis (and above him the Snowman) was known as NIGA, the National Imperial Guerrilla Army.

That explained the information that had been coming into the CIS office regarding burglaries of gun shops, other burglaries and arsons where the initials NIGA had been scratched on doors or other parts of the premises. We had been, unsuccessfully, attempting to identify what this insignia stood for.

Paul went on to say how Christopher Lewis and the Snowman had masterminded the burglaries and arson. Lewis would submit his plan to the Snowman for approval. It was at this point Paul declined to say any more. He expressed a deep fear of Lewis but he seemed even more fearful of the Snowman.

I managed to reassure him that he would have police protection and he then told me how after he, Geoff and Lewis had committed the burglary of the Centrepoint gun shop they had gone to Tomahawk Beach, a rather desolate place on the Otago coast to test fire one of the stolen rifles.

They all took turns firing at seagulls and then the three of them sat in the sandhills. While sitting there out of sight, a man and a boy walked past with their dog. Paul told me Lewis decided then and there to kill both of them. He and Geoff urged him not to but Lewis decided he wanted to shoot them and fired off two or three shots.

The shots missed and the man and boy both stopped in their tracks obviously having heard the shots. They stood looking around for a few seconds before walking on, not realising that they had been fired at.

Lewis was still keen to stalk the two from the sandhills and shoot them from closer range but Paul said he and Geoff managed to talk him out of it. When asked the range, he estimated 150-200 metres.

It was at this point Paul mentioned something about Lewis attempting to shoot the Queen during the recent royal visit. He told me that Lewis was always on about his hatred of the monarchy.

Paul said Lewis had gone to the Octagon to shoot her during her lunchtime 'walkabout'. As he was removing his rifle from his bag, two uniformed policemen left their post in the lower Octagon to get a better view of the royals. They walked towards the Mission building where Lewis was preparing to shoot from. This forced him to put his rifle back in his bag. They then positioned themselves only ten metres from his position. Lewis was forced to abandon this attempt. He was extremely annoyed because he would have had an unimpaired 20-25 metre clear shot at the Queen. Lewis told them that had it not been for the policemen's change of position he would have killed her.

It was Paul's next statement that fully alerted me to the fact that we were onto something big. He said, "Chris was so annoyed he got on his bike and cycled to Geoff's father's office, which was close to the museum where he hoped to get a shot at the Queen." I remembered, of course, the reports of a shot during the walkabout at the museum.

I asked Paul whether Lewis managed to get a shot at the Queen. He replied, "He said he did." He went on to say that Chris told him he went up to a storeroom toilet near Geoff's father's office in the Adams building overlooking the Museum Reserve and fired a shot at the Queen from the window, which missed.

I went to a nearby interview room to speak to Detective Galland who was interviewing Geoff. He, too, was making progress. I told him of Paul's allegation regarding Lewis's attempt on the Queen. He agreed to switch his interview to that subject.

About half an hour later, Galland came back to me to say Geoff was telling a similar tale and had also confirmed the shooting incident at Tomahawk Beach. Galland said that Geoff expressed concern that by talking about this he was signing his own death warrant. He too spoke of the Snowman, the person who gave Chris Lewis his orders, as being the person who would kill him for talking.

By this time Detective Harrod had returned to the office with Christopher Lewis. I went to the interview room where Harrod was speaking with him.

Without a doubt, Harrod had the most difficult assignment as Lewis was cocky and self-assured in denying any involvement at all in the robbery, burglaries, arson and other crimes. Harrod was at that stage unaware of the admissions regarding the attempt on the Queen's life and the attempted murder at Tomahawk Beach.

I left another detective to guard Lewis and I brought Harrod up to date with developments. I then went and spoke with Lewis who was still very cocky.

I told him Detective Harrod would be returning to carry on talking to him and I suggested to him he should co-operate, pointing out that when the detective returned he, Lewis, being an intelligent sort of bloke, would work out from the type of questions being put to him that the game was up.

I also told him we would be searching his home as we had reason to believe vital evidence was there. This seemed to shake him and his confidence was less noticeable as we briefly discussed what we would be searching for.

Detective Harrod then returned to take over the interview. I returned to my office to take a signed statement from Paul concentrating initially on the burglaries, the arson and the robbery. I covered the Tomahawk Beach incident and the shooting at the Queen at the end.

I was very mindful of the fact that Paul had been interviewed for some seven hours and even although his father had been present for much of it the time factor of the interview could affect the statement's admissibility in any judicial hearing.

During the time I was taking the written statement from Paul, I regularly left my office to check on and speak with Harrod and Galland. Harrod was making progress with Lewis and Galland was taking a written statement from Geoff, whose parents had also arrived at the CIB office.

During one of my visits to Harrod, I heard Lewis bragging about how he had invented the Snowman to keep Paul and Geoff in line. He told how he pretended he received orders from the Snowman and painted a picture of a very violent man who would not hesitate to kill if orders were not obeyed or they talked.

It was at this point I decided Lewis's home should be searched in order to confront him with real evidence – proceeds from the burglaries and robbery.

He accompanied us to an address in Forth Street near the Dunedin Teachers' College where he was flatting with university students. It was unusual to hear of a schoolboy flatting and he was asked why he didn't live at home. He replied in a matter of fact way that it wasn't practical because he hated his step-father and had tried to kill him. It was later confirmed that he had tried to take his step-father's life.

Lewis's flatmate was an Indian medical student who knew nothing of his criminal activities. We recovered a cache of firearms that had been buried in the garden along with the proceeds of the robbery and other burglaries.

While at this flat, an incident occurred which gave an insight into the mental make-up of Chris Lewis. He had, in his room, two pet white mice. They were in an unusual type of metal cage, shaped like a wheel which the mice attempt to climb. He was displaying his coolness by playing with the mice while detectives carried out the search of buildings and garden. A detective searching the room was asked by Lewis if he thought he would be going away for a long 'stretch'. When the detective replied that was likely, Lewis said, "Well, I won't be needing these any more." Before he could be stopped, he pulled the heads off the two mice.

I later spoke to the detective concerned who told me he had been sickened by what he had witnessed.

Lewis also commented during the search of his flat and gardens that he would have liked to see how good the police really were if he had been ready for them when they had arrived. He indicated the cache of firearms and said, "I reckon I would have taken a few of you out."

It was at Lewis's flat that his diary was found. In it were notations regarding how he intended to kill the Queen. A map of the Octagon clearly indicated his intended position for the assassination, the Mission building. He had drawn a dotted line indicating his line of fire and her position on the roadway at the time he intended to shoot her. It was quite obvious that had his original plan not been thwarted by the arrival of the two police officers, the Queen would have been killed or seriously injured.

The interviews of Paul, Lewis and Geoff were completed at around 2 a.m. the next morning. I charged them jointly with the robbery of the Andersons Bay Post Office and they were advised that the other charges would be laid at a later date. All three were then lodged in the police cells.

By the time the file had been prepared and checked it was 3 a.m. I arrived home some time after 4 a.m.

At 7 a.m. I was woken to take an urgent phone call from our leader, the head of the Dunedin CIB. He was in a state of panic. He told me he had to ring the Crown Solicitor and the Commissioner of Police in Wellington and he needed me to be present during the telephone calls.

After having had a hectic fortnight averaging 16 hours' work a day and having just put in a 20-hour day with just three hours' sleep, I was not really functioning too well. A cold shower and breakfast seemed to bring me right, however, and I arrived at the CIB office at 7.50 a.m.

I noticed our leader seemed rather agitated but I briefed him and stayed in the office while he telephoned the Crown Solicitor, Dennis Wood, and the Commissioner's office. He seemed to concentrate mainly on the robbery and glossed over the attempt on the Queen by saying more inquiries were necessary before we would be in a position to say exactly what had happened.

After completing the phone calls, he leaned back and said to me, "This could be treason we are looking at here." I told him that in my opinion we already had enough to be looking at attempted treason.

He asked me to go to the Crown Solicitor's office and brief him personally. Before I left, I gave Harrod and Galland some inquiries to complete and I also instructed them to get Lewis from the cells and take him back to the scene. They were to do a reconstruction with Lewis to check whether his statement of the previous evening lined up.

I gave the Crown Solicitor a quick briefing and returned to the CIS office to complete outstanding paper work. I had been due to go on leave for two weeks that day but I had warned my wife that would have to be cancelled.

It was particularly galling because I was to compete in the Winstone Marathon in Southland. We were also intending to go to Wanaka to finalise buying a holiday home. Our leader had advised me that my leave was cancelled but he did agree to give me the weekend off to compete in the marathon.

Around 2 p.m. that afternoon, our leader came into my office and said, "You can take your leave now. I have decided you have had a tough couple of weeks so I'll get John Kelly to take over the attempt on the Queen." This offer made me suspicious because he usually cared little for the welfare of staff.

Kelly, an immature man, was extremely ambitious and was the leader's right-hand man, despite the fact that when he got drunk and was around women he had been known to indecently assault them. He had been returned to the uniform branch in Wellington as punishment for an indecent assault on a policewoman.

His wife was a policewoman and his young son of five was usually dressed up in a police cap or helmet. Although he would always introduce himself, no matter where, as 'Kelly of the Police', his nickname among junior staff was 'Chookfeeder' because he specialised in writing detailed reports on anything and everything.

He was without doubt very good on paper and this was the reason our leader had brought him to Dunedin. Lacking a CIB training, he realised his limitations were Kelly's strengths and he used him to prepare complex orders and detailed reports.

Kelly had been present when we brought Paul, Lewis and Geoff in the previous day and although he had not been involved he was aware of what had gone on.

Initially I believed that Kelly wanted to grab some glory as it was obvious the case would receive maximum publicity once the attempt on the Queen's life became public. In the light of later events, I now believe that Kelly and our leader may have had other reasons.

Later that day I went to court and heard Paul, Lewis and Geoff remanded while inquiries were being carried out in relation to other charges. Lewis had been remanded in custody to the men's prison above the Dunedin Central Police Station

It was early November 1981 before I returned from leave. I had arranged to begin training a new surveillance squad before going on leave and I started on that immediately. Because of the covert nature of surveillance work, squad members were kept away from police stations for obvious reasons.

I had had a long association with the Dunedin Rugby Football Club both as a player and coach. In 1981, I coached their Colts team. The clubrooms were out at Middle Beach, between St Kilda and St Clair beaches on a private road. It was a perfect place to hold the training lectures and I had arranged the hire before going on leave.

John Kelly was also one of the lecturers and he joined me on a lunchtime jog along the beach and over the nearby Chisholm Park golf links. During our jog, I mentioned the file on Lewis's attempt on the Queen, and I asked him how it was progressing.

He was rather noncommittal and made a deliberate attempt to steer the conversation onto another topic. I was not going to be put off so I asked him when I could expect the file back as I wanted to read it fully before laying the additional charges. Once again he was evasive, so I told him that time was running out and I required the file back immediately in order to complete it for prosecution.

After lunch our leader unexpectedly arrived at the Dunedin Rugby Football Club. Initially he pretended to be there solely to see how the training programme was progressing but after I had finished my lecture he came over to me and said, "Grab a cuppa and come outside."

I accompanied him out onto the steps and he said, "You have got too much on your plate. I don't think it's fair to saddle you with the Andersons Bay file so I'll give it to someone else to finish."

I replied, "Like young Kelly, eh?"

I was now convinced that Kelly must have phoned him after we had returned from our jog reporting that I had asked for the file back.

Our leader was quick to point out that as the officer in charge of CIS I should not be carrying files anyway. He never ceased to amaze me – here was a man who had his own set of rules.

I finished by saying, "Young John must think there is going to be some glory in it to be hanging onto the file so grimly. However you're right. I have other things I can be doing rather than being bogged down with court files."

The leader was obviously relieved, something that even then I thought was rather strange.

That Friday, the surveillance course finished and I went into the police station for the first time since returning from leave.

After work I went to the police bar for a drink and I ran into Detective Harrod. After exchanging pleasantries he asked if he and Galland could speak to me as they were disturbed about the Andersons Bay inquiry.

I went out into the corridor with them and Harrod advised me that Chris Lewis had been re-interviewed and some sort of deal had been struck with him. As a result of that deal, the attempt on the Queen was to be played down. Both of them told me they did not really know what was going on as they were being kept in the dark but they thought a deal might have been done to get a guilty plea on all the other charges.

I told them that was ridiculous as one did not plea bargain with the most serious charge. Harrod then said, "Well, you won't believe this but they are only charging him with discharging a firearm in a dangerous manner."

Both were annoyed and disillusioned. I assured them I would find out what was going on.

As our leader was present in the police bar, I took him aside and said, "I've got two rather upset detectives. They seem to think Lewis is being charged with a minor offence in relation to shooting at the Queen and they are bewildered and concerned."

He grabbed my arm and said, "Let's go up to my office, get yourself a drink." When we reached his office he told me he had meant to tell me the full story but he was waiting until the surveillance course was over and I returned to my office.

He said, "This has come right from the top. It's an executive decision and I don't mean the Commissioner. This is a political decision and you and I are just pawns in the game."

He then talked about how royal tours were an important tradition in New Zealand and we would be in danger of losing future tours if it got out that our police security was so lax we didn't even hear the shot and we even ignored reports that a shot had been fired.

For some strange reason he lowered his voice and said, "We had no one on the roof tops. Not that it was our fault – our briefing papers had been okayed by headquarters, but the New Zealand police will be the laughing stock of the world if the Fleet Street mob get hold of this. The kid wouldn't have got the death penalty anyway because he's only a 16 or 17-year-old."

He then told me Kelly had taken another statement from Lewis along the lines of Lewis going to the Adams building and after looking out the window and seeing he didn't have the range with the .22 he fired a shot at the floor in frustration.

I told him that overlooked the fact that he had drawn a detailed assassination plan for an earlier attempt and had been about to carry that out when interrupted by two uniform police. I added that I did not believe anybody would be so naive to accept that after going to all that trouble to kill her he didn't try and merely fired a shot at the floor.

Our leader said, "All I'm asking you to do is keep your mouth shut and the mouths of those two detectives. I will take care of any murmurings among the rest of the staff. We all have to cover our arses."

I told him that I would have nothing more to do with the file and left his office.

People have asked me why I went along with it. I certainly anguished over that cover-up and it never left me. In 1984, when I spoke out over another matter, this cover-up was also in my mind.

When the three offenders, Paul, Lewis and Geoff, appeared in the Dunedin High Court for sentencing in February 1982, most of the blame for the robbery and other crimes was heaped onto Lewis.

The shooting at the Queen was mentioned virtually as an afterthought, as discharging a firearm which could endanger carried only a three-month sentence. In relation to that charge the summary read out was far removed from the events as outlined by Lewis on the night of his arrest.

I was, by this time, aware that Kelly had apparently taken a second statement from Lewis and the first one had been destroyed. That second statement was designed to fit the reduced charge and the summary of facts read to the court.

Counsel for Paul and Geoff described Lewis's evil influence over their clients. They described how they feared Lewis and the fictitious Snowman to such a degree they would have done anything he instructed them to. I agreed with their summation that Lewis was clearly the ringleader and he deserved to be treated as such.

His lawyer, J. (Murray) Hanan had an impossible task attempting to keep Lewis from a custodial sentence. He certainly tried hard but Lewis was sentenced to borstal training. Paul and Geoff, quite rightly, received far lesser sentences.

Counsel appearing for Paul and Geoff respectively both expressed their concerns to Detective Harrod about Lewis 'eyeballing' them during court appearances. Not only was he apparently giving them the evil eye but he also made gestures.

Lewis did it the hard way. While an inmate of the Invercargill borstal (youth prison), he was continually in strife.

To the best of my knowledge, Paul and Geoff have never re-offended and have proved model citizens since the incident.

In 1982, I was in Invercargill on another police matter when I was called to the Invercargill police station where I was told Lewis had escaped. The local police requested I compile an intelligence report on Lewis for distribution as I knew his modus operandi.

Before I had completed the report I was told he had been recaptured. His bid for freedom was short-lived.

Later that same day I spoke to a senior warden from the borstal. He described Lewis as the worst criminal he had met and he told of how Lewis had caused a complete rift between the white and coloured prisoners in the borstal.

The warden was particularly upset over threats Lewis was making to staff at the borstal. He told me Lewis would approach a warden who had disciplined him and he would ask about his wife and children, taking great pleasure in letting the warden know that he knew personal details about his family. On some occasions it was veiled threats but on others he had actually threatened to kill them, their wives or families.

The borstal authorities later gave up on Lewis and he was transferred to the Lake Alice Security Mental Institution to serve out the remainder of his sentence. This was an establishment known to break the toughest of criminals.

It was some eighteen months later that Lewis came to our notice again. I was still in charge of the Criminal Intelligence Section and we were required to update dossiers on radicals, anti-monarchists and extremists before the visit to New Zealand by Prince Charles and Princess Diana.

Although we knew Lewis was still in Lake Alice, I responded to a request from CIS headquarters in Wellington for an update on his dossier with particular emphasis on his behavioural patterns and activities in there and how effective the security would be at the time of the royal visit. They also required updates on the dossiers of Paul and Geoff.

I visited Paul at Burnside, south of Dunedin. He was very nervous, particularly when Lewis's name was mentioned. He said, "I honestly fear for my life should he ever be released."

Paul's employers spoke highly of him, and they regarded him as completely reformed. He was heavily involved in his work and study and I reported that although we would continue to monitor him, Paul did not represent a threat to the royal couple.

I spoke with Geoff at Unicol, a university hostel adjacent to the University of Otago. He was arrogant in the way law students tend to be and initially adopted a "nothing to say to the police" attitude but when I reminded him that he might need us when Lewis was released he was immediately co-operative.

When I went with him to his room I was shocked to find a firearm against the wall. When questioned about it, Geoff produced a recently issued arms permit. He had walked into the Dunedin Arms Office, applied for a permit and despite the fact he had a recent conviction for armed robbery had been given a permit for a firearm!

That apart, after questioning him and making inquiries I was able to report that Geoff also appeared to have reformed and would not pose a threat to the royal party. He was achieving good results in his examinations and the master at Unicol spoke highly of him.

Geoff was also fearful of Lewis. He told me both he and his lawyer feared retribution when Lewis was finally freed. Geoff stated that Lewis had given his lawyer and him the evil eye treatment when Geoff's lawyer was blaming Lewis during his plea of mitigation for his client.

I was aware that Lewis had unnerved lawyer Russell Duell and I had no doubt that he might try to exact some sort of revenge against either Geoff or his lawyer.

I had already arranged for the Wanganui CIB to make inquiries about Lewis at the nearby Lake Alice institution. They reported that he was heavily sedated but was still considered extremely dangerous. As requested, they had obtained for me the name and contact number of the doctor treating Lewis.

Our leader had requested being present while I spoke to the doctor and when we met the doctor advised me that Lewis had already come before the parole board but that just before his appearance his behaviour had improved markedly.

When he was not granted parole, he again became a serious problem at the institution. The doctor described Lewis as an extremely dangerous and cunning criminal, especially for one so young.

He believed that Lewis should never be released, but he acknowledged that he was not on the parole board and eventually Lewis would be paroled.

I later interviewed Lewis's mother, Louise, a fine lady who had tried to help her son through all his troubles. She knew his behavioural traits better than anyone and I wanted to hear from her how she thought he would act when released.

She was co-operative as usual and as a result of inquiries carried out I was able to complete a very full and comprehensive dossier on Lewis. The finished article was sent to CIS headquarters in Wellington and to all CIS offices throughout the country. The SIS (Security Intelligence Service) was also forwarded a copy as Lewis was by now considered a terrorist.

Lewis made his move about two weeks before the visit of the Prince and Princess of Wales. I was telephoned by the Wanganui CIB outlining how Lewis had just attempted to escape from Lake Alice. He had manufactured a knife, overpowered a male nurse and taken him hostage. With the knife at the throat of the nurse, he had attempted to escape but another nurse managed to overpower him from behind.

A search of his cell revealed a written plan outlining how he intended to steal a motorcycle (which he had been keeping his eye on for some time) and travel to Wellington. He planned to stowaway on the interisland ferry and once in the South Island he intended to steal a car and travel to Dunedin. What was especially significant was his intention to arrive in that city the day before the royals.

It was clear from his plan that he intended to lie low for the first ten days after his escape and to make his move to Dunedin only after the search for him had died down.

Also found in his cell was a book he was writing similar to Mein Kampf (the book written by Adolf Hitler when in prison in 1923). Lewis wrote that he planned to assassinate the then Prime Minister, Robert Muldoon. He also wrote of New Zealand becoming a pure Aryan race, with all coloureds, Maoris, Islanders, Chinese and so on deported to the Chatham Islands.

Lewis acknowledged in his writings that his plan for New Zealand to be populated by pure people of European descent might prove difficult to implement. He wrote, "The alternative is to declare the South Island independent and banish all the blacks and coloureds to the North Island." He intended to be President of the

South Island and his reformed NIGA army would be used to implement his ideal.

One thing I was pleased to learn was that he had been transferred to the maximum security wing from where escape was virtually impossible. I was also convinced that the medical people at Lake Alice, having read his latest notes and bearing in mind his escape attempt, would be even more convinced that he was mentally deranged and represented a real danger to the community.

I really did believe that Lewis would be kept in Lake Alice indefinitely but unfortunately I was wrong. Approximately eighteen months later, he was a free man.

In 1984, I was horrified to learn that Lewis might be paroled to Cherry Farm mental hospital, a minimum security hospital 40 kilometres north of Dunedin.

The head of the Dunedin CIB and I decided to make strong submissions on behalf of the police that he be kept at Lake Alice. I telephoned the doctor who had been treating Lewis and he confirmed Lewis was being considered for parole. I relayed to him the concerns of the police should Lewis be paroled to a minimum security mental hospital.

The doctor, however, told me that, since his escape attempt, Lewis had been a model patient/prisoner. On his last appearance before the parole board he had impressed the members with his account of how he had found God and hoped to leave his criminal past behind him and start afresh. The doctor said that he had not been fooled by this but other members of the parole board had.

He also made the point that Lewis was not a committed patient but a prisoner transferred there who had almost served his sentence and was eligible for parole. He could not be held there after his sentence had been completed and he could not be committed from within Lake Alice because he had done nothing during the past few months to indicate any mental instability. On the contrary, he had appeared to be in full control of his faculties.

That being the case, his transfer to Cherry Farm was a formality according to the doctor.

I immediately instructed Detective Harrod to contact Dr Faed to make her aware of our concerns and to brief her on Lewis's criminal history.

Harrod had an excellent rapport with Dr Faed and I felt that after reading Lewis's dossier the doctor would have a better appreciation of our concerns.

Harrod reported back that Dr Faed had appreciated our information but had indicated she preferred not to pre-judge her patients and would make her own assessment.

It was soon apparent that Dr Faed had been conned by Lewis. Within weeks he was walking around Dunedin on day release without an escort.

When spoken to, he was more than co-operative and it was obvious he did not intend to blot his copybook.

A short time later, Dr Faed released Lewis. He returned to crime almost immediately and when I retired from the police in 1986 he was back in prison on burglary charges.

10

Lewis on the Run and on Holiday

I next heard of Christopher Lewis in May 1987. By that time I had moved to Australia and I was living in Perth. On Friday 9 May, I returned home for lunch to find a telegram from a journalist acquaintance, Fred Tullet, of the *Dominion* in Wellington. The message read, "Please call me urgently collect at Wellington 727 893, Fred Tullett."

I telephoned Tullet and he told me that an old friend of mine, Christopher John Lewis, was on the run from the police on the West Coast. He outlined how Lewis had committed a series of bank robberies in Christchurch and had been identified. After escaping to the West Coast, he had been recognised and in the ensuing chase he had crashed a stolen car in a remote part of the Buller Gorge and had 'gone bush'.

Tullet said that he and some other journalists were already aware that Lewis was an extremely dangerous criminal, yet whenever they approached the police they attempted to play that fact down. The catch-cry was, "What's all the fuss about? He's just another bank robber."

Tullet said he had heard about the attempt on the Queen's life and he was sure that had something to do with the strange attitude of the police. However, his main concern was that the police attitude meant the public were being endangered, particularly as he was on the run in an area where many people lived on isolated farms.

He told me that if Lewis was, in fact, as dangerous as the

rumours suggested he would need my help to let the public know the rumours about him were true.

I told Tullett that I had dealt with Lewis from the time he first came to the notice of the police. I explained in detail how he had masterminded the robbery of the Andersons Bay Post Office. I also gave him details about the other criminal offences he had been charged with, such as burglaries and arson.

Tullet then asked about the rumours concerning the attempt on the Queen's life. I told him the story Lewis had related to Detective Harrod and also what he had told me in conversations. Tullett immediately asked why Lewis had not been charged with something more serious such as treason. I merely repeated to him the reason I had been given at the time. He did not ask me who had told me the decision was a political one.

I later spoke to a reporter from the same newspaper, Chris Bishop, whom Tullet had sent to the West Coast to cover the story. I went over with him the story I had told Tullet.

By this time I had spoken to a serving police officer in New Zealand who had advised me that the police were worried that if Lewis received too much publicity it would jog people's memories about the attempt on the Queen. It was the media they were particularly concerned about because they had experienced some difficulty selling the party line to them in 1981.

The man who had been in charge of the Dunedin CIB at that time had been transferred to Christchurch where the operation to capture Lewis was being run from.

Chris Bishop told me he would be writing a story for the *Sunday Times* issue of Sunday, 10 May 1987.

At 10 p.m. on that Sunday, I received the first of a number of telephone calls from English journalists wanting to know details of the assassination attempt. I did not know what had been printed in the *Sunday Times* so I merely referred them to Tullet and Bishop who, I told them, had all the facts.

Two journalists told me they had been accompanying the royal party for their respective papers and had heard the shot at the Museum Reserve. They said that when they later tried to report hearing the shot to police they were told that what they had heard was a car backfiring or a metal sign falling to the ground.

One of them told me he had been in Northern Ireland for some years and he was used to the whine of a bullet in residential or confined areas. He had been appalled at the lack of security, and not just at Dunedin, during the royal tour.

The next morning, Monday 11 May, I welcomed the first of three television crews. They arrived on my doorstep unannounced and asked for an interview. They were persistent and I was in a hurry so I told them I would do one interview and they could film it together. A number of radio stations had also sent reporters so they also sat in.

At lunchtime that day I spoke with three newspaper reporters. I merely repeated what I had told Tullett and Bishop but they were keen to hear more about the cover-up. Once again, I repeated what I had been told at the time.

On Tuesday 12 May, I was contacted by John Mort of the Willesee television programme. We met for a late breakfast at the Merlin Hotel and he asked me to do a live interview that afternoon and said that would also get the 'Pommy' press off my back as Willesee would give the interview to ITV in Britain.

Another reason Mike Willesee wanted an interview was because the New Zealand Prime Minister, David Lange, had said at a press conference that there had not been an attempt on the Queen's life. However, later that day, former Police Commissioner Bob Walton, who had been Commissioner at the time, insisted to the press that a shot had been fired at the Queen. Lange then retracted, adding that he would go back to the police who, he insisted, had given him the wrong advice.

Mike Willesee, a very astute journalist, smelled a rat and John Mort told me that they believed they were onto a major cover-up.

I did try to point out that Lange would not be part of it as he was not the Prime Minister at the time of the attempt. His mistake had been to believe what the police had told him.

I agreed to the interview and we went to *Channel Nine* studios in Perth and Mort telephoned Willesee in Sydney. He came back and told me that Willesee was unwell and that Jana Wendt would do the interview.

It became apparent to me early in the interview that Wendt was after something I could not give her. The Willesee programme had, the previous evening, interviewed the Queensland Minister of Police. They had put the state government and the minister under pressure over police cover-ups in that state and were obviously keen to do the same to the New Zealand government. She seemed hell-bent on proving that this was a cover-up involving David Lange.

Wendt was obviously disappointed that she could not elicit from me the controversial answers she so obviously wanted and as a result only part of the interview was shown.

I learned details of what had happened in New Zealand. Once again, National Police Headquarters, courtesy of Assistant Commissioner Stuart McEwen, had led with their chin and received a solid right cross for their trouble.

McEwen, who knew nothing of the incident, had decided he would be spokesman – a decision he later regretted as he received a rocket from the Prime Minister's office for the embarrassment he caused the Prime Minister by incorrectly briefing him.

Initially, McEwen publicly stated the whole affair was a nonsense and the Queen was never at risk. He said that all the facts had been given to the court at the time. Lange at his press conference the same day expressed a similar view.

Before day's end both were retracting. The Commissioner at the time, Bob Walton, had been interviewed and he acknowledged that Lewis (then 17 years old) had drawn up elaborate plans on how he was to assassinate the Queen.

After Walton had also confirmed that at least one shot had been fired as well, McEwen tried to extricate himself from the mire by stating that the events of 1981 were not within his personal knowledge. The papers (file) had been requested from Dunedin and should be in Wellington later that week.

Prime Minister Lange was then forced to call another press conference at which he stated, "My briefing on this matter came from the police as can be demonstrated by my statements, consistent with those of Mr McEwen. I have now been advised that further discussions took place this afternoon and there is some conflict between the advice received from the police and the recollections of former Police Commissioner Walton. Police Headquarters have now decided to go back to the basic file in Dunedin. They will issue their statement in due course."

Lange had obviously decided to distance himself from the police after the embarrassment of Walton's statement and the subsequent admission by McEwen that he really had no knowledge of the events.

Ex-Commissioner Walton was a man whose reputation for honesty and attention to detail was unquestioned. He had been head of the New Zealand Criminal Investigation Branch before becoming Commissioner and was one of New Zealand's highest ranking Army officers.

The police administration in Wellington, and particularly McEwen, must have been rocked by another article, headed **Lewis police plea**, in the *Christchurch Star* on 12 May 1987. It outlined how Allan Dick, news editor of Radio Avon in Christchurch, alleged that while news editor of Radio Otago in Dunedin in 1981 he had been approached by two senior police officers after his reporters had begun making inquiries about the alleged assassination attempt on the Queen.

He was summoned to a meeting in Detective Chief Inspector Laurie Dalziel's office where he was told that the police did not want this assassination business going too far. They later offered to do a deal with him giving him an exclusive story on a gold robbery.

Dick said, "I now regret complying as I did not get the information on the gold story either." He had also been present when Dalziel told a number of reporters that there was no substance to the allegation of an assassination attempt on the Queen.

On 12 May 1987, the *Otago Daily Times* also got into the act with Robin Charteris's account headlined:

Claim man tried to shoot Queen in Dunedin

Cover-up by police alleged

Charteris quoted the English papers the *Daily Express*, the *Daily Mail* and the *Daily Telegraph*. But then he stated, "However, the incident was not hushed up as the story in the *Otago Daily Times* of 19 October suggests (see above)."

There, we find a copy of an article from the *Otago Daily Times* of 29 October 1981 headlined:

Incident during royal visit to Dunedin

Gun investigation

Leaving aside the content of the article, the heading does not make sense. The police were not investigating a gun! The first few paragraphs state that the police were investigating a firearm incident in connection with the visit by the Queen and Duke of Edinburgh earlier this month.

The article goes on to mention a loud bang being heard by a number of people as the royal couple stepped from their car. It also mentions the then head of the Dunedin CIB, Detective Chief Inspector Dalziel, stating that the police initially believed the bang was caused by someone near the Medical School letting off crackers.

Dalziel, according to the article, went on to say, "As a result of inquiries, police are now investigating an incident involving a firearm in connection with the report . . . Detectives are quite satisfied that a shot was not fired at the Queen." He was, however, unable to say whether a shot was fired during the incident.

He declined to give details of the event but said detectives were continuing investigations.

The report stated that Mr Dalziel last night (28 October 1981) denied a Television New Zealand report that a youth was being held in custody in connection with the incident. He said, "No one is being held in custody in connection with the firearms offence and no charges have been laid."

It is now obvious Dalziel misled the *Otago Daily Times* by that denial. His job of misleading them was made all the easier by the blind acceptance of his statement by the reporter concerned.

Lewis was, of course, in custody and charges were being formulated in relation to the shot fired at the Queen even if they were not the correct charges. Dalziel, as the head of the Dunedin CIB, was a principal player in all of this and must have been fully aware of the details.

It would appear that the *Otago Daily Times* did not ever bother to inquire about the result of the police inquiries Dalziel alluded to.

Worse still, his comment "Detectives are quite satisfied that a shot was not fired at the Queen" was later shown to be untrue as was the statement that he was unable to say whether a shot was in fact fired during the incident. He was briefed fully by me on 23 October 1981. He contacted the Commissioner in my presence and relayed that information to him. Former Commissioner Walton's subsequent remarks confirmed this.

If Robin Charteris had carried out even basic research he, too, would have realised that the *Otago Daily Times* reporter who interviewed Dalziel on 28 October 1981 had been misled by him. He would have then been able to request, under the Official Information Act, police remand records for that date which would have shown Christopher Lewis was in custody at that time and the incident concerning the Queen was one of several he was being held in custody for.

Dalziel was also quoted as stating that no charges had been laid. Surely the obvious question was, "Will any charges be laid?"

It appears that the *Otago Daily Times*, its journalists and editorial staff, were content to accept whatever the police administration fed them. Former Queensland Premier Joh Bjelke-Petersen was famous for his comment before press conferences, "I'm going to feed the chooks."

The Fitzgerald inquiry in Queensland later illustrated how the media can and do assist corrupt administrations by not doing their job properly. Was this an example of media, namely the *Otago Daily Times*, failing the public?

The *Otago Daily Times* ran another article on Thursday, 14 May 1987.

This time the headline read:

Inquiry into royal tour shots after youth seized for robbery
Diary led to revelation of kill plot

The article began:

Inquiries made by the Otago Daily Times *show that police concluded Lewis could not see the Queen from the top floor toilet in the*

Medical School's Adams building about 183 metres from her motorcade.

He most certainly would not have been able to see the Queen if she was in the royal car in the motorcade.

However, in its 29 October 1981 article, the *Otago Daily Times* wrote that a loud bang was heard as the royal couple stepped out of their car.

Six years later, they seemed to be trying to say he was firing at the motorcade.

The truth is Lewis clearly stated on the night he was apprehended that he fired at the Queen while she was in the Museum Reserve. Reporters, with those from the *Otago Daily Times* excepted, also said they heard the shot as the Queen and Duke were going walkabout.

It has always been accepted that Lewis was not a fool. He would not have fired at a motorcade. Why risk exposure for nothing?

We later have the police alleging he fired at the ground in frustration and that he fired at the floor in the storeroom.

The *Otago Daily Times'* inquiries were also remiss regarding where he fired from. It was not the top floor.

The article then states, "Reporters covering the tour did not hear a noise although they were nearby." This is disinformation of the worst kind because without exception the British and Australian reporters who I spoke to heard the shot and were adamant it was a shot.

They reported the fact to the police who fed them a variety of stories from fire-crackers to metal signs falling. This was one of the reasons given to me for hushing up the matter as the British press would have had a field day after having reported a shot to the police and having that information disregarded and then later learning they were right. The New Zealand police obviously did not know the difference between the crack and whine of a bullet and crackers going off or a sign falling over.

Once again in this 14 May article we find inaccurate statements, the most glaring being that the diary found at Lewis's flat was the sole evidence of his intentions that day. His detailed plan of the line of fire at the Octagon is not rated worthy of a mention nor were the admissions made by Lewis to the police.

The police were not questioned at length. A few obvious questions such as:

1. Had the rifle been test fired? What was the condition of the rifle and sights? What ammunition was used?
2. What was the rifle's range?
3. What was its range if fired under the conditions of the day (i.e., from a second-floor window at a range of 183 metres)?
4. Was a search carried out for the bullet? If not, why not?
5. Did Lewis's actions that day fall within the ambit of "attempted treason" as was being alleged?

In the next paragraph, the *Otago Daily Times* refers to an inquiry team being formed to investigate the incident. This "team" consisted of Detective Senior Sergeant Kelly plus, as I later learnt, Detective Murray Lewis. None of the basic police tests referred to above were carried out.

Kelly had his own reasons for playing down the attempt on the Queen's life as did Dalziel.

In effect, the *Otago Daily Times* was asked by the police to accept that Christopher John Lewis, an acknowledged and calculating criminal, allegedly realised he could not hit the Queen so he fired a shot, or two, in frustration either at the ground outside or inside the storeroom. With numerous police as well as the crowds of onlookers, Lewis would have risked drawing attention to himself unnecessarily. Also, there would have been a very real danger of killing or seriously injuring himself as a result of the bullet ricocheting.

The *Otago Daily Times* makes a brief reference to the Octagon attempt and even then manages to screw up by mentioning a balcony, something no one else, Lewis included, ever mentioned.

They also state that he aborted that attempt when he found he did not have an escape route. Another untrue statement, because Lewis aborted that attempt when two uniformed police officers moved up from the Octagon to higher ground by the Mission building and disturbed him as he was about to take aim.

The paragraph concludes with, *Lewis then got onto his bicycle and rode to the Adams building*.

That statement, although almost correct, was at odds with the statement made by Deputy Commissioner Stuart McEwen the previous day: *"After having studied the file at length, the plan found by the police showed that an attempt in the Octagon would have taken place in a position not on the Queen's route so Lewis went to a toilet in an adjacent building from where it would have been next to impossible to hit the entourage even with a suitable firearm."*

Lewis had a clear line of fire at the Queen from a distance of only 20-25 metres in the Octagon. When thwarted there, he rode at least a mile on his bicycle to get to the Adams building, hardly an adjacent building. The remark that it was next to impossible (but obviously not impossible) once again is at odds with the *Otago Daily Times* "inquiry".

McEwen concludes by stating, "Lewis admitted that in spite of a wish to shoot the Queen he could not see the area where she would stop so he fired an aimless shot onto the road below."

A noticeable omission in Charteris's articles is any reference to the allegations made by Allan Dick, news editor at *Radio Otago* at the time of the assassination attempt.

Dick, of course, had alleged that he was asked to play down the attempt on the Queen's life by two senior detectives after being summoned to the Dunedin CIB. This was only a day or so before Charteris did his 'investigative' journalism bit.

Dick has always alleged that a reporter from the *Otago Daily Times* was offered the same deal if that newspaper agreed to drop the Queen story. Dick also states that the offer of a story about a gold heist, promised by the two detectives, never eventuated.

One would have thought such a serious allegation, coming from someone independent of the police, would have warranted some inquiry, or at the very least a response from Charteris and the *Otago Daily Times*.

Fred Tullet later told me that the High Court judge who sentenced Lewis, and who had by 1987 retired, had agreed to an interview. In that interview, he told their reporter that the facts then begrudgingly acknowledged by the police were never made known to him in Lewis's court summary.

In 1987, the media for some reason did not pursue Lewis's

escape attempt from Lake Alice and his plan to make it to Dunedin the day the Prince and Princess arrived in that city.

Also his plan and diary notes showing he intended to attempt to assassinate the Prime Minister, Robert Muldoon, was mentioned only by the *Sunday Times*. It does also have to be acknowledged that it was as a result of the publicity initiated by the *Sunday Times* that Lewis was finally captured.

The police had been advising the public and the media after the *Sunday Times* exposure that there was nothing to worry about as Lewis was trapped in a police cordon. While they played the waiting game, apparently convinced Lewis was trapped, he turned up in Auckland. He was recognised by a car salesman while attempting to buy a second-hand car there after an amazing escape from the police cordon on the West Coast.

He outsmarted the police and in doing so demonstrated just how determined he was and how – due to his martial arts training – impervious to pain and discomfort. Police acknowledged that Lewis had escaped their cordon by riding under a bus holding onto the undercarriage. He travelled from the Buller Gorge to Picton in this manner, a distance of at least 250 kilometres, an amazing feat even allowing for the fact he would have had some respite when the bus made a number of stops.

Christopher Lewis was sentenced to a lengthy term of imprisonment in 1987 for armed robberies and other crimes he committed in and around the Christchurch area. From contacts within the police I learned that he was released in the early 1990s but continued his life of crime and was in and out of prison as a result.

In November 1995, I was a guest speaker on Radio Pacific Talkback with Allan Dick and Jenny Anderson. It was the week of CHOGM, the Commonwealth Heads of Government Meeting, and Radio Pacific had been inquiring into the whereabouts of Christopher Lewis. It would seem they were the only media outlet who remembered his history and recognised the danger he represented to heads of government, the Queen and the Duke of Edinburgh.

When I heard Nelson Mandela was to be present, I immediately recognised the danger he could be in if Lewis was on the loose. Lewis might envisage even greater notoriety for himself by killing Mandela rather than the Queen, a motive likely to be intensified by his deep hatred for blacks and coloureds.

When I spoke to Jenny Anderson and Allan Dick, they told me the police were being very smug about Lewis's whereabouts. They had been told by a police spokesman, "Let's just say we have taken him for a little holiday." Anderson told me that he was out of the country, possibly in Queensland.

The talkback show exceeded all expectations according to Radio Pacific, with tremendous interest from right around New Zealand.

I had been asked to allow for a half-hour discussion but I was on the programme for almost three hours. During that time, people rang in from all over New Zealand with support and additional information on Christopher Lewis.

The only dissenters, you guessed it – the police! They actually did themselves no favours as they were more obsessed with putting me down than debating the issues.

Jenny Anderson asked me what I thought of a police spokesman from Police Headquarters in Wellington who insisted he remain anonymous but who had stated, "With regard to the apprehension of Christopher Lewis and his co-offenders, it was as a result of good detective work but not by Tom Lewis."

My response was to have a chuckle and say, "This is so typical [of] the pettiness and the lies the police department puts on anybody who speaks out. Whistleblowers [police who have spoken out] have faced this time and time again. It would be amusing if it was not so pathetic."

The truth of the matter is that I was in charge of the suspects squad and we got our men. It was as simple as that. I did no more nor less than the others when it came to the interviews. The three of us got admissions and signed statements. I have always acknowledged the contribution made by the late Tony Harrod in spotting Paul and bringing him back to the CIB for questioning.

My role was to supervise and assist in the interviews and to ensure that all evidence and admissions that could be obtained were obtained that night. Because of a lack of staff, I ended up interviewing Paul as well as running the operation.

At the time we were all commended for our efforts and I remember the report ending with the comment that Detective Sergeant Lewis was to be commended for his supervision and leadership throughout a difficult inquiry.

I think most intelligent people realise that if a team has been successful then the leader has, as a general rule, contributed towards that success, usually more than individuals. Likewise, if a team fails then it is usually the leader that comes in for a larger share of the blame.

As this operation was very successful, in the end most people, judging by the calls of support, recognised the police response for what it was — an attempt to shoot the messenger rather than to debate the facts.

The talkback on Radio Pacific had me outlining the facts of the attempt on the Queen, the subsequent changing of Lewis's statement and the events surrounding the shooting after I had been sent on leave.

To give the programme balance, Radio Pacific had Bill Wright, the Dunedin Crown Solicitor, speak. I know Bill Wright well and over the years I have had a lot to do with him. I regard him as an extremely honest man.

Unfortunately for Bill, the discussions I had at the time Lewis, Paul and Geoff were arrested were with Dennis Wood, the then senior Crown Solicitor. Bill did grudgingly acknowledge that the Crown Solicitor's office relied on the police for their information and that the police were in a position to decide what they should and should not give them.

His memory of the incident was not good, which was understandable, and he had some difficulty recollecting range, distance and even what floor the shot had been fired from.

Callers telephoned in disputing his contention that a .22 rifle would not be accurate over 100 metres and Allan Dick had him admitting the incident had been 'played down'.

It was not a convincing performance from Bill Wright but, as I've said, it was not his fault. He had been put in a difficult situation by the police.

It was at this point that Jenny Anderson announced that she had spoken to J. Murray Hanan, Christopher Lewis's lawyer, who represented him in the High Court in Dunedin in early 1982 when he was charged over the incident with the Queen. Hanan had said protocol did not permit him to speak on talkback radio but he did wish to make it known that he agreed entirely with the comments of ex-Detective Sergeant Tom Lewis.

It had not been a good morning for the police and it was about to get worse. For some reason they decided to allow former Detective Chief Inspector Laurie Dalziel to speak.

Until then, they had kept Dalziel out of the firing line, no doubt aware of his tendency to lead with his chin and his vitriolic style of communication. He immediately started on the offensive, telling talk back host Allan Dick that it was "that old-fashioned detective who ran his office like a fiefdom speaking". This was in response to Dick's remarks earlier in the show that Dalziel 's approach was old fashioned and the CIB office was run like a "fiefdom".

When Dick stuck to his guns and said, "I'm sorry, Laurie, but your style was most unusual," Dalziel's response was to switch to a personal attack on me. He told Dick that he needed to understand that he had inherited problems when he took over the Dunedin CIB office as there were two cliques, the Tom Lewis clique and the rest. He said some of Lewis's fellow NCOs had cause to question his judgment. This was a most amazing statement considering that Dalziel used me to head his major inquiries, including staff (internal) inquiries.

It is also worth noting that when Dick put it to me that Dalziel ran his CIB office in an unusual way I responded that Dalziel had been put in a difficult position as the first person to be placed in charge of a CIB office without having qualified as a detective. This had created problems for him in that there was some animosity among the older CIB types at having to take orders from a person they considered to be inferior.

I had gone out of my way to be fair to the man and here was he responding with a personal attack on me. It certainly confirmed what I had stated at the beginning of the broadcast, namely the fact that the police do not debate the issues but prefer to attack the man.

But Dalziel wasn't finished with me. He then decided to follow the line of our anonymous messenger from Police Headquarters who had stated that the arrests of Lewis and colleagues had been a result of good detective work, but not by Tom Lewis.

He acknowledged the arrests followed as a result of good detective work by Detectives Harrod and Galland, the implication being that Detective Sergeant Lewis, the officer in charge of the inquiry, had done something wrong or not done his job.

Dalziel was then put on the spot by Dick who reiterated his story that he had been offered an inducement in the form of another story from Dalziel if he did not pursue the matter regarding the attempt on the Queen. Dalziel pleaded loss of memory and when Dick attempted to remind him of certain things that had been said he resorted to bluster and attempted to bulldoze his way out of trouble.

When that didn't work, he stated that he had telephoned to talk about the attempt on the Queen not to be sidetracked, so he rather conveniently changed the subject.

He then spoke for about fifteen minutes on air to explain his version of what had happened. His line was that he allocated a team of detectives to inquire into the allegations that shots had been heard at the Museum Reserve.

This was, of course, untrue as he and the rest of the police higher up the hierarchy had rejected those allegations out of hand, as verified by the newspaper article by Australian journalist James Oram.

He said the inquiries revealed that students had been letting off crackers at the Medical School, some 400 metres away! He also came up with the theory that a sign had fallen down and yet another that workmen were using nail guns nearby. He would not acknowledge that the claims by respected overseas journalists of having heard shots had been summarily dismissed when they approached police at the scene.

Dalziel then moved on to the actual attempt and started with a classic blunder by stating, "When Lewis confessed to going there to kill the Queen, I mean going there to take a shot at her, the fact that he fired a shot or shots is only his assertion. We had no actual proof."

This statement, apart from having to cover up his first comment, is an indictment on the police handling of the case. Had a search been made for the bullet there may well have been additional 'real' evidence. Had ballistic tests been carried out there may have been additional evidence. Had basic area inquiries been carried out there most certainly would have been corroborative evidence. People in the buildings, offices and shops nearby were not canvassed as would normally happen in any serious crime scene. Why?

The diary notation and detailed plan were also conveniently forgotten.

If journalists, members of the public and even some police heard the shots in the Museum Reserve some 150 metres away, then those people working in the building where the shot was fired from would have surely heard something, as would those working nearby.

The other very obvious reason for inquiries in the area would be to discover whether anybody had seen Lewis in the vicinity, entering or leaving the building.

It is now apparent that Dalziel and John Kelly did not want any corroborative evidence. Their reason was not obvious to me at the time but after speaking to other police and drawing my own conclusions based on my knowledge of them, I now believe it was a police cover-up to avoid the inevitable inquiry that would have followed had the press become aware of the security botch-up in Dunedin.

The planning of security and the operational orders for the Dunedin leg of the royal tour was the responsiblity of Laurie Dalziel. Because he was deficient in these areas, he assigned the task to the ambitious Kelly. Here was a man who would produce pages and pages of operational orders which looked impressive at first glance but which would often prove to be hopelessly inadequate in crucial areas.

Had the true facts emerged, both of these ambitious men would have had career setbacks, setbacks they would not have been able to live with. Both considered themselves high-fliers and were aiming for the top.

Reason enough to organise a cover-up perhaps?

After Dalziel exited the talkback show, a number of calls came in supporting my allegations, some from former police officers.

The biggest impact, however, came from the last two callers, one of whom was Lewis's ex-fiancee. She said that she had heard on the show that police and others were alleging her former fiancee had changed, but she rejected that opinion. In her few moments on air, she painted a picture of a dangerous, calculating criminal who could be charming one minute, lethal and dangerous the next.

She also mentioned the fact when she had first met Lewis he was embracing religion and she found him to be a kind and loving person. She later realised that this was a front and he had been committing bank robberies during this time.

Unfortunately, for reasons best known to herself, Jenny Anderson cut Lewis's fiancee short just at a time when the information about this strange man was beginning to flow. Before that happened, it was obvious to all listening that it had taken a lot of courage for her to telephone in to warn the public about her ex-fiancee. Her speech was quavering and she sounded close to tears throughout.

The next person to call was a man called Warren, who owned a house on the Port Hills near Christchurch in 1987 when Christopher Lewis was on the run after committing a number of bank robberies in and around Christchurch. Lewis had crashed his getaway car in the Port Hills after a chase by police. He escaped on foot and hid out in the area.

The police did not mount a large-scale search for him, they merely left him in the area, according to Warren. The public were not advised that a dangerous criminal was about and it would seem the police, for some strange reason, pulled out and left Lewis in the area.

After Lewis left that area he went to the West Coast and later to Auckland, where he was finally caught.

Warren was interviewed by police after Lewis's capture. They showed him a plan Lewis had drawn of the interior of his house after he had broken in while Warren, his wife and children were asleep. He had eaten food, drunk beer and wandered through the house. Lewis had made notes of his plan to kill Warren and his family when he next returned.

The police interviewed Warren as they were considering charging Lewis with the burglary of the house.

As can be imagined, Warren's reaction was one of horror. He told listeners he considered himself and his family lucky to be alive, no thanks to the police. He went on to say that, firstly, he was fortunate neither he nor any member of his family awoke during Lewis's burglary and, secondly, they were fortunate the publicity emanating from the *Sunday Star-Times* caused him to leave the area before he was able to implement his plan to kill him and his family.

Warren was scathing in his criticism of the police in playing down the danger Lewis represented to the community. He pleaded with them to acknowledge just how dangerous Lewis was before someone was killed. He said, "They say he's cured. Well, if he's cured why do they consider him so dangerous they have to get him away while CHOGM is on?"

Jenny Anderson then offered me the last word and I merely repeated what I had been saying for eight years – that Lewis was a dangerous criminal and it was only a matter of time before he either killed or seriously wounded someone. The losers out of this cover-up would be the public.

During 1996, I heard Lewis was wanted for questioning regarding a number of armed robberies and that he had been a suspect when taken 'overseas' for his paid holiday at the time of CHOGM. These facts were a source of annoyance to a number of police who knew of his background and were aware of the cover-up in 1981. As one police officer said to me, "Not only is he a danger to the public, he represents a real danger to the police because if he is ever cornered I have no doubt we will have a shootout."

In late 1996, I was told by a police contact that Lewis had been arrested in Christchurch and charged with theft of a passport. I was also told he was the suspect for the murder in August 1996 of Tania Furlan, at Howick in Auckland.

I was extremely angry when I heard this because my prediction that it was only a matter of time before someone was killed or badly injured had become a reality. The police had continued with their game of playing down the potential danger of this psychopath to keep him away from the media in order to maintain the cover-up of 1981.

Despite my warnings and the plea of the man whose family were stalked by Lewis on the Port Hills of Christchurch, the police refused to take measures which could have prevented the tragic murder of a young mother.

I received a number of calls from the press in New Zealand in early December 1996 but I could not make any comment as the matter was sub judice. At the time I was also completing a long-term project, a book about cover-ups and corruption in Australia and New Zealand. The cover-up over the Queen and subsequent downplaying of Lewis's danger to the community was the subject of a chapter of that book. Naturally, I was not keen to pre-empt that.

In January 1997, I broke my silence on the matter when I spoke to Brisbane reporter Peter Hansen. Hansen had exposed the New Zealand police when they assisted a convicted criminal to illegally enter Australia after an early application had been turned down by Australian immigration authorities.

The man, a crucial crown witness in the Ross Appelgren murder trials, was a protected witness and a criminal. He had been under New Zealand police protection in 1985 and 1986. In 1986 the New Zealand police gave the man $30,000 to relocate to another country under another name.

The case came to light in Australia when the man was convicted of attempting to set fire to his ex-wife and her boyfriend while they were in bed together. He subsequently received a nine-year jail term.

As a result of some excellent investigative journalism by Peter Hansen it was shown that the New Zealand police clearly knew the man was illegally living in Australia and that New Zealand police were in fact communicating with him regularly. The man, courtesy of false identification papers allegedly supplied by the New Zealand police, was able to make numerous trips between the two countries and on at least one occasion a senior New Zealand police officer travelled to Australia to meet him.

Hansen was able to show the New Zealand police's denials were lies and the New Zealand press picked up on what was another cover-up. The *Sunday Star-Times* of 26 January 1997, carried the headline, **Papers prove police role**. They quoted the police denials and then stated unequivocally that official documents showed that the police knew a convicted Kiwi conman was living illegally in Australia after being denied entry by immigration authorities.

The documents also showed New Zealand police kept up regular communications with the man while he was in Australia, even though they knew the Australians had refused to allow him to settle there.

Janet McIntyre of TVNZ's *60 Minutes* produced an excellent piece of investigative journalism which culminated in the Assistant Commissioner of Police in New Zealand having to acknowledge his original statements were incorrect.

The Minister of Police, Jack Elder, a rookie in the job, stated he was briefed by senior police officers and he was satisfied there was no wrongdoing. "It would be absurd to think police would jeopardise a close working relationship with the Australian police by going behind their backs," he said.

When 'our Jack' was shown internal police documents which proved otherwise, he reverted to sending messages through a spokesman saying that he still accepted assurances from police that they had acted responsibly in the case. He then found a way out by stating it was 'not appropriate' for him to comment further as Appelgren's lawyers had lodged an appeal for a pardon with the Governor-General. 'Our Jack' was learning fast that to be Minister of Police one had to be quick on one's feet and ready to break a promise or two.

Janet McIntyre, of *60 Minutes*, flew from Auckland to Wellington to carry out an arranged interview with Police Minister

Elder only to find when she got to Parliament that Elder had cancelled the interview. Perhaps Jack had been watching as McIntyre put Assistant Commissioner Ian Holyoake through the wringer or perhaps it had suddenly dawned on him that briefings from senior police officers could be often seriously flawed.

It was against this background that Hansen and I chatted about the possibility of Christopher John Lewis being brought into Australia illegally during CHOGM in November 1995. I told Hansen that at the time of CHOGM a number of reliable people had told me that Lewis had been taken out of New Zealand for an all-expenses-paid holiday. Great Barrier Reef was the destination according to two sources and the other source told me that police had said he was in Queensland.

I had no doubt that the police would have to get Lewis as far away as possible during CHOGM because not only would the Queen be at risk but Nelson Mandela would probably represent an even bigger trophy.

Hansen and I also discussed the murder of Tania Furlan and how the cover-up of the attempt on the Queen's life had come back to haunt the police over the years. I was adamant that had the police not been so obsessed with keeping Lewis out of the limelight in case he talked to the media, he would have, and should have been committed to a mental institution years earlier.

Hansen told me he would like to print a story as a follow-up to his previous story regarding police illegally assisting convicted criminals to get into Australia. After I gave Hansen background information on Lewis, he told me he would contact the New Zealand police before running the story in order to get their reaction.

The following Saturday he told me that he had contacted the police concerning Lewis's whereabouts during CHOGM only to be told that he had been under surveillance. That was all they would say, according to Hansen.

That morning my wife was contacted by Janet McIntyre of *60 Minutes* who had read the article at Brisbane Airport while awaiting a return flight back to New Zealand. She had been given my phone number by Hansen and she had been in Australia compiling the background to her story about the New Zealand police assisting convicted criminals to illegally enter Australia. She was able to elaborate on the Furlan murder and I agreed that I might be able to assist her further at a later date.

The next day I was contacted by Kim Hurring and Bill Ralston of TV3. I declined to be interviewed by them.

During the next week a number of the media organisations attempted to contact me including the *Sunday Star-Times*. My wife politely told them that I was not prepared to talk to them.

Later that week, Peter Hansen telephoned me. He told me that a former policeman from New Zealand, Graham Perry, had written a letter to the *Sunday Mail* stating my claim that Chris Lewis went to the Great Barrier Reef was incorrect. Perry, a former Assistant Deputy Commissioner from Auckland, stated that he had inside information that Lewis was, in fact, on Great Barrier Island during CHOGM. He did not say how he came to know this, because he was not a member of the police at that time, or what proof he had.

I found it quite amazing that a retired policeman was making a statement of denial rather than an official from Police Headquarters. A loyal member of the brotherhood undoubtedly but a bizarre way of getting the official message across.

The plot thickened, however, when retired Superintendent Rowe, who claimed to be the officer in charge of security at CHOGM, made a press release to an obviously tame journalist at the New Zealand Herald a few days later. Rowe stated that Lewis had agreed to an all-expenses-paid holiday at Great Barrier Island with his girlfriend during CHOGM. He went on to say that Lewis had gone there unescorted but airlines and tour boat operators had been alerted as had the local police constable.

There he stayed for the duration of CHOGM, free to do as he pleased, with the New Zealand police apparently content in the knowledge that New Zealand's most dangerous criminal was on an island only an hour or so away with numerous unattended boats, large and small at his disposal.

Of course I have overlooked the island's lone police constable. He must have been some guy, a virtual superman who never slept for a week. A man who was expected to do what squads of specially trained police apparently could not do over the years – control Lewis.

11

Protecting the Prince and Teddy

Not all royal visits were as fraught as the Queen's in 1981. Prince Charles' visit to New Zealand just before his marriage brought more than just a few laughs for those of us close to the action.

These were the days before Diplomatic Protection Squads and the CIS (Criminal Intelligence Section) was assigned duties close to the royals and their personal bodyguards. As well as briefing the VIPs' personal bodyguards, we were required to be close to the royals during walkabouts or when they attended civic functions.

Other duties were checking the royal accommodation before they moved in. This was always done before any of their personal belongings were brought into their suite. An explosives sniffer dog accompanied us and once the suite had been cleared the batman and ladies-in-waiting would move in with the royal luggage.

The entire floor of a hotel or travel lodge was always reserved for the royals and their entourage with their personal bodyguard in the room next door and CIS officers in the room at the other end of their suite.

Armed police were positioned outside their door, and guarded the stairwell and lift. In addition, all exits and entrances were under police guard.

The biggest enemy in these tasks is always boredom and I attempted to overcome this problem by sending staff away for a jog during the small hours. I would send them off in pairs and on their return they would have a light meal. This made them mentally and physically alert for the rest of the shift.

In the early eighties, Prince Charles arrived in New Zealand for his last visit as a single man. On his arrival in Dunedin, my CIS squad joined his personal bodyguards and I assigned two detectives and the explosives sniffer dog to thoroughly check the royal suite at the Southern Cross hotel in Dunedin.

I had a floor plan of the suite and each detective was allocated a room to search before they would swap rooms and check each other's work.

While I was out in the passage arranging the search of that area, I heard laughter and banter coming from the royal suite so I went to find out the cause of their obvious mirth.

One of the detectives was something of a wit and he enjoyed a prank and a laugh. When I walked into the room I found him 'knighting' the other detective. He had an impressive sword in his hand, the scabbard around his waist and a pair of boxer-type underpants around his head, which bore the insignia of the Prince of Wales. I immediately asked them where they had obtained the royal sword and the royal underpants.

They indicated the wardrobe where I could see suits and uniforms and some drawers that were open containing other underclothing. It immediately became apparent that someone in the royal entourage had bungled by placing Prince Charles' personal belongings in the suite before it had a security clearance.

I was about to call the personal bodyguards when a detective brought a teddy bear to me and said, "This must have been left here by the previous occupiers." It was a normal teddy bear although it did look old and somewhat bedraggled.

As I was examining it, a small man in a black lounge suite burst into the room. He was grabbed by a detective but continued screaming and struggling. We attempted to quieten him but he was still shaking with rage and trying to grab the teddy bear. Finally we calmed him and managed to establish that he was in fact the Prince's batman.

I introduced myself and he said, "You're not supposed to be here. There will be trouble over this."

I escorted him out into the passageway and showed him my

orders, telling him in no uncertain terms that he, in fact, had erred as he was not permitted to enter the suite until it had a security clearance.

He requested the teddy bear and after a cursory examination I agreed to give it to him. But before doing so, I asked him who it belonged to. When he did not answer immediately, I became annoyed. I felt I had put up with enough from this upstart so I said, "Is it your teddy or the Prince's? I have to know."

In a voice barely audible he said, "It belongs to His Royal Highness."

I handed the teddy bear to him and he stalked off without so much as a thank you.

After giving the suite and the entire floor a security clearance my squad settled in to guard the floor for the next 48 hours. I detailed the armed guards at each end of the corridor to cover the lift and the stairwell until the Prince arrived to take up residence. The rest of the squad and I went to the suite we had next to the royal suite to relax and have a meal.

At about 5 p.m. I was in our suite finishing my meal when I received a call from an Inspector Nichol. Nichol was the Police Commissioner's aide and was the liaison between the British police who were guarding Prince Charles and the New Zealand police.

Nichol requested that I come immediately to the Commissioner's suite, where I was introduced to a very agitated man, Paul Officer, the Prince of Wales' personal bodyguard.

Officer said, "It's about the teddy bear." My initial reaction was to assume he was upset because we had not checked the teddy bear thoroughly. I had thought of cutting it open at one stage but once the Prince's batman had identified himself that was not necessary.

I said to Officer, "Yes, that has been returned to the Prince's batman. He'd arrived at the suite early and had partly unpacked before we had cleared the room."

Officer glared at me and said, "I want you to understand this is bloody serious. His Royal Highness has done stints in the Navy and the Air Force but his secret has stayed just that until we come to New Zealand and a half a dozen of your nosey bloody detectives find out about it."

By this time I was getting annoyed. I pointed out to Officer that my men were merely doing their job and someone had stuffed up badly on their side by not ensuring that the batman was properly briefed.

I also told him that my staff had virtually forgotten the incident and I suggested he do the same.

He said, "I just can't take that risk. If your chaps blab about it and it gets to the newspapers it could ruin the Prince's image. I want them all up here now."

I told him that was impossible as they had been assigned their duties for the next 24 hours and if they were to be removed from their positions relief staff would have to be brought in to cover. I reiterated that in my opinion it would be better to leave the matter as my staff were not even discussing it among themselves but if an issue was made of it someone might leak the information to the newspapers.

He would have none of it so Nichol and I arranged relief staff to cover while my men were brought up to Officer.

On entering his suite, I found him pacing the floor. When I had left him an hour earlier he had been in his shirt sleeves and had looked rather bedraggled. He had rearranged his tie and had his suit jacket on. Paul Officer was very much on edge.

He asked me if the men were ready to be paraded before him. I told him they were all detectives and they were not there for a parade. They were there to hear what he had to say. I turned on my heel and left the room.

When I brought my staff in, Officer asked them to remain standing as he had something extremely important to announce. His jaw set, he began a most amazing lecture: "We all have our little quirks and idiosyncrasies but as you well know they are things we like to keep to ourselves. Unfortunately you men have stumbled upon one of his Royal Highness's little quirks or idiosyncrasies.

"He has served in the Air Force and Navy in Britain and this thing has been kept a secret. Now a half a dozen of you know about it and it will remain among you lot. It will go no further. It will not be repeated or discussed, ever.

"Should the press get to hear of this, your Commissioner assures me he will stage the biggest witch-hunt ever in order to identify the culprits.

Not only will those responsible lose their jobs but other more drastic action will be considered."

Officer then repeated his warning, adding, "You can imagine what a field day the gutter press would have over this as this man is the future King of England.

"That must not and will not happen. God help any of you lot if this gets out."

He then asked the detectives to leave and asked me to stay behind. He was still extremely agitated and asked me if I thought any of them would attempt to sell the story to the press.

I assured him that the New Zealand press would not pay a penny for the story and I knew of only one newspaper which might be interested and even they would not pay.

He seemed genuinely relieved at this and as we shook hands as I was leaving the room, he said, "Let me know if any of that lot are laughing, joking or even discussing this and I'll have them."

On returning to our suite, I heard the sounds of raucous laughter and one detective stating, "No bloody wonder it took such a long time for the Queen to find a wife for him. How do you explain to a chick that she will have to share the matrimonial bed with a bloody teddy bear?"

It was quite obvious Paul Officer's pep talk had merely served to rekindle discussion about the incident.

The staff were advised by me that I had discussed the matter with the New Zealand police attachment to the royal bodyguard and he had also informed me any leaks to the press would be ruthlessly investigated. I advised my staff to forget the incident.

It was obvious over the next few months that not everyone had adhered to the instruction. I was asked by several members of the Dunedin CIB if the story was true and a TVNZ journalist also asked me if there was any truth in the rumour that the Prince of Wales still slept with his teddy bear.

Some months later I read in a newspaper that Paul Officer had been replaced as the Prince of Wales' personal bodyguard. Later still,

I read about the sacking of Prince Charles' batman and the newspaper report hinted that the Princess of Wales, Diana, had been behind the batman's sacking.

A colleague at Police Headquarters in Wellington later told me he had heard that both had been replaced when the Prince learnt of the incident with the teddy bear back in Dunedin.

I found it rather ironic that later the police, and allegedly the government, would go to so much trouble to hush up an attempt on the Queen's life so that they would not be embarrassed over a lack of security, yet the teddy bear incident was treated as a major threat to the royal family.

Over the years I had been involved in a number of royal tours and I had the opportunity to study the royals at close quarters. The Queen was always friendly and although she acted with decorum she would occasionally exchange a word or two or merely acknowledge a presence with a smile or nod.

The Duke of Edinburgh often found an opportunity to lighten up proceedings. He always acknowledged his bodyguards and often looked for an opportunity to question staff about local customs or landmarks.

He caused consternation in the ranks one night when he emerged from his suite in his dressing gown and asked for the officer in charge. At that time I was the officer in charge of internal security during the night shift so I stepped forward.

He said, "There's some bloody chap having a shower and singing his blasted head off in there," indicating the suite we occupied. "Ma'am's none too happy so can you get him to put a bloody sock in it?" With a wink and a grin, he returned to the royal suite.

I immediately checked our bathroom and found a young detective who had been for a jog around the streets having a shower, singing with great gusto the Abba song *Waterloo*.

He couldn't understand what all the fuss was about when told to shut up. A product of the defunct cadet system, he is now on his way to the top!

Prince Charles was different to his parents and, indeed, his sister Anne. I had the opportunity to study him closely, particularly at unguarded moments. He had obviously been trained to do a certain job and he carried out his duties unenthusiastically.

At the end of a day of engagements, he returned to the royal suite looking as though he was carrying the worries of the world on his shoulders. He never seemed to joke or even talk to his private secretary or personal bodyguard, retiring to his room as quickly as possible.

Prince Charles always seemed to dine alone and he certainly ate sparingly, which was great news for the police guarding his floor and the royal suite. When he left to attend an evening engagement, greedy detectives would descend on his suite like a swarm of locusts. Grapes, pineapples, exotic fruits would all disappear as would various nuts, chocolates and cheese boards.

The hotel staff thought Prince Charlie had a voracious appetite and accordingly they would place even more food around the suite and it too would be consumed by his New Zealand police bodyguards.

The future King certainly appeared to be a troubled man and it did not surprise me when I later heard his personal life was in disarray.

12

Nursemaiding the VIPs

The first experience I had with overseas dignitaries was when Lyndon B. Johnson, President of the United States, visited New Zealand in early 1967.

I was well and truly in the background but I did attend an address by one of LBJ's bodyguards, who kept repeating ad nauseam, "I would die for my President," and went on to describe circumstances how this might occur.

A few years later, in 1975, Robert Muldoon, an abrasive character to say the least, was barnstorming his way around New Zealand with what turned out to be his winning election slogan, "New Zealand the way you want it".

The anti-Muldoon faction were becoming concerned. The radicals, left-wingers and trendy lefties saw him as a real threat. New Zealand has had more than its fair share of radicals, left-wingers and trendy lefties over the years so a reasonable number of the population were starting to feel threatened.

Anonymous threats were made against Muldoon's life and a colleague of mine nicknamed 'Buddah' started sending out situation reports ('sitreps') about an alleged buildup of Ananda Marga and PLO agents in New Zealand.

Buddah was a master of the art of disinformation. An avid reader of *Time* magazine, he spent hours studying articles on the PLO, Ananda Marga and other terrorist groups. From all this he prepared 'sitreps' in which he stated unequivocally that these groups were in New Zealand and represented a threat to security. He endeared himself to the SIS, an organisation which was under threat of staff cutbacks from the Norman Kirk-led Labour government.

Buddah was a master of subterfuge as well and when some headquarters personnel likened his detailed intelligence reports to Grimm's fairytales some strange things happened. Just before Muldoon hit the campaign trail in Otago, Buddah's home province, a mysterious phone call was received by the owner of a South Dunedin gun shop. The caller, speaking with a foreign accent, stated he wanted to buy six high-powered rifles with telescopes. He was told that these could be supplied but he would need a permit from the police.

The caller stated he was prepared to pay a kickback of $5000 if the proprietor would sell them without a permit. The gunshop proprietor refused.

About the same time, someone with an Indian accent telephoned the news editor at 4ZB radio station in Dunedin and stated Muldoon was to be killed.

The result was that Buddah's intelligence reports and his predictions were vindicated and from that time on Robert Muldoon and the then Prime Minister, Wallace Rowling, were always accompanied by plainclothes police.

Buddah and I accompanied both Muldoon and Rowling around Otago and Southland when they were electioneering in those provinces. One night, over a few beers, I put it on him that he had orchestrated the threats to Muldoon. Naturally, he denied all knowledge but I have always suspected him of being the mystery caller.

It was not uncommon to use such ploys in the CIS. When drug squads or CIS wanted more staff, equipment or money, taped conversations allegedly between criminals, drug dealers or radicals (but really between undercover officers) spelled out a story of planned bank robberies to finance drug habits or deals, massive drug importations, drug murders, political assassinations and more.

When these tapes were played to parliamentary select committees, they sat there open mouthed, completely taken in by what they were hearing. I was reliably informed that it never failed to work and was done in collusion with high-ranking officers. One such officer was removed from the CIS in the late 1970s after being caught out.

The incident was played down and he was found to have just exaggerated the facts but this same officer was the brains behind this scam from the outset.

Robert Muldoon did not like being under armed guard 24 hours a day. He gave the impression he was not frightened of anyone and in fact such was his ego he actually believed everyone liked him and therefore no one would want to kill him.

I will say he treated us very well, always making sure that drinks and snacks were available for us. He also ensured we were well looked after at functions. One of the party faithful was always given the task of seeing that we were well provided for afterwards.

In 1975, he was at his best. His meetings were packed and they were always entertaining as he was brilliant at scoring points off interjectors.

In 1982, I accompanied Muldoon on a visit to Central Otago and I was amazed how much he had deteriorated mentally and physically in the space of seven years. He was overweight and I suspect he had a drinking problem as he sat in his room and consumed a bottle of spirits on his own.

Wallace Rowling, who became Prime Minister after Norman Kirk's untimely death, was a likeable man. He had been thrust into the job of Prime Minister and at times it did appear to weigh heavily on him. Following a populist like Kirk was never going to be easy.

Because Otago and Southland had been Labour strongholds, Rowling performed quite well on the hustings but he did not have the rapier-like wit of Muldoon.

Although different types, both Muldoon and Rowling were unpretentious and they made our job easier by their co-operation in matters of security.

Muldoon's successor, David Lange, was something else. I first observed him at close quarters during the 1984 election campaign. He waddled into view with his stomach bursting through his shirt, trousers and suit jacket. After hearing him speak, I considered him to be a pompous buffoon who spoke in riddles. Over the years, my opinion of him has not altered.

At a Labour party function before the 1984 election, I spoke with a party stalwart who was obviously very concerned about the way the party had dumped Bill Rowling for Lange. He told me that it had been a coup led by Auckland politicians after Richard Prebble, Michael Bassett and Roger Douglas had decided the party could not win back power with Bill Rowling as leader. So they decided to 'manufacture' one. What they really required was a frontman, a person who could match Muldoon in the cut and thrust of an election campaign.

To the amazement of many party followers, David Lange was that man.

Overnight he was transformed from a scruffy, grossly overweight, former small-time lawyer with lank greasy hair from unfashionable Mangere, into a well-dressed but still grossly overweight man with carefully coiffured hair and now a political party leader.

Lange was a raconteur of note, a master of the glib one-liner. The journalists of the time, used to being either ignored or abused by the now power-crazy Muldoon, were enraptured by the new Labour leader. His lack of political nous was overlooked as journalists and the public welcomed him.

My friend, the party stalwart, said to me in 1984, "This bloke won't last. There is no substance to him. These blokes think they have a puppet but mark my words this guy's a megalomaniac."

Lange proved to be a man long on rhetoric but short on solutions.

Some months before guarding Muldoon and Rowling, Buddah and I were given the job of guarding Robert James Lee Hawke, then the Secretary of the ACTU and later to become Prime Minister of Australia. Bob Hawke had been invited to New Zealand as the guest speaker at the Combined Social Workers Conference at the University of Otago Campus in Dunedin.

Buddah and I were not exactly enthused at the prospect of having to attend the Social Workers Conference as we anticipated a boring week with a bunch of trendy lefties. It turned out to be anything but.

Because Hawke had been openly critical of the Palestinian Liberation Organisation, and openly supportive of Israel, he was on the PLO's death list. This meant that whenever he travelled overseas he required at least one personal bodyguard, 24 hours a day.

We were not very well briefed but we were told never to leave his side; at least one of us was to accompany him at all times.

Although headquarters was not overly enthused either about having to provide an armed escort for an Australian trade unionist, we were issued with the very latest snub-nosed pistols, with the small clip-on holsters. When we asked if we could use them at the range to familiarise ourselves with this new type of firearm we were refused on the grounds that the police department could not afford to waste the ammunition as they only had one box!

Having had considerable experience firing a normal issue police .38 with the longer barrel, I was aware of how difficult it was to achieve accuracy even with that type of pistol, so I certainly had misgivings about how we would perform with an untried snub-nosed pistol.

When we met Bob Hawke at Dunedin airport we were immediately made to feel like life-long friends. He impressed as a chirpy, good-natured guy and he made it obvious early on that he liked a drink and intended to enjoy himself during his stay. He was not convinced his life was in danger but he acknowledged we had a job to do and he would respect that.

Our first problem came when we arrived at University College (UniCol) in Dunedin where the conference was to be held and where the delegates were to stay. We had booked a double room for Hawke and one for ourselves. Our brief was that one of us would sleep in the room with Hawke and the other in the adjoining room.

Hawke made it quite clear, however, he was not keen to have a detective sleep in the room with him, and he insisted on having a room of his own. In the days that followed we came to understand why.

After much discussion and quite a few beers, we reached a compromise.

He agreed never to draw the drapes and by opening his window at a certain angle we could, at all times, see into his room via the reflection. He also conceded that we would check his room out each night.

We then took Bob on a tour of the city and it soon became obvious that he was not much into architecture or scenic beauty as he suggested a pub crawl. I remember him saying, "You get the feel of a place by visiting its watering holes." He certainly did his best to get the 'feel' of Dunedin.

Buddah and I had an agreement that one of us could have a drink (or two) with Bob while the other, the driver, would abstain. It was my turn to drive that first day and I was quite glad it was as Buddah was a bit of a mess by 6 p.m.

I was starting to get a little worried myself as Bob was to be one of the opening speakers at the conference, which was due to begin at 8 p.m. When I mentioned this fact to him he merely replied, "You're quite right. I'll knock off the beer now and have a few wines instead." This he did during his meal with no obvious ill effects.

When we reached the conference, it was agreed that one of us would stay close to him at all times and the other would mingle. Well, that's how it started off.

When Bob made his opening address, he introduced us and told the conference, "They are bloody good blokes and I want them looked after." From that moment on we were certainly looked after, many of the people at the conference assuming we were from Australia and were his permanent personal bodyguards. Hawke did not go out of his way to correct this assumption as this added to his celebrity status.

He also gave a command performance in his opening address and received a standing ovation. Considering the amount of alcohol he had consumed during the afternoon and evening, it was a truly amazing performance.

As soon as the formal part of the evening was completed, the dance and cabaret commenced. Bob was in his element. He drank copious quantities of alcohol, got up on the stage, told jokes and even sang a few Labour Party songs.

The author (second from right, front row) at the Trentham Police School for the first ever surveillance course held in New Zealand, 1973.

The author (far right, back row) poses with other members of the Dunedin CIB in 1974.

The author as an undercover cop.

Dealing with the 'Mr Asia' syndicate,
1974-75.

Former Police Commissioner K.O. Thompson.

Former Police Commissioner Bob Walton.

Mal Churches, who rose to become NZ Police Commissioner.

Detective Inspector Dick McDonald in 1977. He was later to become NZ Police Commissioner.

Detective Sergeant John Scott in 1977.

Chief Inspector Laurie Dalziel, known to many of his underlings as 'Dazzle Fawlty'. (Otago Daily Times photo)

Cuffed and in custody, the notorious Bassett Road machine-gun murderer Ron Jorgensen. The author believes he is alive and living in Australia. (NZ Herald photo)

Christopher John Lewis in police custody for the alleged killing of Tania Furlan. Lewis committed suicide in his prison cell before his trial began. (NZ Herald photo)

"Give me the money" . . . Christopher John Lewis caught on a security camera during his armed holdup of a BNZ branch in Auckland, in August of 1997. *(NZ Herald photo)*

'Audrey' – identified by John Lewis as the recruiter of young girls in the Dunedin Sex Ring.

The author with former beauty queen Christine Griffin (nee Antunovic) pose together on Queensland's Gold Coast 30 years after first meeting in Dunedin during her reign as Miss New Zealand.

The Lewis family during the harrowing days of the Dunedin Sex Ring inquiry. Back row (from left): Tony, wife Teresa and Tom. Front row: Tania and Chris.

At about midnight, he made a serious move on a young social worker who had been hanging on his every word. After dancing cheek to cheek, he whisked her off to his room. This was, of course, contrary to our agreement as we had no time to check his room out.

By the time we got to the adjoining room and took up a position at the window so that we could see into his room, Bob had stripped the young woman. We were able to confirm, at a glance, that she was not carrying a weapon.

After they settled down for the night, Buddah and I took turns at keeping watch. Around 6 a.m. Bob yelled in the direction of our window, "Hey boys, she's not staying here. She's staying in the town so we'll have to get her home."

We all piled into the unmarked police car and drove Bob and his lady to a motel in the city.

After breakfast, Bob decided he wanted to go for a walk. For starters we walked around the university campus. Otago University is New Zealand's oldest university and this time Hawke did take an interest in the architecture and the old buildings. He told us he had been a Rhodes Scholar at Oxford University in the late forties.

Over a cup of coffee in a local coffee bar, our Bob casually announced that as he was not required for the day-to-day business of the conference he would like to continue with the pub crawl of the previous day. He said, "We can do the ones we missed yesterday or get out in the country and do a few of the country pubs."

We decided a pub crawl in the country would be preferable to driving around the city again so just before lunch we set off down the Otago Peninsula.

After spending an hour or two at the Shiel Hill Tavern, a quaint little hotel overlooking the ocean, we headed off to the Portobello hotel for lunch. As it was my turn to be Bob's drinking companion, I was most relieved to find he was drinking at a more sedate pace than the day before when he had virtually written off Buddah.

Hawke was in his element among the lunchtime crowd at the Portobello. He found a partner and took to the pool table. The two of them beat off all challengers and by 3 p.m. they were undisputed champions. From my point of view, his obsession with the pool table challenges from the other hotel patrons meant drinking became a secondary consideration so Buddah and I enjoyed our meal over a quiet ale.

In those days, the name Bob Hawke meant nothing to the average New Zealander so he won people over with his personality. As I watched him playing pool, laughing and joking with the bar patrons, I was amazed at just what an unpretentious, uncomplicated person he was.

After the Portobello, we went on to the fishing village of Port Chalmers on the other side of the Otago harbour. It is rumoured to have more hotels per square kilometre than any other place in New Zealand.

We checked them all out and he and I had a five-ounce beer in each pub. The hungover Buddah, our driver, was on lemon squash.

On returning to Dunedin, we went to the university hotels, the Captain Cook, the Bowling Green and the Robbie Burns. After a meal, we returned to Unicol where Bob Hawke was to take part in a debate. He freshened up with a shower and when he took his place at the debate nobody would have guessed he had spent the previous eight hours drinking. His capacity for beer absolutely amazed us.

Bob Hawke was the star of the debate without a doubt. He injected some much-needed humour and received a huge ovation at the end.

What amazed Buddah and me was he was the only one involved who did not have notes. He hadn't had time to prepare while he had been with us and he later confirmed it was an impromptu performance.

That night we took off from Unicol with a couple of ladies who had been offered a tour of the city night spots by Bob Hawke. After visiting a night club, we went out to visit the proprietor of a suburban hotel whose brother was a rather famous Melbourne criminal.

It was certainly interesting listening in on the conversation between Bob Hawke and the publican about the Melbourne underworld and who controlled it, the various politicians and other public figures who were suspected of being corrupt. It was obvious that through his union contacts Hawke knew a number of unsavoury characters.

We arrived back at Unicol around 1 a.m. and Buddah said, "You get some sleep. I'll put Bob to bed."

Around 3 a.m. I was woken up by Buddah who said, "He's been at it again but the action's all over. They're both asleep. It's your turn on duty."

When I took up my position by the window I could certainly see evidence of Bob's latest conquest. Clothes, male and female, were strewn everywhere. Both participants were, by this time, fast asleep in bed. Fortunately, this lady was living in for the conference and we did not have to take an early morning trip across town.

Amazingly, he kept this pace up for the remainder of the conference. He would have been lucky to average three hours' sleep a night but it was obvious that he was thoroughly enjoying himself.

On the final night of the conference a huge party was held and everybody seemed to be drunk. Bob was in great form, either up with the band singing, dancing or shocking the female social workers with raunchy tales.

At about 9.30 p.m. I noticed him disappearing with a young social worker. I checked her out in the prescribed manner via the reflection in the window. This was a rather quick liaison and Bob was back on the dance floor within an hour.

He then proceeded to liven up the show. I had mentioned to him that Buddah was the unofficial SIS agent in Dunedin and how he was forever sending off 'sitreps' to SIS and Police Headquarters alleging that Dunedin was a hotbed of communism and that the Ananda Marga and PLO were active in the city.

Bob had, for some days, been exchanging friendly banter with Buddah about socialist philosophy. He told me it was his intention to get Buddah drunk and to get him to perform. A drinking game was organised and poor old Buddah was no match for our Bob. Before long he was a mess.

Bob got the band to play socialist songs and he had most of the radical social workers up on the stage, arm in arm, singing such songs as *The Red Flag*. Right smack in the middle of them was

Buddah. A photographer had been engaged for the final night and I quickly arranged a photo to be taken during the song's rendition. I later got hold of the photo and there right in the middle of the country's worst socialists, radicals and trendy lefties was our ace spycatcher for the city of Dunedin, Buddah.

Some weeks later at an NCOs' meeting, the head of the Dunedin CIB, a real character, produced the photo and said, "Sergeant, what would Brigadier Gilbert [head of the SIS] say about this?"

Buddah, never one to be lost for an answer, replied, "I should think he would be bloody pleased, sir. To infiltrate that lot in just five days was no mean feat."

Bob Hawke's sexual exploits were not over, however. In the early hours of the final day he managed to get an attractive, middle-aged, matronly woman up to his room.

It was obvious as we watched he was having some difficulty disrobing her. Finally he said, "What's wrong with you?" She nervously replied, "Oh look, I don't know about this. It's just that I'm happily married and I've never done this sort of thing before."

Bob Hawke replied, "I'll let you into a secret. Neither have I. Let's relax and help each other."

She soon became another notch on the belt.

When we drove Bob Hawke to the airport he told us the holiday had revived him and he was looking forward to getting back into work. We looked at him in amazement because after a week with him all we wanted was a couple of days off to catch up on sleep.

His final remark to us just before boarding the plane was, "Have either of you boys ever had to feign premature ejaculation? It's not easy I can tell you."

13

Casualties of War

Early in my career I was singled out as having the attributes considered desirable for an undercover officer and a large part of my police career was spent in the seedy world of undercover policing.

While I was at Trentham Police College I was approached by Detective Sergeant Robin ('Cocky') Thompson, officer in charge of the Wellington vice squad. He had been giving a lecture at the college and he told me the chief instructor had recommended three trainees as possible undercover agents and I was one of them.

I told Thompson that as I was married I was not interested in working undercover. He agreed that my marital status was a problem for vice work but he was interested in using me as a short-term undercover agent in the drug scene (which the vice squad covered then as part of its duties).

In those days, the main offenders in the drug scene were the elderly opium-smoking Chinese but Cocky Thompson knew that there were more illicit drugs around than the police department was prepared to concede. He seemed to know the Australian scene and he told me that his contacts there had warned him that it was just a matter of time before drug use and abuse became a major problem in New Zealand.

I received a detailed briefing on cannabis. What it was, what it looked like and more importantly what it smelled like. He did not have any samples – this was, after all, New Zealand of the mid-sixties – and I was briefed from a book.

My interest was aroused when he told me that New Zealand

police would soon have specialist drug squads and people who had worked undercover would be the first recruited onto these squads.

Finally, I agreed to what he described as 'intelligence gathering undercover work' in Wellington.

The following Saturday evening, I travelled into Wellington and I met Thompson outside the railway station. He gave me £10 and told me which hotels and clubs he wanted me to visit. We agreed on a cover story. If asked, I was Tom Collins from Dunedin, a railway worker staying with my sister in Wellington.

I spent the next six hours in the inner city visiting a couple of hotels and a number of strip joints. I struck up a conversation with a couple of guys in a city hotel and I accompanied them to another hotel. They were pretty straight so I decided they were no use to me and I went on alone.

The inner city hotels, although rough and full of criminal types, did not seem to me to be the type of place where cannabis would be bought or sold. These were the days of six o'clock closing and the clientele were mostly concerned with how much beer they could consume before 6 p.m.

After having a meal, I made my way to the strip clubs. I had never been inside a strip club before so I was unsure what to expect. It was certainly an experience watching dozens of middle-aged men, and one or two women, pushing and shoving to get a beter view of the 'girls' doing the strip.

The place was so full of people and smoke that someone could have smoked cannabis beside me and I doubt if I would have been aware.

The first 'artiste', as she was described, bounced down the boardwalk to a raucous rock tune. She was about 5 foot tall and weighed around 11 stone, most of it around her buttocks and breasts.

After bouncing around on the stage for ten minutes or so, she removed her bra top for about a second before the lights went out. When the lights came back on, she left the stage to tumultuous applause.

I was certainly grateful the police department were paying my admission fee as I would have demanded a refund for what turned out to be a very boring evening.

The shows did become more daring later in the night with some of the strippers calling the 'front-rowers' up on the stage. One old bloke was delighted when his necktie was made to seemingly disappear in the vicinity of the stripper's private parts. Later a pair of glasses belonging to another middle-aged front-rower disappeared.

Around midnight I reported back to Thompson. I told him I had not seen any signs of cannabis or even smelt the drug. As I had never smelt it, that was going to be a big ask anyway!

He was happy and seemed quite relieved to know his patch was apparently drug free. It was hardly an auspicious start to my undercover career.

Arriving in Dunedin, I did my brief stint working undercover to detect licensing and gambling offences. For the next eighteen months, I worked in the uniform branch.

It was not until I joined the CIB that I was used in an undercover role again. The head of the drug squad was aware that I had done some undercover work so he used me for mainly surveillance roles. I was allowed to grow my hair longer than police regulations permitted and I grew a moustache. Wearing clothing typical of students at the time, I was able to mingle with the crowds in the university hotels, particularly when the rock bands were playing.

The Dunedin of the late sixties and early seventies was a swinging place with many of New Zealand's top bands getting a start there. A number of them had a 'druggie' following and cannabis and LSD were freely available. I was always on the alert during the bands' breaks as they liked to have a 'toke' (smoke a joint) during that time.

The usual scenario was for me to check out a hotel before the drug squad raided it. I would do this by slipping into the hotel while the band was in full swing and positioning myself in a darkened corner of the bar, as near to the toilets and exit as possible. From that position I could note any suspected dealers heading for the toilets to do a deal. Alternatively, I could see anyone regularly going outside to the car park, another favourite place to do a deal, particularly a large one. Before the drug squad raided the hotel, I would brief them about who was dealing.

This method worked reasonably well for nine months or so. We would get a couple of arrests each night and everybody was happy. The small-time dealers we were catching soon caught on and we had to revert to other methods.

At that time, the police were, by and large, untrained in drug detection and no one was sure exactly how much cannabis was around. Drug squads were formed in the late sixties but little thought and even less training went into these squads.

I then became more involved in mobile surveillance, following suspected drug dealers in my private car and calling in the drug squad when a deal appeared to be about to go down.

This was exciting at the time but in retrospect I have to acknowledge that it was hit and miss stuff. I learnt a lot from my experiences and I was probably one of the first police officers to work in an undercover capacity in the drug scene.

I also had an undercover role when it came to investigating radicals and dissidents.

Because the SIS did not have an office in Dunedin, the CIS (Criminal Intelligence Section) carried out some work for them. We did have some intelligence-gathering functions to carry out on their behalf but it was mostly mundane stuff like hiding in bushes all day, or worse all night, taking photographs of people entering and leaving the suspected headquarters of Ananda Marga. It later transpired that the building concerned was a yoga centre and the people we had been photographing were merely yoga students.

We kept dossiers on all kinds of people – ethnic groups, civil libertarians, trade unionists, university lecturers, foreign fishermen, anti-police lawyers and politicians (only Labour Party members of course).

For these 'adventures', we adopted a variety of disguises with wigs and various types of spectacles available. My particular favourite was a waist-length black wig with a sweat band. With granny glasses, it changed my appearance so much so that even local police did not recognise me.

The compiling of dossiers on people became ridiculous. My friend Buddah had dossiers on all kinds of people, mainly based on gossip and innuendo. They were called our 'dirt files' and they were kept on people because they belonged to groups or organisations not because of anything they had done. It became difficult to distinguish between dissenters and criminals and many of the officers employed in CIS at that time lived in a world of make-believe.

In the 1970s, I remember the District Commander coming to our office with what he described as "confidential information on communists". After locking the office door, he told us that he had been at a mayoral function and had noted a well-known local Chinese family in animated conversation with the Russian ambassador. When he went and stood beside them, they ended their conversation!

Funny that. What did he expect? They probably knew he was the local police chief and would be wondering just why he sidled up and stood beside them, a big florid-faced man with size fourteen shoes!

I couldn't resist asking, "Were you in uniform, sir?"

He glared at me and said, "I'm not a fool you know, young man."

Of course, another neatly bound dossier was compiled. Buddah garnished it up as only he could and the Chinese family became suspected Soviet spies.

Our district commander was 'mentioned in dispatches' when the information was sent off to the SIS.

I then returned to normal detective duties until I had completed my training and the detective qualifying course.

It was 1973 when I next became involved in undercover work.

I attended a course in Wellington run by the American Drug Enforcement Agency (DEA) on undercover duties, static and mobile surveillance. Because the Americans were paying for it, we wanted for nothing. For the mobile surveillance they apparently did a deal with a car hire company and we had the latest and fastest vehicles available.

The American lecturers were very interesting and we were certainly left in no doubt regarding the drug problem they maintained was about to engulf New Zealand.

I found the lectures on undercover work extremely interesting and at the conclusion of the course I was told that I had been one of the detectives chosen to be an undercover operator.

Because nearby Christchurch had been chosen as the venue for the 1974 Commonwealth Games, I was too busy with CIS duties to run any undercover operation. Our squad was heavily involved in intelligence gathering and arranging security for the many visiting dignitaries.

As soon as the games were over, I was told that I would be given an undercover agent. The head of the Dunedin CIB, Emmet Mitten, was concerned that many criminals had become bookmakers and organisers of other types of illegal gaming. Our intelligence indicated that some of the lucrative profits were being used to finance cannabis deals.

Stolen property was also being received as payment for drugs and these same criminals were heavily involved in that trade, mainly in the public bars of inner city hotels.

The national head of the CIS in 1974 was Colin 'Cyril' Wilson. He chose my undercover agent and it turned out to be a good choice. This was always a difficult decision for the head of CIS because he had to be sure the agent and his operator would be compatible. They have to work very closely and trust is paramount. The operator has to provide the intelligence and direction for the agent. Their lives are in your hands and they must trust you explicitly.

The daily meetings with the operator are extremely important as only during that time can they can return to normality, at least for an hour or so.

My man, James Bernard Ryan, was from a small North Island town and he had been in the police for about eighteen months. It soon became obvious to me that he had been chosen for undercover work because he was an extrovert. Unlike the drug scene, the gaming and criminal scene required an agent with an outgoing personality. But although he liked to be the centre of attention, Ryan was also a good listener.

Because I had been working undercover I did not take as gospel all the theory we had been fed at the undercover operators' course. I was prepared to stick to the basic rules, and of course the police regulations, but I believed I knew, from my own experience, what was required to make the operation a success.

For a start, I did away with having Ryan visit me at my home in the dead of night to be debriefed and to get his mail and money. He was a keen sportsman and a good golfer so I bought him a set of clubs and at an arranged time he would be at a certain hole on a certain golf course when I would jog past on my daily workout. If no one was about we would arrange to meet nearby.

Sometimes it was at a nearby cemetery, sometimes a deserted beach, sometimes a church. We varied it. What did not vary though was his weekly meal at my home on a Sunday night. I would pick him up at an arranged spot and he would lie down on the back seat while I drove to my home. When it was time to leave, I drove him out in the same manner.

Ryan and I had an excellent relationship. As keen sportsmen, we shared much the same interests, and he was popular with my wife and children. Most importantly, he was honest and trustworthy.

It was the first time a long-term undercover agent had been used in Dunedin and the operation was a resounding success. This was at least partly because, unlike many of my fellow operators, I did not push my agent to get instant results. Nor did I come up with any elaborate plan for the operation.

I waited to see what sort of person I had as an agent then I allowed him a month or so to establish himself before we sat down and formulated a plan. To succeed I knew that he had to feel he had a say in the way the operation was to run. As it transpired, Ryan's input was vital but the most important thing was that the guidelines were established and agreed to by both of us.

Our long-term plan was for Ryan to get a job as a barman in one of the seedier inner-city hotels. He was a brilliant pool player and he was never short of a partner when playing pool. He made it known that he was down south looking for work as a barman.

Within a week or so the manager of the hotel, who often

partnered him at pool, offered him a part-time position. That turned to full time within a fortnight.

Ryan was able to associate with the bookmakers and criminals operating out of that hotel. On his days off, he would go around the other hotels with one of the barmaids. His pool-playing prowess ensured he became very well known in a relatively short space of time.

As a result, he was able to place bets in other hotels, purchase stolen property and gather valuable intelligence on criminals and the rapidly escalating drug problem.

After three months we had a clean-up. Approximately thirty people were arrested simultaneously and once they realised they had been exposed by an undercover operative most pleaded guilty.

Within six months I was given another undercover agent, for a drug operation. A number of fishermen operating out of remote areas of Fiordland and the West Coast of the South Island were allegedly acting as pickups for drug dealers. They were meeting container ships and transporting the imported cannabis to shore. One of these fishermen was bringing the cannabis (imported buddah sticks) through to Dunedin where it was distributed through a prominent city musician.

Pat O'Brien was my new agent and he was a shock to the system. He phoned me to say he was in town and I met him near St Clair beach. As he approached, I realised that I had the complete opposite to Jim Ryan to work with.

O'Brien was the son of former prominent politician Gerry O'Brien, the leader of the Social Credit party. He had long, flowing hair, a large diamond stud in his nose and a dangling earring. Although it was late spring, he was wearing a converted women's fur coat, leather sandals, jeans and a muslin shirt. He was carrying a large leather handbag.

As I walked toward him I thought, "This guy will be a challenge."

I was wrong. O'Brien was the consummate professional. He was an extremely experienced and successful undercover agent and within a month he had our drug ring in jail for Christmas.

I strongly suspected that he was a user rather than someone who simulated using cannabis but he showed none of the traits of a heavy cannabis user.

During the next four years I had a number of other agents. It became apparent to me after a year or so that the police department was not looking after these agents and many of them were becoming drug dependent.

At one of the undercover seminars, the drug sample bag of the visiting lecturer, Detective Sergeant Norm Cook, was rifled and hard drugs and cannabis stolen. It was obviously the work of one of the trainees or the former agents instructing them. I was shocked when the incident was kept in-house. There was no inquiry, no attempt to identify the offender or offenders and the excuse given was that any exposure could adversely affect the undercover programme.

The other area of concern for me was the department's policy of placing an agent with an informant. Many of these informants were not just drug dependants but were in fact drug addicts. Some of the young police officers placed with them also became addicted to drugs, and not just cannabis but hard drugs.

In early 1976, I was told that I would have at my disposal the top informant in New Zealand at the time. He was known as Shorty. I was aware of Shorty's reputation having heard all about him at drug squad conferences and seminars. I was also aware that he was an addict.

Shorty was an evil-looking little man with a swarthy complexion and long greasy hair.

At all times, winter or summer, he wore the same clothes – a sheepskin waistcoat, jeans and leather sandals. He was always bare chested and never wore socks. He also carried a sacking shoulder bag.

I did not take to Shorty from the start. I had not requested an informant and I heard through the grapevine that CIS headquarters had to get him out of a North Island town quickly hence the transfer to Dunedin.

Because police regulations did not allow us to pay an informant a weekly wage, headquarters sent me a young undercover agent to accompany Shorty. The idea was that I would draw extra expenses for the agent to pay Shorty.

The young man sent down to me was known as 'Football', a nickname he had aquired after being viciously kicked by a group of Maoris in a pub brawl. Football was a clean-cut, decent young man with no previous experience as an undercover agent. He was a big boy and the cover for him was to pose as Shorty's 'heavy'.

The idea might have been okay in theory but the two were not compatible. After a week or two it became obvious to me that something was seriously wrong when Football began complaining about Shorty's behaviour. He told me that he was carrying a knife and he frequently flashed the knife when they were among druggies. His heavy cannabis use was also concerning Football.

Then there was the matter of cleanliness. Having lived at home before joining the undercover programme, Football would have found it difficult sharing a flat with Shorty who was grubby and untidy.

I telephoned CIS headquarters and relayed Footy's complaints to Sergeant Phil Spackman, one of the CIS co-ordinators. He telephoned me back a few hours later and stated that Shorty would have to remain in Dunedin because there was a contract on his life as a result of his previous work for the department. He agreed that the situation was far from ideal but he gave me an assurance that as soon as the court cases were over and the offenders imprisoned Shorty would be shipped out.

I decided to sort Shorty out. I told Football to bring him to our next meeting at Tomahawk Beach. When I told him that while he was working for me he would have to obey the law as well as the ground rules agreed to, he became extremely angry. He told me he was going to ring Mal Churches, head of the New Zealand CIB, at Police Headquarters.

I did not take him seriously and I continued to berate him over his heavy cannabis use and the fact he was carrying a knife. I pointed out that he was of no use to me or the police department if he was busted on drug charges or caught with an offensive weapon. He remained surly during the remainder of the meeting but I felt I had at least spelled out the ground rules under which we would be operating in future.

A short time after arriving back in my office, Spackman phoned. He said, "I thought you understood that you were to lay off Shorty. He's telephoned Mal Churches complaining that you are getting heavy with him."

I told Spackman exactly what had been discussed at the meeting but he was still agitated. He told me again that Shorty was an expert in his field and if I let him have his head he would clean up Dunedin.

He said, "The beauty is he's not a cop Tom, so if he does anything not quite according to the book then it's not our problem. Let him jack up the buys and Football can hand over the cash and give the evidence in court." He finished by reassuring me that Shorty would be out of Dunedin as soon as practical but he had to be utilised in the meantime.

Although I had serious misgivings, I allowed the operation to proceed as I had been instructed. By this time I had been promoted and I was head of the drug squad covering the Otago and Southland provinces. As this entailed responsibility for the cities of Dunedin and Invercargill as well as the tourist resorts of Queenstown and Wanaka, I considered I was busy enough without the added responsibility of running two undercover agents. It was becoming virtually impossible to devote the necessary time to the undercover operation with drug squad staff to supervise and train as well.

After a week or two, I had a change of heart about Shorty. His intelligence in relation to the Dunedin drug scene was proving to be excellent. He and Football had also made a number of drug buys and Football now seemed reasonably content.

After another two months, the two of them had around thirty drugs buys and a number of Dunedin's prominent burglars were ready to be arrested as a result of their efforts.

I had noticed a decline in Football's physical appearance over that time, but I put it down to the lifestyle he was leading. Then I noticed mental deterioration. He was becoming forgetful, late for meetings and suddenly unable to account for his expenditure. I knew the significance of this and I suspected he was using cannabis.

When I questioned him alone he was evasive but I knew the signs. I telephoned headquarters and requested they terminate Football.

As usual they tried to stall but this time I was adamant and it was finally agreed his operation would be terminated within a fortnight. It was also agreed that Shorty would also leave Dunedin after doing a short-term assignment in Invercargill.

Shorty's short-term Invercargill assignment proved an embarrassment. I was told that he had infiltrated a druggie wedding reception as arranged and when the police raided they found hard drugs exactly where Shorty told them they would be. What concerned them, however, was the allegation being made that he had planted the drugs himself.

Although he denied it and the police proceeded with the charges against the people arrested, some police officers had misgivings.

A week or so later we had operation 'Cleanup'. We raided the flats and houses of the various people Football and Shorty had made buys from, as well as the houses and flats of criminals they had received stolen property from.

The operation itself went without a hitch and a variety of drugs were seized as well as proceeds of burglaries. About forty people were arrested that day, some on serious drug charges.

After their initial court appearances and after they had briefed their solicitors, I had the first of a number of complaints about Shorty and to a lesser extent, Football.

Maurice Knuckey was the first solicitor to approach me. He said he had an horrendous story to tell me. He proceeded to relate how his clients would be alleging that Shorty carried a firearm and a knife, how he had this heavy with him who stood over people in the drug scene to such an extent that they were frightened not to sell drugs to them.

Knuckey was known as an anti-police lawyer so although I listened to him and noted his complaints I was somewhat sceptical, although the knife allegation did worry me.

The next solicitor to complain was J. Bruce Robertson, now a High Court judge. He was certainly not one to make frivolous complaints so when he began his allegations I sat up and took notice.

He alleged that his client, a pizza shop proprietor charged with selling a number of imported 'buddah sticks' (high-grade cannabis), told him that he had sold the buddah sticks to the two 'agents' but he was adamant that they had sold him a quantity on an earlier occasion before returning in the evening and asking to buy some back. What they bought back, according to Robertson's client, was part of the original amount he had purchased from them.

This was a very serious allegation and I assured Robertson I would have the matter fully investigated, although I was sceptical. He told me he was employing a private detective to look into the matter.

The allegations made did not stand up to scrutiny and Robertson's private detective could not find any proof of wrongdoing by the two agents. Robertson's client eventually pleaded guilty to the selling charges but Maurice Knuckey's client elected trial by jury.

The trial was held in the Dunedin High Court and was presided over by Sir Richard Wild, the Chief Justice of New Zealand. Sir Richard, and the jury, after listening to the witnesses, dismissed Knuckey's claims and his client was convicted and sentenced to imprisonment before being deported.

That was not the end of the story, however. During my inquiry, although I found no evidence of criminal conduct, I did find that Football, a police officer, had been compromised by having to work with an informant, particularly one with a criminal background and drug dependency.

To protect his cover, he had to stand by on occasions while Shorty broke the law and he could have been forced to smoke cannabis rather than simulate because of situations Shorty got them both into. Not to do so may have endangered their lives.

I reported to CIS headquarters that I was concerned at the department's policy of putting an undercover police officer with an informant because of what had occurred during this operation. I also expressed my concerns about the effect it had had on Football and I recommended that because of his use of cannabis he should be removed from the undercover programme.

My recommendations were ignored and I was sad to learn that Football's police career ended ignominiously. Later, at a conference in Wellington when I expressed my disgust at his treatment to the head of the CIS, he said, "Tom, it's a war out there and he was always going to be a casualty after Dunedin so we just got a bit more mileage out of him."

My response was to withdraw from the undercover programme as an operator.

I did briefly return in 1982 to run another undercover constable only to find things had not improved. Undercover police officers had become even more expendable, particularly if they were 'straight'.

My frustrations with the undercover programme had been festering for some years. In 1975, while working on the infamous Mr Asia drug ring, I was appalled at the lack of security and also the lack of protection I was given in what turned out to be an extremely dangerous operation. Later events clearly demonstrated that the Mr Asia drug ring was responsible for many brutal murders throughout the world.

My first cause for concern was the lack of information I was given by police headquarters when the operation was first discussed. Although they knew all the leading players I would be dealing with they chose, in their wisdom, to keep the names of the more dangerous members of the drug ring from me because they were concerned I would refuse the assignment.

The most basic requirement in a successful undercover operation is honesty. If the agent cannot trust his operator then it is usually a disaster. The ambitious commissioned officer who was running my operation wanted the operation to succeed for his own glory and was not really interested in my welfare. I did have contacts in the Auckland drug squad and CIS, however, and I belatedly received an honest briefing from them. Only then did I decide to continue.

While at the NDIB (National Drug Intelligence Bureau), an

incident occurred that illustrates the fantasy world Police Headquarters people live in. A Detective Sergeant Norm Cook briefed me about headquarters requirements in relation to the large amount of money I would have in my possession over the next two or three days. Twenty-five thousand dollars was a large sum of money in 1975 and he was quite right to emphasise my responsibilities in safeguarding the money.

At the conclusion, Cook mentioned, almost as an afterthought, that some members of this syndicate were dangerous and for that reason the Director-Crime, Mal Churches, insisted I carry a firearm. I was agreeable until he produced a police service revolver. I told Cook that I would not under any circumstances carry a police issue revolver on a drug undercover operation and that I would go unarmed.

He went away to telephone Mal Churches. When he came back he told me I would have to carry the firearm because Churches considered that if the money was ripped off at least the department would have 'covered its arse' by taking every precaution possible to prevent that by having the undercover agent armed.

I didn't mince words. I told Cook that he wasn't dealing with a rookie undercover cop. I had run undercover operations as well as being an agent. In drug buys, the sellers as well as the buyers can get ripped off so it was common practice for both parties to carry firearms and even have armed backups standing by. I pointed out that at any time I could be frisked and while it might be considered cool and enhance one's cover to be carrying a 'piece', a police issue pistol was a ridiculous proposition.

If they could not obtain an appropriate firearm then I would go unarmed.

Cook grudgingly acknowledged that the instruction to carry the firearm had been made not with my safety in mind but because of departmental concerns for the $25,000. A typical example of departmental thinking! They were prepared to risk my life and jeopardise the operation with a stupid last-minute requirement just to – as they so typically put it – cover their collective arses.

That incident merely confirmed what I had suspected all along

– undercover agents were just a number as far as the gurus from Police Headquarters were concerned. Necessary but expendable.

I flew from Christchurch to Auckland as Greg Knox, part-owner of a car sales operation in Christchurch. A cover identity had been arranged so that any subsequent check would show that Greg Knox was indeed the part-owner of a Sydenham car sales.

I had with me $25,000 in cash and I was to meet a Maori known as Dick. This had been arranged by an informant who was out of the country. He had, before leaving, told the Mr Asia ring that he knew a Christchurch businessman who was dealing but wanting more 'gear', particularly imported buddah sticks. They had taken the bait and a meeting was arranged at Auckland airport.

I was to arrive on the 11.30 a.m. flight from Christchurch and go to the shoe-shine stand. I was to have with me a copy of *Truth*, which I was to pretend to be reading. I would be approached by a large Maori who would introduce himself with the statement, "I hear it was a rough flight." I was to reply, "Piece of cake, mate." He would then introduce himself as Dick and I would introduce myself as Greg.

I would go with him, either to the bar or to his car, to negotiate a buy. I was told that I was to show him the cash and he would produce one of the buddah sticks for my inspection.

I had already been told that the former head of the Auckland drug squad was now in charge of airport security. I had also been told he had been removed from his previous position because it was suspected he was corrupt. This was a major concern to me because I had been at drug and undercover courses with him.

Although my appearance had changed since then, I was still concerned.

I decided that I would insist on going to the Maori's car despite the danger of a cash ripoff.

The next morning before catching my flight to Auckland, I heard a radio news flash that a large consignment of buddah sticks had been seized by Auckland waterfront police. It had been a fluke catch in that the officers were driving around the waterfront when one got out of the car to stretch his legs. As he gazed out on the water, he noticed two frogmen towing two huge plastic bags. He

alerted his offsider and the drug squad were called in. The result –
millions of dollars of buddah sticks were seized and two men
arrested.

I listened with interest, mindful that the seizure could impact on
my operation. It wasn't long before I found out.

The flight to Auckland was uneventful. I was carrying a briefcase
with a change of clothes and $25,000 in cash underneath those
clothes, and of course the copy of *Truth*.

To me this was not a particularly dangerous mission although it
did have the potential to become one. When I worked undercover,
I was invariably cast as a businessman. This meant I usually dealt
with the upper echelon of the drug or criminal world and our
meetings would take place where danger was minimised.

The adrenalin was still pumping, however, because I realised
factors beyond my control could affect the outcome of the
operation. One of the big problems in arranging meetings at public
places such as airports was the very real danger of being sprung by a
fellow police officer. If one did recognise me, they would probably
start with the line, "Well now, how long have you been out of the
job then?"

No matter how much they are lectured at the police college
about being cautious, when they think that they have recognised a
fellow officer they still tend to blunder in as only the police can.

These were the thoughts racing through my mind on the flight.
What if? What if? As the plane approached Auckland, I composed
myself and went through my normal routine of selecting the more
likely problems I could encounter and then selecting a strategy to
cover those eventualities.

On arrival in Auckland, I made my way to the shoe-shine stand
as arranged. I pretended to browse through my newspaper and then
I heard a voice behind me say, "Rough flight, mate?" I turned and
replied, "Piece of cake, mate."

As I turned, I saw a large Maori with his hand outstretched. He
said, "Greg, I'm Dick." I shook hands with him and I noted that he
was clean cut and well dressed. He said, "Let's go over to the bar. I
hope you brought the bread."

I told him it was in the briefcase and I offered to show it to him although I insisted that I do so in the carpark as there were too many cops around.

I was still worried about the former head of the Auckland drug squad and although the carpark would be more dangerous with the possibility of a ripoff I had been assured that the Auckland surveillance squad would have me under surveillance at all times.

Dick agreed to this and as we walked towards the exit he said, "I've got some bad news for you. That big haul the cops grabbed at the wharf was ours. Things are bad. The two pings [Chinese] won't talk but everyone's paranoid."

I said, "I guess this deal's off then?"

As I spoke I noticed another Maori appeared to be following us. I purposely dropped my newspaper and as I bent to pick it up I recognised him as Zak Ratana, a member of the Mr Asia ring.

Dick then suggested we go for a drive. He said, "I want to eyeball the bread. If I can tell the boss you had the bread then we can maybe do business at a later date."

I just nodded. When we reached his car, I decided I would not go for a drive with him. It was a Mustang, a real souped-up job. I knew if he took off in that the ex-public service Falcons, Toyotas and Datsuns of the surveillance squad would not be able to keep up.

I said, "Listen, mate. I'll show you the bread but I'm not going anywhere with you. There's no point. You haven't got the gear and I have to be careful."

Dick shrugged his shoulders and said, "That's cool."

As I went to get into the car, I checked to make sure no one was hiding in the back then I got in and left my door open. I was nervous as I couldn't see Ratana but I knew he was watching.

I unlocked the briefcase, removed the clothing and allowed Dick to view the money. The bundles were in thousand-dollar lots and I quickly pointed out to him that there were twenty-five bundles.

Dick relaxed and seemed much happier. Once again he said that he was sure we could do business in the near future as what the cops had got was only a small amount compared to what they were bringing in.

I gave him my telephone number at the Christchurch car yard and also a number in Dunedin. It was the special line into the Dunedin CIS office. I explained to him that the second number was where I stayed while doing business in Dunedin. I then asked Dick to give me his number, handing him my airline ticket so he could write the number on it. He did it without hesitation and I knew then we had him as I now had his fingerprints on the ticket and a sample of his handwriting.

After declining another offer to go to town with him for lunch, we farewelled each other and I returned to the airport bar where I had a relaxing drink and some lunch.

I re-booked my seat on the late flight to Christchurch and then after checking to see I wasn't being followed I caught a taxi into Auckland.

I had the taxi driver stop at a couple of shops which enabled me to check once again that I wasn't being followed. The driver was then directed to take me to the Catholic cathedral where a friend, Father Dennis Farrell, worked. I had afternoon tea with Dennis before asking to use his phone.

I telephoned my operator, a detective inspector at Auckland Central police station, known as 'Boyscout Bruce'. When he came to the phone he was breathless. He gasped, "Shit we lost you. Where's the money?"

I couldn't resist it so I said, "The bad news is I got ripped off. But I'm still alive."

I heard a moan and he said, "Jesus, it's the surveillance squad's fault. They're in the shit over this."

Time to put him out of his misery I thought. I could almost hear his brain ticking over, "Where can I lay the blame for this stuffup . . . anywhere so long as it's away from me."

I told him I still had the money thanks to the fact that I had not accompanied Dick. I said, "Wasn't it you who told me you had the best surveillance squad in Australasia?"

He told me he was not impressed at all with my sense of humour nor my attitude but he would overlook it on this occasion. He then told me to come to the police station for a debrief.

This was the last straw as far as I was concerned. I said to him, "How many undercover operations have you run? If I have to come to a police station during an undercover operation then I pull out. It's my bloody life at stake here not just $25,000."

I gave him a brief outline of what happened over the phone and said I would report in full to the NDIB in Wellington. His attitude was typical of most commissioned officers. He had already been preparing his press release about how he had run a successful undercover operation and the crime clearances that had resulted. He didn't appear to give a damn about my safety.

I had no confidence in him so I told Police Headquarters that if the operation were to continue I would have to have a new operator. He was replaced with Detective Sergeant Tony Hill, a man I knew and had the utmost confidence in.

Hill gave me the briefing I should have had at the beginning of the operation. He told me that some of the most dangerous criminals and standover men in New Zealand were involved in the operation. Some of the names were known to me and he produced photographs and dossiers so I knew just who I might be dealing with. They included people who became well known in later years as members of the Mr Asia syndicate such as Craig Leslie Brown, 'Scruff' Ralph, John Sydney West, 'Too Fats' Smith, Peter Fulcher, Christopher Martin Johnstone, Terry Clark and Zac Ratana.

Hill suggested a change of plan. He said that with the security problem at the airport it was too dangerous to do the proposed buy in Auckland and in future negotiations with Dick I should endeavour to change the venue.

He recommended I point out that I had already travelled to Auckland only to be let down at the last minute so the next meeting and buy should take place at either Christchurch or Dunedin. I agreed but I was not confident that Dick would agree.

Through February and March 1975, Dick, who I now knew to be Richard Legg, kept in touch on a regular basis. I had to make sure I was in various parts of the country in order to act out my cover which entailed buying performance cars.

Each time I travelled I took with me the $25,000 in case I was contacted at short notice and advised the deal was on. I still had the original cash and the reason for this was that all the banknote numbers had been recorded. When I was at home I hid the money in my house. I was amazed the department never checked on the cash during that two-and-a-half-month period. Later I learnt that they had forgotten I had it!

In the discussions I had with Dick Legg, I gradually increased the pressure for him to deliver the buddah sticks to me rather than me going to Auckland to get them. The trump card I used in the end was to guarantee him that my next drug buy would be a $100,000 purchase, providing the gear was top quality. I also haggled over the price with him and he kept putting me off, telling me he couldn't make decisions on price.

Finally a deal was struck whereby Legg agreed to deliver $25,000 worth of buddah sticks to Dunedin. If I was satisfied with that deal I was to travel to Auckland and meet 'Scruff' Ralph, his boss, and members of the syndicate to negotiate a quantity deal for the $100,000 buy.

This was the breakthrough we had been after. I was to meet the top dogs of the syndicate and negotiate future deals with them.

Headquarters were advised that the $25,000 of imported buddah sticks were about to be delivered, probably by Legg. After the transaction was completed, Legg would be allowed to return to Auckland.

Phase two of the operation would be my trip to Auckland to meet Legg's boss, Scruff Ralph, and other members of the syndicate to finalise a $100,000 buy. After that transaction, police could arrest the identified members, which would effectively remove the country's biggest drug syndicate.

Headquarters' response left us absolutely flabbergasted. We were ordered to terminate the operation at Dunedin when the $25,000 worth of buddah sticks was delivered. The courier was to be arrested there with any follow-up arrests to be made in Auckland. The reason given was that we would have spent $25,000 of undercover money without any real chance of getting it back.

We argued long and hard but we were dealing with idiots. I felt frustrated after all that work to get close to the syndicate and then, when given the opportunity to meet and identify them, some paper shuffler at Police Headquarters made the decision to pull the plug.

As the years went by and the Mr Asia syndicate grew to become an international drug cartel, responsible for numerous murders throughout the world, plus the crime and destruction of hundreds of young lives, I often wondered how many lives could have been saved if that undercover operation had been allowed to run its full course.

In March 1975, the curtain finally fell on the undercover operation. Dick Legg and I agreed on a quantity of buddah sticks for the sum of $25,000 and he arranged for a drug courier to bring it to me.

It really was an anti-climax. I travelled to Dunedin Airport on a Saturday morning and uplifted the courier – a clean-cut young man of about 25 – as arranged. I drove him to my office at the South Dunedin car yard I had at my disposal and we completed the transaction.

While I counted the buddah sticks, he counted the money. After I sampled the buddah, the transaction was complete.

I took him to a inner city bar for a drink while he awaited his flight back to Auckland. It was of course a set-up. The barman was a police officer. A policewoman and another police officer, in rough clothing, were drinking in the corner of the bar. They were pretending to study a race guide, had a transistor radio, and acted like pub bookmakers.

We sat near them at the bar. It had been arranged that after we had a drink or two I would get up to go to the nearby machine to get some salted peanuts. That was the cue for the 'crunch' team to make their move.

As I walked away, they pounced and the drug courier suddenly found himself staring down the muzzle of two police .38 revolvers. Extreme care had to be taken because intelligence we had indicated that most of the couriers in this drug syndicate were armed when making deals.

After the courier had been interviewed in Dunedin, Auckland

drug squad detectives raided the home of Richard Legg, where he was hosting a poolside party for friends. He had earlier received a phone call from his courier in Dunedin to say the buy had been made without any problems so Dick obviously thought it was time to celebrate.

Although Legg made no admissions he had been 'bricked in' during the preceding months with his phone calls monitored and my phone numbers found in his office. He pleaded guilty to dealing and received a five-year jail sentence. His courier was sentenced to two years.

Neither man 'talked' and so an operation that had promised so much just fizzled out.

That night as I watched some of the police officers involved in the arrest at the hotel celebrating the drug bust with the bosses I felt the most frustrated I had ever felt in my entire career. I have never suffered fools gladly and I considered resigning.

I let it be known that I was unhappy and at the debrief was openly critical of the decision that had been taken to terminate the operation at a time when we had penetrated the inner circle of the drug ring.

I had been made aware that I was to be recommended for a Commissioner's commendation for my work on the operation but after I spoke out at the debrief the recommendation was withdrawn. The truth obviously hurt!

A few months later I carried out my last undercover assignment as an agent. I was asked to organise myself and two other ex-agents to attend a gaming evening in Christchurch for businessmen and sportsmen. It was alleged prostitutes had been sold and raffled at previous functions.

To me this appeared to be a simple operation but before I arranged staff I was approached by the head of the Dunedin CIB who asked me to take a trainee detective as an undercover agent. I declined on the grounds that the person concerned was not a trained agent and I had a number of ex-agents in Dunedin I intended using.

The trainee detective was known as the 'Womble' to staff in the

CIB office due to his physical resemblance to the television characters. I had also heard that he was prone to acting like the Wombles, especially after a few drinks.

I was rather surprised at the request but this individual seemed to have the ability to ingratiate himself to the bosses. Not that it was difficult with the commissioned officer in question. A number of staff had found that by buying the boss a drink or two in the police club their futures could be assured.

The Womble lived at home with his mother and father who were very protective of him. When he later worked under me on the drug squad I found they would phone regularly to say he was too ill to come to work. I wondered at the time why he didn't telephone himself. Later, when he was admitted to a mental institution to be treated for alcoholism, I realised why.

Unfortunately one of the officers I had chosen to go on the mission had to withdraw at the last minute and I was forced to take the Womble as a substitute.

The other police officer was an undercover agent I had recruited directly into the undercover programme from university. He had been working in the Auckland area and was an experienced agent.

On arriving in Christchurch we were briefed by the commissioned officer in charge of the operation. Once again I found myself dealing with a police officer who was completely out of his depth when it came to running an undercover operation. His briefing, if one could call it that, lacked any background intelligence.

All he really had for us were the admission tickets and the address of the venue. He knew nothing else. When asked about the layout of the venue, including exits, he confessed that he didn't know.

We were given a bleeper to signal the appropriate time for the raiding party to enter – an arrangement I was far from happy about as these devices were often faulty.

In the end I decided it was a waste of time trying to get a proper briefing from the detective inspector so I briefed the other two officers in the car on the way to the venue. I told them that we would have to play it by ear but the crucial thing to remember when the crunch team came in was the preservation of evidence and the identification of the organisers. Unbelievably, this had not been covered by the detective inspector.

I allocated one officer to watch and track just who made off with the money, another to gather any real evidence such as crown and anchor boards while I would try to apprehend the prostitutes and their minders.

When we arrived at the venue, the carpark was almost full. After parking, we gave our ticket to the doorman and found ourselves in a large hall with a stage at one end. The hall had been transformed into a miniature casino with areas set aside for crown and anchor, blackjack, two-up and so on. Two bars were in full operation and the place was swinging.

The clientele were something of a mixture. Middle-aged men in business suits mingled with younger, more casually dressed males and bouncers were at each exit. It was obvious there was only one way in and out and that was well guarded.

Shortly after 9 p.m. the main door was locked and two guards were posted there. The organisers were clearly happy with the crowd they had and security was now their main concern.

We wandered around having a drink and taking in the games. I decided to play crown and anchor and the other two headed for the card games. As is often the case when gambling with departmental money, you get lucky. I was up around $50 when I felt a tap on the shoulder and a voice whispered in my ear, "We had better get the Womble. He's pissed already and starting to draw attention to himself. He could blow things."

It was the other undercover agent speaking and he looked very agitated.

I followed him over to the two-up and the Womble was certainly making a spectacle of himself. He appeared to be drunk and was shouting and yelling every time he had a bet.

I noticed the heavies watching him. We got beside him and pretended to enter into the spirit of things before inviting him to come down to the crown and anchor. We stopped at the bar and in muffled tones I told him he was drawing attention to himself and that was not how he had been briefed. I ordered him to stay with me and just to act naturally, have a drink, have a bet and relax.

Two things became obvious to me in that short time. The first was that the Womble was scared and the second that he was drunk. I determined not to let him out of my sight and to stop him becoming more intoxicated. Fortunately I succeeded.

For the rest of the night we were just part of the crowd but by 11.30 p.m. I was confident we could identify the organisers. About this time I heard the announcement for live entertainment. I saw a double mattress being placed on the stage and scantily clad women around it.

It was difficult to see through the crowd milling around but from the cheers and occasional glimpses I realised that two of the females were taking part in a lesbian act on the mattress. Both were naked.

The Womble and I were approached by a man and offered a ticket in a raffle for the two performing females. He told us the winners would be announced immediately the lesbian act was over and they could claim their prize on the mattress.

Although we needed the tickets as evidence, it did pose a problem if we won. We had not signalled the police to begin their raid and I did not know just how long it would take them to gain entrance to the place. Obviously not to claim the prize would create suspicion. I was about to intimate that we were queers and not into women, when the Womble thrust $20 out for two tickets. I could have killed him.

I grabbed him and took him to the toilets where I activated the signal for the police raiding party to enter the hall. I said to the Womble, "You had better pray neither of us win this bloody raffle, son." When we returned to the hall, it was obvious that we had not been winners as I could see two men climbing onto the stage.

The three of us positioned ourselves so we could help the raiding party to round up the organisers and preserve evidence.

It seemed an eternity before we heard the raiding party but I was amazed to hear the sound of chopping at the door and the call, "Police, open up!"

This set off a chain reaction. The organisers, as we anticipated, started grabbing the money and heading for the other exits. The on-stage performance came to a sudden halt with the participants frantically attempting to get their clothes on.

I grabbed a crown and anchor board and took off after one of the organisers. I grabbed him as the raiding party entered the hall. My two offsiders also grabbed evidence and offenders while the raiding party apprehended the rest.

Back at Christchurch police station I was still shaking my head wondering why the police raiding party did not have basic equipment such as chainsaws in order to gain quick entry to the hall. I silently thanked my lucky stars that we had not required their assistance in a hurry.

The officer in charge of the operation was strutting his stuff, telling the district commander what a success the operation had been. I remained silent but I made a vow then and there that I would never be involved again as an undercover agent.

More and more I was seeing ex-cadets, commonly known as 'space cadets', running undercover operations. Many were totally incompetent and their only claim to fame was that they had demonstrated an ability to pass examinations.

Police work really involves summing situations up by seeing, exploring and finally judging. I often felt sorry for the ex-cadets because they had been indoctrinated into the police culture at an early age, in fact straight from school. While they may have seen and judged a situation, they seldom explored it.

Because of their police indoctrination many, but not all, had missed out on developing people skills. They really only felt comfortable among their own kind, other police officers. They were the generation of police that invented police clubs, where they could drink and socialise among fellow police. This enabled them to become even more insular. The establishment of police clubs was one of the worst moves the department ever made.

To sum it up, ex-cadets often seemed to me to be okay at solving a problem or puzzle if they had all the pieces. They tended to falter when a situation arose where it required them to find the pieces and assess the value of those pieces.

My final association as a long-term undercover operator came in 1982.

I was reluctantly brought back in as an operator because CIS headquarters would not allow an agent to work in Dunedin unless an experienced operator was available. This was because the CIB in that city had as its head a man who had not even qualified as a detective.

This was Laurie Dalziel, known to all as 'Dazzle Fawlty', such was his resemblance to television character Basil Fawlty of Fawlty Towers fame. During Dalziel's time as head of the Dunedin CIB, local journalists nicknamed the local CIB, Fawlty Towers.

CIS headquarters were understandably nervous about how this man would react to covert police operations when he had no previous experience in even basic detective work. This, plus his propensity for loose talk and interference, was cause for concern And they certainly had good reason to be concerned.

I finally agreed to run the undercover operation, which we hoped would penetrate the Maori gang, the Mongrel Mob. A number of the Mongrel Mob played rugby league for the local Maori league club, Kia Toa, and I requested a Maori agent.

CIS headquarters were unable to meet my request but they did suggest a young Islander policeman, Vula. He was a promising rugby league player in Auckland and with the standard of league much lower in Dunedin it was thought that he would be much sought after as a player. 'Ratz', as he was known, was introduced to me and I realised immediately that he had the potential to do the job.

He was about 21 years old, tall and well built and, what was most essential, a handsome guy who would catch the eyes of the girls. This is an important attribute for an undercover agent because if he can get a girl to accompany him to places like hotels and nightclubs he does not usually rate a second glance, while trying to penetrate the drug scene if alone is virtually impossible.

His dress was very trendy and he told me that his interests were working out in the gym, rugby league and music. I decided he was the agent we needed.

Within a relatively short period, Ratz had been accepted by some of the local rugby league players. His obvious ability had shown at pre-season training and the local Maori club were keen to obtain his services as a player. They had accepted him as one of their own, even letting him know that he should play for them because they were a progressive club who awarded their player of the day a deal bag of cannabis.

All was going well and we were making steady progress after two months when unfortunately I was required to go out of town for a fortnight and a relieving operator was appointed for that period. At that time, the detective sergeant in charge of the drug squad was a person who had worked under me and who had relieved as an operator in the past. I told Dalziel that he was the person who would be relieving me.

Dalziel immediately overruled me. As far as he was concerned, his boy 'Chookfeeder' was the only man for the job. I tried to dissuade him but he was adamant that Chookfeeder Kelly needed to get experience in this aspect of undercover work as it would help his career path.

Ratz was not happy but there was little more I could do as Dalziel had made up his mind.

When I returned to Dunedin I was contacted by Ratz, who wanted to see me urgently. When I met him I could see he was very upset. He told me that he had made a buy of cannabis at a local hotel and had taken the deal bag of cannabis to Chookfeeder the next day and reported the purchase along with details including the offender's identity, time, date and place.

I insisted with all of my agents that they include in their report whether or not they had to use any of the cannabis at the time they made the buy. This was essential because most buyers have a smoke to sample the gear. Ratz included in his report that some cannabis had been used when he 'sampled' the gear. He reported that he had simulated smoking, being able to do so because the buy had taken place in a hotel toilet cubicle in a darkened area.

Chookfeeder had insisted to him that he should not include that in his evidence as a defence lawyer would make an issue of it should the seller plead not guilty. He then proceeded to doctor the evidence by adding more cannabis to the deal bag to ensure the weight of the cannabis was as it had been before the 'sample' was smoked.

I told Ratz I would deal with the matter. Because the allegation was so serious I went directly to Dalziel and told him what Ratz was alleging. I was ready for a cover-up because I had seen it all before but his initial response even surprised me. He said, "Lewis, you surely wouldn't take the word of a black over the word of a fellow CIB NCO? I cannot believe you would be that disloyal."

I replied, "It's not a matter of taking anyone's word at this stage but a serious allegation has been made and the simple way to resolve it would be to get the deal bag of cannabis from the drug exhibit room and have forensic [DSIR] examine the contents. They will be able to tell us whether there are two different strains of cannabis present in the bag."

This incensed Dalziel and he told me he was not going to have a witch-hunt into a tried and trusted NCO just because some druggie undercover cop was trying to make a name for himself.

I was adamant that we could not be seen to sweep this one under the carpet and told Dalziel that Ratz was upset and if the matter was not resoved to his satisfaction he would probably contact CIS headquarters. I left with the matter still unresolved. I also spoke to Chookfeeder who refused to discuss the matter.

After I returned to my office, the officer in charge of the Dunedin Drug Squad called on me. What he told me disturbed me even more. He said that he had been working with an officer of the investigation unit of the Inland Revenue Department regarding a suspected drug supplier. He went on to tell me that the IRD man had told of a conversation with Dalziel where Dalziel had disclosed that the police had, in Dunedin, an undercover agent who was working in the drug scene among the gangs.

The IRD man further stated that Dalziel had promised he would, at the end of the undercover operation, have confidential information that he would pass on to the IRD which would relate to the earnings of certain drug dealers.

This was very disturbing news. Dalziel was running a sheep farm with his brother and he often spoke of how he was a 'Queen Street farmer' and would be able to write off paper losses against his personal tax. He was obviously hoping to ingratiate himself with the local IRD. To risk blowing the cover, and possibly risking the life of an undercover agent, was reprehensible

While I was considering my options, a further development occurred. Amazingly, when I spoke to Dalziel, his response was, "You should learn to co-operate with other Government departments, Lewis."

He telephoned me at home that night and told me that Ratz was the suspect in the theft of a wallet at St Lukes shopping centre in Auckland, the alleged offence having been committed just before he joined the undercover programme.

An Inspector Davidson would be coming to interview Ratz the next day. I was instructed to book a motel for the interview and have Ratz in attendance. I was ordered not to tell him the reason behind this meeting.

It was an extremely difficult situation. While I suspected Dalziel was setting up the agent I could not be sure so I had to obey orders and arrange the meeting.

The next day when I met Davidson outside the motel, he told me a wallet containing cash had been handed into police at St Lukes shopping centre some six months earlier. He said his inquiries indicated that Ratz may have been the constable who had received it. Neither the wallet or the money were ever received by the department as found property. He would therefore be interviewing Ratz regarding a theft complaint, and he was the suspect.

I insisted I sit through the interview as I was Ratz's immediate superior. Davidson was not happy with that but he was forced to agree.

The interview was a sham. It was obvious after only a few minutes that Ratz was not the offender. He was not evasive just completely confused. Davidson's interviewing technique was pathetic for someone allegedly trying to get to the truth. He talked in riddles and never once actually asked Ratz if he had in fact kept the wallet.

I spoke to Davidson outside the motel and I told him that I was of the opinion that Ratz had not stolen any wallet and that to question him about something months later, when he was operating as an undercover agent, was unfair. Ratz had continually requested Davidson to allow him to have his police notebok sent down as then he could say, without fear of contradiction, just what he was doing on a particular day months earlier. I insisted Davidson terminate the interview until that request had been granted. He agreed.

After I had taken Davidson to the CIB office, I went to lunch. On my return, I was met by Dalziel who said, "I'm meeting with Davidson this afternoon. I'll let you know the outcome."

At around 4 p.m. that day, he returned to my office and said, "Ratz is terminated. You are to keep him at your house tonight, and put him on the first flight out of Dunedin to Auckland tomorrow. It's non-stop, here's his ticket."

I told Dalziel that what he was doing virtually amounted to house arrest, and asked, "I suppose he is going to be met by Auckland CIB?"

He acknowledged that he was.

I then decided I would be more use to Ratz by pretending to go along with the charade. Later that afternoon I picked up Ratz and took him to my home. I told him what had transpired and I said to him that I thought he was being set up because of the allegation he had made against Chookfeeder, a superior officer.

Naturally for an honest young policeman this was just too much. He could not understand how he was in trouble for refusing to be party to a crime and reporting the police officer concerned.

How do you explain to an innocent young police officer how the 'brotherhood' works?

I immediately contacted my friend Paddy Finnigan, an Auckland barrister. He agreed to represent Ratz and he told me he would be there at the airport on his arrival and present at any subsequent interviews. My next move was to contact Peter Hilt (later an MP), and I asked him to ensure Finnigan's fees were met by the Police Association (the policemen's union for all officers below commissioned rank). After I explained the background, he readily agreed.

Finnigan later reported to me that the matter had been resolved and Ratz completely cleared of the allegation of theft. He told me that Ratz would have a case against the police department should he wish to pursue it.

I later flew to Auckland where I spoke with Ratz. My suggestion to him was to return to Dunedin and continue the undercover operation, assuring him that I would take up the matter of Chookfeeder's alleged action and the subsequent events at the highest level.

He listened patiently and then told me the police department had told him he could virtually pick his job in the uniform branch in Auckland if he didn't make waves. Having experienced first hand what some people in the department were capable of, he didn't have the stomach to take them on. He was adamant that he could never work undercover again and certainly would not consider working in Dunedin.

When I spoke to Paddy Finnigan he said Ratz had told him much the same despite Finnigan advising him he could be eligible to a compensation claim from the police department for unlawful detention.

The police association were tut-tutting over the incident but were obviously not keen to pursue it, having decided it was too hot to handle.

Their advice to Ratz was, "Pick yourself a good job and forget it ever happened. You can't beat the system."

While the Ratz incident is typical of what went on and still goes on in the police, I have highlighted it for another reason. That is the fact that here was a young police constable living away from his home city, working as an undercover agent, an extremely lonely and dangerous job at the best of times, and his only contact away from criminal elements was his daily meeting with his police operator.

His faith in the system is sorely tested when the police operator acts in the manner that Ratz' operator did.

However, in this case worse was to follow because when he reported the tampering with evidence, a criminal offence, he quickly faced a trumped-up inquiry designed to show his credibility as suspect. This would have assisted greatly in the writing-off of any subsequent inquiry into the allegations made against Chookfeeder.

The Ratz saga was the last straw as far as I was concerned. I had seen just how little loyalty the department had to its undercover agents and I vowed to have nothing more to do with the undercover programme. With the exception of two or three short-term vice undercover operations, I did just that.

I had long been disturbed at how many decent young policemen were coming off the undercover programme with a drug problem. Whenever I tried to raise this, I was cried down by people who quite frankly were not qualified to speak on the issue. The pen pushers and paper shufflers at head quarters had no idea of the physical and psychological damage being inflicted on these young police officers.

Many of the headquarters gurus argued that cannabis was a soft drug and therefore not addictive. However, I knew from my experience as a drug investigator, an undercover police officer, and as an undercover operator that cannabis was psychologically addictive and certainly physically addictive. I also witnessed the memory and attention deficit in officers under my control who were regularly using cannabis.

I was aware that the cannabis I had first come into contact with in the late sixties and early seventies was nowhere near as strong as the cannabis being distributed in the early and mid-eighties. In simple terms, the difference could be compared with drinking a pint of beer to a pint of scotch. Hybrid varieties and hydroponically grown cannabis contain over 18 per cent THC (tetrahydrocannabinol, the ingredient in cannabis which makes the user feel stoned). Compare this with the THC content of early cannabis of 1 and 2 per cent.

Trying to explain the problems of long-term cannabis use to my superiors was an exercise in frustration. To make it simple, I always related cannabis use to alcohol. A comparison I used to illustrate the insidious problem of cannabis use was to show that if one consumed a half bottle of wine the body would secrete the alcohol within a matter of hours. Smoke a joint and your body could be still excreting the THC a week later. That was the problem – THC stayed in the body for so long that regular, heavy cannabis smokers, as undercover agents often were, ended up permanently stoned. The other serious problem was the use of hard drugs among some undercover agents.

We had, even in the late seventies, a situation where the promising careers of many young police officers were being wrecked because of their involvement in the undercover programme. Despite warnings from myself and other experienced undercover operators, nothing was done. The police department put its head in the sand and argued that undercover police used cannabis in moderation, and because they mostly only simulated therefore it was safe!

It is only in recent years that the New Zealand police engaged psychologists to run a cursory check over agents at the end of a term of undercover work. The agents, trained to be experts in lies and deceit in the undercover programme, easily conned these psychologists.

They were also under pressure from police staff at headquarters not to say or admit anything that could adversely affect the undercover programme. So they continued living a lie, using cannabis because they were dependent on the drug, and eventually resigning or being sacked from the police. Some even went to jail for lengthy periods for dealing in drugs.

The police department disowned them as casualties of war but in recent years some of those 'casualties' have fought back, proving that while working as undercover agents they became addicted to drugs, mainly cannabis.

In New Zealand alone there are as many as 50 former undercover police officers who are unemployable as a result of their psychological and physical addiction to cannabis.

Although I did not use cannabis as an undercover agent to any great extent, my involvment in the programme certainly affected my career in the police. Secrecy was paramount and as an agent or operator I worked alone. I was encouraged to drift away from my workmates and instructed to tell them lies. For example, I would say I had six months' leave without pay to go overseas when in fact I would be winging away to another undercover assignment.

When I had an undercover agent working under my control

even the district commander did not know of the operation. The head of the CIB, myself and usually a backup operator were the only people aware that an agent was working in the city and province.

When I was promoted to detecive sergeant I had been working in this twilight zone for some four years. I was immediately placed in charge of the drug squad where I had the responsibility of training, and supervising a number of staff. I was still operating an undercover agent at that time.

The police department certainly erred in not taking me out of undercover work before my promotion. I would be the first to acknowledge that I had become a 'loner'. I had drifted away from my fellow officers and I found it very difficult to be a supervisor and confidant to trainee detectives.

That legacy of my undercover work – being a loner, tending to distrust others, making decisions without consultation – stayed with me throughout my career. One unintended benefit was that decision making without consultation was acclaimed by my subordinates accustomed to the indecision and procrastinating of NCOs and commissioned officers.

14

Whatever happened to 'Jorgy'?

Remember Ronald Jorgensen? He and his co-offender, John Gillies, achieved instant notoriety when in 1964 they carried out an execution-type murder in Bassett Road, Auckland.

Jorgy was what is known in the criminal world as a 'heavy'. He was a standover man and a bad criminal. When he received a life sentence for the Bassett Road murders he became known, within the confines of prison, as 'The Trump'. He was feared and respected by the underworld even while he was in prison.

I had been an interested listener when Bob Walton (former Commissioner) spoke of his dealings with Jorgy in Auckland during the fifties and early sixties. Walton had been one of the arresting team, if not the arresting officer, in the Bassett Road homicide. He rated Jorgensen as one of the worst criminals he had encountered and he predicted he would revert to crime when he was released from prison.

I quizzed Walton about Jorgensen because at that time Jorgy had been in prison for ten years and with a liberal Labour government in power and a radical Minister of Justice, Martyn Findlay, calling the shots I knew it would not be long before he was on parole.

Jorgensen was first released on parole about 1976 and he was immediately in the limelight. At that time I was in charge of the Dunedin drug squad and late one night I received a call from police operations about a serious drug-related assault at the Shoreline hotel.

On arriving at the hotel, I spoke to the manager who told me that Ronald Jorgensen and the victim had been seen arguing at the bar. The victim left the bar to go to the toilet and was found ten minutes later in the men's toilet in a serious condition.

The beating the man received was one of the worst seen during my police career spanning twenty years. When we attempted to interview him, he refused to divulge just who his attackers were.

Jorgensen was unco-operative as usual but his attitude just hardened our resolve to get him behind bars once again. We received our chance when the CIS under my old boss, Ron Bridge, recruited an informant who was close to Jorgy and his drug-pushing operation. Eventually he came up with the goods and as a result Jorgy was charged with drug offences. His parole was revoked and he was returned to prison to serve his life sentence.

Before Jorgensen was released, I received a frightening insight as to just how powerful his criminal connections were. A local criminal, Michael Robert Campbell Dore, had just been released from prison and had returned to live in Dunedin. I was working in CIS (the Criminal Intelligence Section) in Dunedin. The CIS received prior notification of prisoner releases so that front-line staff could be briefed on the more dangerous criminals. Dore was dangerous, an assault and battery man and a potential killer.

His mother and one of his brothers were approachable and they were aware of how dangerous he could be. I contacted his mother and she confirmed that Michael was living at home but was very quiet and withdrawn. I reassured her by stating that was common in people recently released from prison.

I was more than happy that Dore was living at home because under the influence of his mother and elder brother he seldom offended.

A short time later I was shocked to hear that he had turned a shotgun on himself at his parents' address. It was clearly a suicide but as there were no witnesses the CIB became involved.

I received a message that Michael's mother wished to speak to me. During the subsequent conversation she told me that her son believed he was on Ronald Jorgensen's hit list. She said Michael had told her that everybody had to pay homage to Jorgensen in prison and even the screws (prison officers) were careful not to cross him. Michael had been threatened by Jorgensen while working in the kitchen. As usual, he had 'snapped' and allegedly hit Jorgensen with a bread shovel.

Jorgensen was momentarily stunned and prison officers quickly removed Michael Dore to solitary confinement for his own safety.

It quickly went around the prison network that Jorgy had a contract out on Dore.

For the remainder of his sentence, Dore was kept apart from other prisoners. He was granted early release but before he left the prison Jorgy somehow got a message to him that there was a contract out on him and he would be hunted down when he was on the outside.

Mrs Dore told me that Michael never left the family house after his release. He sat all day by the window overlooking the entrance to the property. He even sat there during the night. She said she knew he was waiting for them to come but he had sworn her to secrecy so she just hoped it was all in his imagination. Naturally she was concerned but she knew the consequences of talking to the police so she remained silent.

There were no witnesses to Michael Dore's death at around 10 a.m. when the rest of the family were at work. It was confirmed that the firearm used was the one he had beside him during his lonely vigils at the front window.

A verdict of suicide was recorded yet such was Jorgy's reputation that many of the criminal element believed he had Dore killed rather than just driving him over the edge until he commited suicide.

In the early eighties, Jorgy was paroled once again but this time strict conditions as to where he was to live were imposed. He was paroled to his elderly father's care in the sleepy South Island fishing town of Kaikoura.

This certainly cramped Jorgy's style. He had always been a big-city boy, thriving in seedy bars and clubs but for some time he seemed to be lying low although rumours were rife that he was active in the drug and criminal scenes.

On 17 December 1984, Jorgy's Cortina was found upside down

at the bottom of a cliff near Kaikoura. It was not completely submerged and the keys were in the ignition but there was no sign of Jorgy.

Coincidental to Jorgy's disappearance, Christchurch police began executing search warrants in and around Kaikoura. Many of his former associates ended up in court facing drug and property offences. Perhaps the cruellest twist of all was the plight of an elderly widow who told the press that she had tried to help Jorgy by allowing him the use of her henhouse. Her reward was cannabis planted in the henhouse and her name added to the police hit list allegedly supplied by Jorgy himself.

The whole episode had that 'set-up' stench about it. A little investigative journalism might have forced the police to divulge their part in this unsavoury episode. The word was certainly out among the criminal element that Jorgy had 'topped' his mates for police assistance to leave the country. The story received even more credence when it was revealed a senior police officer had gone to school with Jorgy and in fact had been behind the raids.

The police stood firm. The 'this too shall pass' attitude prevailed once more. They tried to insinuate that Jorgy had died in the amateurishly faked car fatality. No one believed them, however, and there the matter rested until a former schoolmate of Jorgy, Bill Mason, who was holidaying in Perth, recognised him.

Panic in the police ranks! "No," they said, "Jorgy's dead."

His former schoolmate was adamant that he wasn't. The New Zealand police did not want to know.

Jorgy was still alive and well. At the time I was living in Perth and I saw him myself. Even after being identified at the Subiaco Markets and despite the subsequent publicity he still carried on working there.

Would the New Zealand police really assist a man on parole for such serious crimes to leave the country? Did they assist him to enter Australia illegally? When you line Jorgy's case up with Ross Appelgren's illegal entry into Australia and the part police played in that then perhaps the facts speak for themselves.

So where is Jorgy now? In a strange twist, police once again allowed a retired officer, Neville Stokes, to be their spokesman. "There are two possibilities: one that the scene was created to cover for a murder or it was done as a cover for his disappearance. When we weighed up the possiblities, we concluded it was more probable that he was alive," said Stokes.

Jorgensen's lawyer, Auckland QC Peter Williams, believes he is dead.

He maintained he had not heard from Jorgensen since his disappearance in 1984. "He and I corresponded and we talked together so often that if he had been alive I'm sure he would have communicated with me," said Williams.

My information is that Jorgy is alive and well!

15

Paedophiles, Prostitutes, Police and Payoffs

As the evidence of appalling mistreatment and neglect of children flowed out of the NSW royal commission under Justice James Wood, the question on every concerned parent's lips was, "Just who can we trust with our children?"

Certainly not the people we have in the past trusted to look after them.

Teachers, ministers of religion, politicians, diplomats, public servants (including police), even parents themselves have been involved in the sexual exploitation of children.

What used to be regarded as a sexual rarity has been allowed to flourish through lack of action on the part of various governments and bureaucrats. This problem is not exclusive to NSW. Paedophilia is rife worldwide, as well as in all the states of Australia, and New Zealand.

In the face of official apathy, some people have decided to wage their own war against paedophiles. Take Deborah Coddington, who recently compiled a directory of Australian sex criminals, The Australian Paedophile and Sex Offender Index, which follows hot on the heels of a similar publication in New Zealand. The Australian edition is now in its second printing, with a third not far behind.

Child abuse expert Dr Ferry Grunselt has blasted government

funding being used to try and rehabilitate paedophiles. He claims it is an absolute waste of money, which should be used to provide care for the young victims and perhaps to attempt to rehabilitate juvenile offenders before they become adult paedophiles.

The public service has failed to respond to what is now a crisis. As is usually the case with these bureaucrats, the blame is being placed elsewhere.

What of the police? The revelations of corruption and lack of commitment by police at the NSW Royal Commission were most disturbing, but to me, not surprising. Thirteen years ago I found a similar situation existed in New Zealand.

At the NSW royal commission, the extent of paedophilia shocked even Justice James Wood, who in March 1996 described the revelations of "the dark and secret world of paedophilia" as "heinous and disturbing". He is to prepare a special report on paedophilia two months after he issues his final report into corruption in the NSW police.

Already the public have heard how prominent people were involved in paedophile rings, and they still are! Many of them enjoyed the protection of corrupt police and many were never exposed because of bureaucratic bungling.

The paedophile network extended to all spheres of society. Judges, politicians, ministers of religion, and businessmen were all implicated during the NSW royal commission.

Their network even had a secret code. A few examples: S: Sex; Keester bandits: pederasts; Royal party: group of boys brought to Kings Cross for sex; The Royal Mail: payments made to a pimp for the sexual services of young boys; The hut: Kings Cross restaurant where the pimp would take boys for paedophiles; Dr Z: a paedophile doctor who owned a nursing home; 9/10: rating of a boy's sexual appeal or performance.

It took the NSW Wood royal commission to expose the extent of paedophilia in NSW and the corruption and incompetence of police and bureaucrats.

In 1985, in Dunedin, despite public demand, a royal commission into the Dunedin children's sex ring was denied by the

Labour government. Some Labour members of Parliament went to unbelievable lengths to ensure that a royal commission did not take place into the children's sex ring and the alleged interference in the inquiry.

Thirteen years have now passed since that issue dominated public interest, not only in Dunedin but throughout New Zealand. The damage to the police image lingers.

The then Commissioner of Police, Ken Thompson, stated in late 1985, "I doubt whether any recent issue has done the police reputation more harm. Our dirty linen, washed in public, painted a grubby picture of an inefficient operation and internal friction of an unacceptable level."

This was the same Ken Thompson who, in the opinion of a number of investigative journalists, had been actively involved in the cover-up and who, until forced by media and public pressure, refused to order any inquiry into the allegations.

The same Ken Thompson who, when forced by public opinion to appoint an independent examiner to the police team inquiring into the allegations, appointed lawyer John Gibson, who just happened to be a member of the police board and who 'mothered' the police inquiry team allowing them to mount what was later described as a selective investigation, overlooking witnesses and omitting evidence.

The same Ken Thompson who many believed had most to fear from a royal commission and who fought against it using every means at his disposal.

In mid-1984, I was in charge of the serious crime squad in Dunedin, formed as a quick response group to deal with the investigation of serious crime. We did not carry any other investigation files so it was envisaged we would be able to devote ourselves full time to a major investigation, should one arise.

At the time the squad was formed, the only other member was involved on another matter so I was on my own. At that time, the CIB office did not have a serious investigation so I was asked to assist with vice inquiries.

The staff were inexperienced and a backlog of work had built up.

It was made clear to me that I was only there to direct and supervise the inquiries the staff were involved in and I was not to carry any vice files myself.

In June 1984, I was absent from the office for approximately three weeks. During that time, a number of complaints were received about what appeared to be attempts to recruit young girls for sex shows.

One mother of a fourteen-year-old girl went to the Dunedin CIB office to report that not only had her daughter been approached in the street regarding the sex show, she had also been telephoned at home and propositioned.

The fourteen-year-old was able to graphically describe the details of the proposed sex show and describe the young woman she had met in the street who had tried to recruit her.

The mother, Cathy, had also spoken to the woman while she was on the phone. This person, who introduced herself as 'Audrey', told Cathy that, for $1000 a performance, her daughter would be required to dress in a sheer nightie and perform in the private suite of one of the upmarket hotels in the city.

The audience would be mixed, with well-to-do people including members of Parliament, lawyers, doctors, ministers of religion, councillors and businessmen present. She told her that it was essential that confidentiality be maintained at all times even if some of the audience were recognised.

Audrey then said her daughter would be required to lead a naked man, wearing a dog collar, around a small stage. She would be shown how to whip him and later would masturbate him. If she then had sex with him on stage in front of the audience she could earn a bonus. She would also receive a bonus if she had sex with those members of the audience prepared to pay for the privilege.

Although shocked by all this, Cathy decided to play along and managed to obtain a contact phone number from Audrey.

Armed with his information, she approached the Dunedin CIB only to find a CIB clerk who was uninterested. She was advised that the sex/vice squad were unavailable and no one else was available to take her complaint.

Despite the fact that it was the CIB clerk's job to take all complaints, worse was to follow. The clerk then instructed Cathy to carry out additional inquiries of her own!

To instruct a complainant to take on what was a police function was unethical and unprofessional. It could have also put Cathy in danger.

The CIB clerk was also aware that this was not an isolated complaint as by that time other complaints had been received.

Despite being annoyed at the cavalier treatment she had received at the hands of the CIB clerk, Cathy decided to press on in the hope she would be able to obtain more evidence thereby eliciting a more positive reaction from the Dunedin police. Through her own initiative she managed to convince Audrey to supply her with the contact number of her boss, a man known as John.

When she telephoned, Cathy's call was taken by an answering service. John later rang her and she taped the conversation. He suggested to Cathy that a mother-and-daughter act would go down well with the type of clientele he catered for at his sex shows.

She expressed her interest in his suggestion and asked exactly what he had in mind. John told her that for the sort of money he was proposing – $1500 for each show – they would be required to indulge in sex and masturbation.

He explained that the format of the sex show would be Cathy's daughter leading a naked man around the stage on a dog lead while clad in a see-through nightie. She would be required to verbally abuse him and to whip him before masturbating him.

Some females from the audience might wish to masturbate him also and she was to co-operate with them in that regard. Appropriate background music would be played during the performances and they would be video recorded.

Cathy was told that if she "measured up" she would be required to appear on stage naked and to have intercourse with the "slave" while her daughter whipped and verbally abused him.

In the latter stages, a dog would be introduced to the act and she would be paid a substantial bonus for having sex with the dog.

After the main show was over, male members of the audience

might request sex with her on stage. The price would be $150, of which she would receive half.

John reiterated Audrey's warning about the need for confidentiality as many prominent people attended these sex shows – lawyers, members of Parliament and the like – and they could be ruined by loose talk.

Cathy told John she was interested only because of the large amount of money being offered. She told him she would discuss it with her daughter as they could do with the extra money.

When Cathy reported back to the CIB in early July 1984, I had resumed duty. She was escorted to my office and introduced to me by the CIB clerk. She was an attractive woman in her mid-thirties and she impressed me as being a very intelligent lady.

She outlined to me in detail her daughter's meeting with Audrey and the events that followed. I asked her to bring her daughter to the CIB office so I could interview her and take a statement from her.

As she was leaving, I apologised for the treatment she had received from the CIB clerk, advising her that I would deal with that individual. I told her to leave the inquiry in my hands and should either Audrey or John contact her she should tell them she was still considering their proposition.

A day or so later, Cathy brought her daughter to the office to be interviewed. She was a pupil at Otago Girls High School and she looked older than her fourteen years. As I recollect, she was modelling part-time, and she certainly was an attractive young lady.

She gave me details of her meeting with Audrey, who used the same modus operandi with all the young girls she approached. She picked out attractive girls between fourteen and fifteen years of age and offered several hundred dollars to take part in a modelling show.

At the first meeting she merely inquired if they were interested and if they were she would get their home phone number for a follow-up call.

I took a signed statement from Cathy's daughter. When Cathy expressed concern about Audrey or John making further contact I again assured her that I would take action within a week and advised them both to say that they were still considering the proposition.

I knew I had to move quickly so I checked the other complaints made to the police. What I found was disturbing indeed – pieces of paper recording alleged incidents outside Otago Girls High School, in many cases without even the name or phone number of the complainants. Those I could contact I did and I found the approaches that had been made were similar to that made to Cathy's daughter.

When Audrey had telephoned the other young ladies, or their mothers, they had told her they were not interested. However, one of my inquiries did bear fruit. This was a mother who, after speaking briefly with Audrey, had told her she would not let her daughter model. Later, however, an advertisement in the personal column of the *Otago Daily Times* for young girls to take part in modelling shows caught her eye. The mother was convinced that Audrey had placed it.

I decided on an undercover operation to identify and prosecute the persons behind the sex ring. Police officers cannot be ordered to carry out undercover work, it is voluntary, but I had no difficulty at all in deciding on the policewoman I would ask. Constable Judith Devlin was a petite brunette who could certainly pass for a teenage girl.

Whenever I approached staff to take part in an undercover operation I liked to be completely up front and I also gave them 24 hours to go away and weigh up the pros and cons. I recommended they also discuss it with family, boyfriend or girlfriend before coming back to me.

After fully briefing Constable Devlin, I told her to report back to me in 24 hours with her decision.

The next day, Constable Devlin reported back to me. After asking a few more questions, she agreed to go undercover on 'Operation Audrey', the code name I had chosen.

She attended a meeting where I briefed the head of the Dunedin CIB, Laurie Dalziel. At that meeting, which lasted approximately an hour, I told Dalziel of the possible criminal charges we could be looking at in respect of Audrey and John. Being a uniform branch police officer, most of this was over his head and he had little input into such discussions.

I also raised the issue of the clerk's unprofessional behaviour at the front desk when Cathy tried to make the original complaint. Dalziel's reply was typical of the police attitude: "That's why I have a uniform branch police officer on the front desk, to sort the wheat from the chaff," he said. "It was a victimless crime, they hadn't been hurt, it's low priority as far as I am concerned."

On leaving his office I telephoned Cathy to advise her of progress and I intimated we were confident of making an arrest in the near future.

Constable Devlin was instructed by me to respond to the advertisement in the *Otago Daily Times* and she was briefed on just what to say in the initial stages. The advertised number turned out to be that of a telephone answering service which requested the caller's number so the advertiser could contact them when suitable.

Constable Devlin gave her home number and later that day she received a telephone call from a woman who introduced herself as Audrey. The constable told her she was interested in the modelling position advertised.

Audrey was cautious and she questioned the constable for some time before giving her a brief outline of what would be required. She mentioned the show as an adult show which regularly took place in private suites at top hotels in the city.

The audience would comprise men and women, many of whom were well-known professional people. The admission fee entitled them to free drinks from a well-stocked bar, a buffet meal and the show. Constable Devlin told Audrey that she was out of work and needed money so she was definitely interested. The call ended with Audrey telling the constable that she would discuss her application and others with her boss and get back to her.

A few days later she telephoned back to tell her that she was still checking all the applicants and she needed some more information for her boss. Audrey then proceeded to ask the constable her age, her measurements, in particular the size of her breasts, and then she told her that they had a show organised for Christchurch that weekend. She asked her if she was prepared to travel to Christchurch to perform.

Constable Devlin told Audrey she was unable to travel out of Dunedin but was prepared to do the shows there. Audrey commented that her boss would prefer her to do out-of-town shows in case she recognised people in the Dunedin audience.

Over the next two or three weeks, the constable was contacted by Audrey on a number of occasions. Each time, she revealed a little more about what was expected of the 'models'.

At the end of three weeks, the constable had been given virtually the same story as Cathy. She was told she would lead a naked male around by a dog collar while whipping and abusing him. She would masturbate him and invite female members of the audience to assist. She was then to have sexual intercourse with the slave, who would adopt a passive role.

Audrey also told the constable she could double her fee by having sex with as many of the audience as she could manage. The more she serviced, the more she would be paid. She was, like Cathy, told that if she had sexual intercourse with the dog she would receive a large bonus.

Constable Devlin had been well briefed and would have given the impression that she was not shocked at what had been put to her. Audrey then offered to meet the constable at a coffee bar to 'check out her statistics'. The venue was the Little Hut coffee bar in Dunedin's main street, George Street.

I arranged for the surveillance squad to photograph everyone entering or leaving the coffee bar from the time it opened until after the 10.30 a.m. meeting. This was not only to obtain photographic evidence of Audrey's attendance but for identification.

I also wanted to see if we could establish who else was involved as I suspected that Audrey would have a heavy checking the coffee bar out.

Surveillance was to be set up in the coffee bar.

At the meeting, Audrey was obviously very impressed with Constable Devlin's physical attributes. She said, "I'm sure my boss, John, would like the look of you. He will want to meet you and he usually has sex with the girls to see if they are suitable for our show."

Constable Devlin did not answer and Audrey quickly added,

"Look, he will pay you for the sex. He doesn't expect it for nothing."

The constable then agreed to a meeting with John, and Audrey told her she would phone the next day with John's contact phone number.

She kept her promise and the next morning, 8 August, Constable Devlin contacted me to tell me she had John's phone number and he would be expecting her to make phone contact that morning.

I arranged for the phone call to be made from a special telephone in the CIB office and the conversation was taped. We had checked the telephone number and as a result we did have a suspect but the taped conversation would be additional evidence.

When Constable Devlin called, the phone was answered by a man who said, "Good morning, Parkside Hotel." The constable then asked to speak to John. The man said, "Speaking." She introduced herself as 'Jenny', the code name she had been using.

John got straight to the point. He went on to repeat what Audrey had said about the sex show but went into even more detail, telling her it was based on a book by the Marquis de Sade. He said the people attending were right into bondage and perversion but she must promise to maintain secrecy about the shows as prominent people such as members of Parliament, doctors, lawyers and the like would be present.

He then discussed with her the part the dog would play in the performance and ended by saying that he would make it worth her while financially to carry out indecent acts and have sex with it. The call ended with Constable Devlin agreeing to meet John for a chat at the hotel at 1.30 p.m.

As soon as she hung up, Constable Devlin told me she believed the man she had been speaking to was John Lewis, the proprietor of the hotel and the father of Detective Murray Lewis of the Dunedin CIB.

I confirmed to her that he had been our suspect from the moment we had learnt that the phone number was that of the Parkside Hotel, but I decided against telling her before she had made the call because I wanted her to give her opinion without any influence.

When I listened to the tape, I recognised John Lewis's voice.

By this time it was almost midday and, although through no fault of her own, Constable Devlin had committed us to staging an undercover operation within a very limited time frame.

I had warned the head of the CIB the previous day that the operation might go down at short notice but he was uninterested, stating that he was going to his farm for a few days. He said, "You organise the undercover operation and John Scott can organise the rest."

Scott's nicknames were 'Rigor Mortis' or 'Poulan'. 'Rigor Mortis' because he was so slow he often seemed brain dead, and he was the last person I would have chosen to organise the crunch team.

His other nickname was used by those who had worked with him before his transfer to Dunedin. 'Poulan' was a well-known brand of chain saw. Scott had apparently been carrying on with a young woman in a South Island country town when her father and brothers learnt of the relationship. They accosted Scott in a barn and started up a chainsaw while threatening to remove a certain part of his anatomy. Scott fled in disarray.

The story spread rapidly throughout the relatively small district where he was stationed forcing the police department to transfer him. His district headquarters at Christchurch did not want him so unfortunately the Dunedin CIB ended up with him.

I had warned him the previous day that I would require at least six CIB staff for a crunch team, at short notice. When I went to his office at midday on August 8 he was at lunch and I learnt that nothing had been arranged. He did not have any staff on standby. He was finally located in the canteen and requested to return to his office immediately.

After thirty minutes he had still not arrived, so I went looking for him. I found him in the street watching a fire drill. Naturally, he had finished his lunch!

The disorganised Scott came up with only three police officers to assist in the operation. Because I was briefing the surveillance squad and Constable Devlin, I could not brief the crunch squad until the last minute.

It was then that I learnt from Scott that I would have to go with the crunch team as officer in charge as the staff he had given me were inexperienced. That meant that I was effectively running both the undercover operation and the crunch team. This was a ridiculous situation and had time not been running out I would never have agreed to it.

When I remonstrated with Scott, he argued that it was not his fault. He said, "Dalziel's gone off to his farm again and Kelly is away. It's an administrative fuck-up."

He assured me that he would run things back at the CIB but I would just have to do the best I could running both phases of the operation.

By 1.30 p.m., the surveillance squad reported to me that they were following Constable Devlin, who was travelling by taxi, towards the Parkside Hotel. I told them that my staff were in position despite another last-minute cock-up. Constable McLachlan, who had been allocated as part of my crunch team by Scott, was off duty so I ended up with one detective, Detective Kevin Marlow.

Because of the time factor, I had organised a simple operation with the objective being to firstly identify John Lewis as the principal behind the sex ring and secondly to record an admission through his conversation with Constable Devlin. We would be in a position to hear the entire conversation between them courtesy of a small microphone hidden in the constable's bra.

At 1.35 p.m., surveillance reported that Constable Devlin was entering the hotel. On our radio receiver, we heard John Lewis greet her and ask her to accompany him upstairs.

After offering her a drink, which the constable accepted, we heard Lewis say, "I'll come straight to the point." He then launched into a further description of his sex shows and on this occasion he was more descriptive. He talked at some length about the Marquis de Sade and said the show he staged was based on the book. He also told the constable that many of the guests shared a love of bondage, group and kinky sex.

Lewis added that although she might not like it she would be well paid for her participation. It was at this point he mentioned again that he would pay her well if she gave an exhibition of sexual intercourse with the alsatian dog, which had taken part in the previous shows. He said the act was a favourite with audiences.

It was at this point Lewis said, "You look young and pretty good to me but I like to inspect my merchandise closely. Here's $40 to let me see you naked. I want to look you over closely. Take off your clothes."

It had been arranged that Constable Devlin was to make an excuse to go to the toilet when things were getting difficult. When she told Lewis, "Okay, I will, but I need to go to the toilet first" we did not wait to hear any more. Detective Marlow and I sprinted from the car, into the hotel and up the stairs. We went straight to the door of the suite and began smashing it down.

As the door burst open, I saw Lewis standing near the door. He was quite calm and said, "What's going on boys?"

As my main concern was Constable Devlin, I left Lewis to Detective Marlow and checked the toilet to see if she was all right. She assured me that although it had been an unpleasant experience she was okay.

I escorted her out the door before returning.

When I returned, Lewis was still standing in the same spot clutching a bottle of baby oil and a whip. Nearby on a double bed was a Marquis de Sade book and a dog collar and lead. A video was plugged into the television set above the bed.

An inspection of the tape showed it to be sexually explicit. It included sex scenes similar to those described by John Lewis to Cathy and Constable Devlin. One local man was recognisable. This film was later placed in the custody of John Scott. It subsequently disappeared without trace.

Lewis quickly composed himself. He said, "I've been a fool, Tom, picking up a prostitute at my age. Still there's no law against it, is there?"

I said, "I will discuss it with you down at the station, John, and we will also discuss these items we are seizing under warrant," indicating the whip, book and other sex items.

On the way to the station, Lewis said, "I hope Murray [his detective son] won't get to hear of this as it would hurt him. It would kill my wife."

On reaching the station, I took John Lewis to another building, well away from the CIB office as I did not want him seen by other detectives for the sake of his son.

I told Detective Marlow to go back to the CIB and give Scott a situation report, and as soon as I had elicited Audrey's address from John Lewis I would relay that to them so that a search warrant could be obtained for her address and she could be interviewed.

While I was speaking to Marlow, Lewis was nervously chattering away stating that the girl we had found him with in the hotel room was a prostitute. He said he had been having trouble with his wife and had been using prostitutes for some years as a substitute.

He then requested he be allowed to phone his lawyer. I agreed that he could but I told him that before he did I wanted to make him aware of the fact that I knew he had used a woman named Audrey to recruit young girls to participate in live sex shows.

He slumped into a chair and put his head in his hands. I asked him if he wanted to make a clean breast of it. He was shaking and sweating profusely so I gave him a glass of water.

After a time he said, "Yeah, it's true she did recruit them for me but it was just for me to screw. I paid Audrey to get young girls for me as I enjoy sex with young girls. It's just one of those things, a lot of men do."

I asked him how many young girls Audrey had arranged for him. He said, "I can't remember. Not many. I only remember the name of one, Bonnie. I think she was over sixteen but you can't be sure these days. I admit I've had sex with a few but honestly I can't remember their names, Tom."

Lewis then said, "Shit, Tom, I'm obviously in trouble. I'd better get a lawyer." He was given the phone and a phone book but he pushed them away and said, "God, I can't ring him, he's our family lawyer. He's a close friend of my wife, Audrey, and the kids."

I told Lewis that I would like to ask him a few questions and I cautioned him in accordance with the Judges Rules. For the next 45 minutes, I chatted with him in an informal manner trying to elicit from him details of the sex shows he had spoken about to Cathy and Constable Devlin. He was very evasive and only admitted what we already knew, acknowledging that he had spoken with a lady called Cathy, and that he employed Audrey to recruit girls for him.

I asked him about the money he had offered Cathy and her daughter as payment for participation in a sex show. He acknowledged that he had.

I pointed out that Cathy's daughter was only fourteen years old. He denied knowing that.

I told him I had a tape recording in which he had stated to Cathy that the fact that her daughter was only fourteen did not bother him when it came to participation in the sex shows.

He initially denied this but then said, "I've had nightmares about this. Now it's run its course. I'm finished. I've ruined my family's name. Yes, I did say that."

He went on to acknowledge that he offered them $1500 and that he had said they would be expected to have sex with "people in high places".

Lewis would not name those who attended the sex shows nor disclose the venues and then he attempted to change the subject. He tried to tell me that he had sex mostly with Audrey and the young girl Bonnie.

When I attempted to question him about the MPs and other dignitaries who had attended the sex shows he became very nervous and refused to answer.

I then questioned him about his conversations with Constable Devlin.

Once again he became evasive.

I asked him about the dog's part in the act. He said, "I was exaggerating. I don't want to discuss it any more, I want a lawyer."

John Lewis asked me to telephone Michael Guest, a well-known Dunedin barrister and solicitor who later became a District Court judge. Guest was not available but his secretary said he would phone on his return.

I then asked Lewis to make a written statement but he refused.

When I attempted to question him about Audrey's real identity he again became agitated. Finally he gave me her contact phone number.

I sent the phone number over to Scott to have the Post Office confirm the address. I instructed him to ensure that a search warrant was obtained for her address and after evidence had been seized she was to be brought back to the station for questioning. I briefed him on the extent of Lewis's admissions and I also pointed out that if we interviewed both of them simultaneously we could play one off against the other.

The Otago representative rugby team, of which my son was a member, were playing Canterbury that afternoon and I had to compete with the radio broadcast when attempting to get Scott's attention.

When I returned to the interviewing office, John Lewis was pacing the floor. Once again I asked him to make a signed statement and I was surprised to hear him agree. He was very careful when making the statement and only reiterated what he had said earlier.

Because John Lewis was getting agitated over his solicitor's failure to phone back, I decided his son should be told of his father's predicament. Detective Murray Lewis was, with some difficulty, finally tracked down. He was at Carisbrook Park watching the Otago and Canterbury rugby game, as were most of the Dunedin CIB that sunny afternoon.

With Rigor Mortis focused on the rugby broadcast and most of his staff absent at a rugby union game, it was little wonder that inquiries made later in the afternoon were carried out in an inefficient and unprofessional manner.

After I had told Detective Murray Lewis of his father's situation, I left them both together and returned to the CIB office to find out how Scott and his team were progressing.

I met Scott in the corridor and he advised me that he had just been to see the District Commander, Ross McLennan, to advise him of the situation. I was annoyed to hear this as Scott had not even bothered to get an update from me. This, however, was vintage Scott – always getting in first, trying to impress the bosses with his involvement.

He told me McLennan had suggested that John Lewis be released into the custody of his son, Murray, while we carried out additional inquiries. When those inquiries were completed, we could ask Murray Lewis to bring his father in so that he could be arrested and bailed immediately.

I told Scott in no uncertain manner that we were putting the cart before the horse as we had not yet located Audrey. When I asked him what was happening in relation to that aspect of the inquiry he confessed that he did not know as he had been busy briefing the District Commander.

He did tell me, however, that he had assigned Detective Sergeant McQueen and Detective Marlow to the 'Audrey inquiry' but they had not returned. This disturbed me greatly as McQueen was one of the less able detective sergeants in the office. He had been a patient in the Ashburn Hall mental institution some years earlier and was still, in the opinion of many, mentally unstable.

Scott then returned to the District Commander's suggestion that John Lewis should be released meantime and when Audrey had been interviewed and arrested he could be brought back in and arrested and bailed. The reasoning behind this was that as most staff would be off duty not so many would be aware Murray Lewis's father had been arrested. It illustrated the naivety of the District Commander as police are the biggest gossips around and the news of the arrest would have spread like wildfire around the station.

I was also aware that John Lewis was the 'host with the most' among the hierarchy of the Dunedin police. I had been to his hotel on more than one occasion, with the head of the Dunedin CIB, and partaken of his hospitality as he curried favour with his son's bosses. I also knew that Scott was a regular visitor to the hotel and I suspected that this was the start of a campaign to minimise the seriousness of the charges against Lewis.

When I disagreed, Scott threw in his punchline. He said, "The District Commander is concerned that Lewis may attempt to take his own life."

I told Scott that I had been discussing charges with the Crown Prosecutor, Dennis Wood, and he thought that Audrey and John

Lewis should be interviewed simultaneously.

Scott was adamant, however, that the District Commander had insisted Lewis be released into his son's custody. I had no choice but to comply.

John Lewis was advised by me, in the presence of his son, Murray Lewis, that he would be released into Murray's custody pending the outcome of the interview and arrest of Audrey. We would then require Murray to bring him back to the police station where he and Audrey would be charged jointly.

Murray Lewis told me that he had been talking to Michael Guest in my absence and Guest had requested I telephone him. He then thanked me for the way I had treated his father. I told him that I would continue to treat his father fairly but I would not make any concessions because he was the father of a police officer. He told me he understood.

I then telephoned Michael Guest myself. At his request, I outlined the circumstances of John Lewis's apprehension. He asked me details of my conversation with Lewis and as well as telling him of Lewis's admissions I mentioned that I had been unable to get any admissions from him regarding the sex shows, the guests and participants.

I told him I believed they had taken place although Lewis had been very evasive when it came to dicussing the sex shows.

Guest asked to be notified when Lewis was arrested later in the evening as he wished to be present. Guest also asked me if I would object to name suppression and bail in court the next day. He said, "I'm requesting this on behalf of the family not Lewis." I agreed that I would not object because of the circumstances.

I returned to the CIB building expecting to find Audrey being interviewed and Constable Devlin awaiting her operational debrief.

Instead I found Rigor Mortis Scott and absolute chaos. Scott told me that Audrey had been located and was in the CIB but she was demanding that she either be arrested or released immediately.

I asked him just what evidence had been seized at her flat. He replied, "Nothing because McQueen forgot or neglected to get a search warrant so she would not let them search the flat."

My next question was the obvious one: "Why didn't they radio up and get a search warrant sent up to them?"

Scott shrugged his shoulders and said, "Who knows with 'McQueer'? You know what he's like. He even let her ring her lawyer, Kelvin Marks, and he's here now demanding she be released." He then told me Audrey had refused to answer any questions so we had nothing on her.

I said, "Why didn't you get Constable Devlin to identify her, then Cathy's daughter? She could, at the very least, have been charged with attempting to procure a girl under sixteen to have unlawful sexual intercourse."

Scott's reply almost sent me into orbit. He said, "Oh, I sent Devlin home an hour or two ago. Didn't know you still required her."

By this stage I was roaring at him. I said, "You have to be fucking joking! She hasn't been debriefed nor has she written up her notes for evidential purposes."

Scott replied, "I was busy and saw her sitting around so I said she could go. I thought you could get her later if you wanted to."

It was pointless arguing any more and my last remark to him was, "Jesus, you are fucking hopeless."

A few minutes later, I saw him with his overcoat and briefcase sneaking out the door. When I asked him where he was going he told me he was off to a rugby function at the Mornington Tavern.

After he left, I went to his office to telephone police operations requesting they send a car to bring Constable Devlin back to the CIB office. While making the phonecall, I noticed the exhibits Detective Marlow had seized from Lewis at the hotel lying about the office. Marlow had been instructed to label the items and place them in the exhibits room. The book on the Marquis de Sade had a pen inside it as a book mark. Obviously Scott had been very busy during the afternoon. With both the rugby union and the lurid sex of the Marquis de Sade on his mind, police work obviously rated a very poor third.

I locked the exhibits in the Chief Detective's safe and went to face solicitor Kelvin Marks. Marks was jumping up and down demanding I either arrest his client or release her.

After speaking to Detective Marlow, who placed all the blame for the debacle of the afternoon on Scott and McQueen, I was forced to release Audrey as Constable Devlin had not been located at her home. It was believed she was visiting friends. Without her I could not positively identify Audrey.

Murray Lewis was advised that we would not be arresting his father that night.

On arriving home, my wife told me Scott had telephoned from the Mornington Tavern asking if Audrey had been arrested. He was keen to get to the head of the CIB first to give him a situation report and to deflect any criticism that he thought might be coming his way.

He told my wife that he was still at the Mornington Tavern and requested I phone him on arriving home.

After my experiences with Rigor Mortis that day I was in no mood to speak to him so I ignored his request.

The next day, Thursday 9 August, I called Detective Marlow to my office. He was instructed to obtain a search warrant for Audrey's address and also a search warrant for the *Otago Daily Times* advertising department. I wanted to obtain handwriting samples of the advertisements placed in that newspaper by Audrey.

The search of Audrey's address would concentrate on locating address books, anything connecting her to John Lewis, Marquis de Sade literature, hand-writing samples, an alsatian dog or any other evidence which would corroborate the staging of previous sex shows.

It was anticipated that Audrey would have destroyed evidence after being released the previous evening but it is often surprising what can be overlooked when people panic.

I planned to have Constable Devlin accompany us to identify Audrey as the person she had met at the Little Hut coffee bar. Kelvin Marks, Audrey's solicitor, had grudgingly acknowledged the previous evening that she would be in big trouble if identified by Constable Devlin and Cathy's young daughter.

I had Cathy available for an identification parade if absolutely necessary. It was an ordeal I did not want to put the young girl through unless it was unavoidable.

Just before leaving the office, Scott approached me and said, "I've been talking to Laurie [Dalziel] and he told me that the sex inquiry is to be stopped until he gets back tomorrow."

I told Scott that was ridiculous as after the previous day's debacle it was imperative we act quickly otherwise more valuable evidence would be lost.

He said, "Laurie's quite emphatic. No further police action until he gets back. He just wants a short report on what's happened so far."

By this time I was convinced there was to be interference and I said to Scott, "John, this had better not be another snow job by Dalziel because this is a serious matter whether it involves one of his mates or not."

Scott shrugged his shoulders and said, "It's nothing to do with me. You know what he's like."

It was at this stage that I suggested to Scott that we travel to the farm to speak to Dalziel and explain the situation to him. Scott wasn't interested. Once again he said he did not want to be involved and he added that Dalziel was already aware of the situation because Murray Lewis and his father had been speaking to him the previous night.

It was obvious that I was wasting my time with Scott and if Dalziel had been speaking with the Lewises without even seeking my advice there was little point in travelling to his farm to speak to him.

I returned to my office and told Marlow to cancel the search warrant meantime and to advise Constable Devlin we would not be requiring her.

My frustration had reached boiling point. After the previous day's bungling I now had to deal with interference from Dalziel. It was also becoming obvious that he was deliberately trying to slow the inquiry down. Knowing him as I did, his next steps would obviously be to minimise and eventually bury it.

Later that morning, I went with Constable McLachlan to a local video shop where we watched the video seized in the raid at Lewis's hotel.

It was a pornographic movie featuring group sex and bondage.

The filming was amateurish to say the least but I recognised Audrey in the video. She was having sex with another person, who I recognised as a local shopkeeper and male model. There was an audience in the background but it was impossible to identify anyone because of the poor quality of the tape.

It had always been my opinion that the $1000 to $1500 Lewis was offering for women and girls to have sex was generous in the extreme. However, if he was producing blue videos then everything fell into place. Pornographic videos were fetching big money on the black market in New Zealand and Australia and I was also aware John Lewis's business connections in Asia would mean he would have little difficulty in finding a market for them there.

The next day, Friday, 10 August 1984, Dalziel came to my office.

It was around 10 a.m. and he was clearly nervous. He closed the door and said he needed to talk to me urgently. He wanted me to report the John Lewis offences along favourable lines, even to the extent of changing my report to say there was insufficient evidence to charge him.

He told me Murray Lewis was a good and valued member of the office who he was hoping to promote to sergeant in Dunedin. His father, John Lewis, had merely had a temporary falling from grace. Dalziel said, "It happens to otherwise decent citizens at that age."

He then suggested that he would make the decision whether or not Lewis was charged but my report would be crucial if he was to help John and Murray Lewis. He said, "Look, just remember Lewis, it could be your father. How would you feel? You'd want and expect a bit of help from your workmates. This thing is just about on the same level as bookmaking. John Lewis tells me he has learnt his lesson. You don't normally charge a person who bets with a bookmaker, do you? Look, the point I am making is we don't need to charge John Lewis."

I told Dalziel that the evidence was there and I would recommend Lewis be arrested and charged. I also added that I did not appreciate any suggestion that my father would be involved as a paedophile.

He replied, "Bullshit, don't you understand? It's a victimless crime."

I said, "Correction. We have two complainants who have spoken with Audrey and Lewis and other complainants whose daughters were approached by Audrey alone."

By this stage, Dalziel had realised he was losing the battle and he started to get agitated. He told me he would take care of the complainants, stating, "Look, I was over at court when you prosecuted those girls for soliciting. We were laughed out of court for charging them. [District Court Judge] Jamieson said it was not worth bringing vice matters to court. Let's give John Lewis a break."

We argued for a further 15 minutes before I told Dalziel that I would not be party to a cover-up but would in fact be recommending in my report that Lewis and Audrey be arrested for attempting to procure a girl under 16 years for the purpose of unlawful sexual intercourse and possibly conspiracy.

He became incensed at this and stormed from the office shouting, "And you just remember, Tom Lewis, it could be your bloody father or your bloody wife!"

His last remark enraged me and I leapt from my chair and went after him down the corridor. As I caught up with him the manager of State Insurance walked through the door and rather than create a scene in front of him I decided that for the time being Dalziel would keep.

I then began putting the file together and I decided to speak to the Crown Solicitor, Dennis Wood, once again to discuss the charges we would prefer against Audrey and John Lewis.

When I had last spoken to Wood, I believed that McQueen and Marlow had executed a search warrant on Audrey's address and that they would have had her identified by Constable Devlin, then arrested her. In fact, none of this had been done thanks to the bungling of Scott and McQueen.

I went to Dennis Wood's office at 11.05 a.m. only to be met by him at the door. He said, "Your Mr Dalziel has just been on the phone to me, Tom. For some reason he says you are not to show the file to me nor discuss it with me. He wants you to return to the office forthwith."

I was embarrassed by such an approach by Dalziel to a man who everybody in the Dunedin police district greatly respected; it almost sounded as though we did not trust Wood. Dennis Wood was a man of the utmost integrity.

I mentioned to Wood that Dalziel's behaviour was rather strange as I was merely there to discuss in more detail the charges we had agreed could be appropriate the previous Wednesday.

Wood shrugged his shoulders and said, "I don't know what's going on with your Mr Dalziel. He never ceases to amaze me. However, let me know when he's sorted out his problem with the file and we can get on with discussing the appropriate charges."

I went back to the CIB office and headed straight for Dalziel's office.

He was not there but as I walked past Chookfeeder Kelly's office I noticed that the door was closed. Knowing that if there was any conspiracy going on Dalziel would be in conference with Chookfeeder, I went into the office. Dalziel was seated at the desk with Chookfeeder and Rigor Mortis Scott.

I said to Dalziel, "I want a word".

He replied, "In here then, Mr Lewis."

I said, "Alone."

He then became agitated and yelled, "I said in here, Mr Lewis."

I told him I was not prepared to discuss a serious matter with him unless he got rid of his two stooges, Chookfeeder and Rigor Mortis.

This sent him into orbit and he screamed, "In here, Mr Lewis, and that's an order!"

Because he had obviously lost it and because of his previous conversation with me when he attempted to influence me to let John Lewis off, I decided enough was enough. I said, as I began walking towards the lift, "I have nothing more to say to you. I will lodge a complaint against you with the District Commander."

Dalziel was screaming behind me, "You're finished in the CIB, Lewis!"

When I reached the foyer and was waiting for the lift, Dalziel came racing through the door. He was still screaming as he skidded to a halt on the polished floor, "All right, I'll see you in my office."

Even though it was a serious situation, I had to smile as Dalziel by this time was unintentionally doing an excellent impersonation of Basil Fawlty. His facial and physical resemblance to Basil were only one part of it. Whenever he panicked or lost his cool, he acted as Basil Fawlty would.

I returned with him to his office but again he tried to get the two stooges to join us. Once again, I repeated that I would discuss it with him alone or not at all.

He lost his temper completely then, waving his arms about and screaming, "I can't trust you. You went to the Crown Solicitor to try and set me up."

He then said, "You are not a fit person to be in charge of this inquiry, you have become emotionally involved. I am removing you from it forthwith and handing it over to John Scott."

I replied that I would not be a party to an attempt to pervert the course of justice and I was not prepared to let him get away with protecting his mates.

He said, " That's it! You've gone too far. You're out of the CIB."

When I walked away I knew I had to report the matter to the District Commander but I did not expect much of a response from him as he was a close friend of Dalziel. He also rated as one of the worst District Commanders I had worked with.

Chief Superintendent Ross McLennan was also known as 'Cookie Bear'. He and another commissioned officer had a contact in a bank opposite a local cake shop where, every afternoon at varying times, depending on how business was going, the cake shop would put a sign in their window reducing all cakes and sponges to cost price to clear them before closing.

Just before afternoon tea was the most important part of the Bear's day because if the phone call came from his bank contact between 2.30 and 3 p.m. he would send 'Bashful Brian' (the other commissioned officer with the sweet tooth) down to get him a half-dozen cream buns or whatever was going cheap.

These would be consumed with gusto in his office before going to the police canteen for afternoon tea. He was grossly overweight and his addiction to cream cakes, and indeed all food, did nothing for his physical appearance.

The Bear was typical of many commissioned officers heading to the top. He just didn't want to know anything that might have an adverse effect on his planned career path.

Enroute to McLennan's office, I stopped and spoke briefly to the Welfare Officer, Detective Sergeant Ron Bridge. Bridge was an old friend and he offered to come with me to see the Bear.

McLennan was defensive from the start. As I was telling him of my conversation with Dalziel in my office, he was saying, "Look, it's obviously a personality clash. I'll speak with him and fix it up." It soon became apparent that I was wasting my time so Bridge and I left. I told Bridge I was far from happy with McLennan's attitude.

When I returned to my office I was met by Rigor Mortis Scott. He said to me, "Thank God you didn't talk to him in front of Chookfeeder and me. He was trying to set you up and we were to be his witnesses. He's a bastard but you won't beat him."

Rigor Mortis told me Dalziel had cooled down and had requested I go to his office. He said, "You are both on a collision course. For God's sake do as he says. You can't win against the system and, what the hell, if John Lewis gets off it's not worth losing your job and pension for."

I went to Dalziel's office. He was obviously shaken and worried and said, "I've never been spoken to like you spoke to me in my twenty-five years in the police."

I told him that I had had enough of his coverups over the years and this was the last straw.

He then asked me to apologise to him for accusing him of perverting the course of justice. He said, "You apologise and I'll apologise for what I said about your father and your wife."

When I refused, he became aggressive again stating that the CIB was a disciplined organisation and he would have to decide whether or not I could remain. However, if I was prepared to apologise and file my report along the lines he prescribed then he told me we could get our relationship back on course.

My reaction was to tell him that the conversation was going nowhere. I would not apologise and I would file my report accurately and honestly.

His response was to tell me that his door was no longer open to me and that my position in the CIB would be reviewed forthwith.

I walked out of his office.

After returning to my office, I made a record of the conversations I had with Dalziel that day. It was obvious when I read through my notes that he was determined to ruin the inquiry and write the file off without any arrests being made.

At lunchtime I took my concerns to Senior Constable Paul Stevenson, a very experienced and respected police officer. He had been a member of the Police Association for over twenty years and a prominent member of the national executive.

We sat down and discussed the whole episode and he examined the notes I had made of my conversations with Dalziel. He was very disturbed and warned me, when I said I was intending to make a complaint of perverting the course of justice against Dalziel, that any such complaint would be investigated by a fellow commissioned officer and from previous experience he was concerned about how honestly such complaints were inquired into.

He advised me to prepare the file honestly and accurately and to talk to my wife and family before formally making a complaint against Dalziel as the ramifications would certainly affect them. These were truly prophetic words.

During the weekend, I discussed my proposed complaint against Dalziel with my family. They agreed that to stand by and do nothing would be wrong as the matter involved children and was extremely serious. Despite the possible damage to my career, it was decided that I had to take a stand and make a complaint.

I telephoned Paul Stevenson and told him of my decision. He advised me that McLennan was on leave and Superintendent Lance Bardwell was relieving as District Commander.

When I telephoned Bardwell at his home seeking an appointment for the next day he asked about the nature of my visit.

When he had heard the details of my complaint, he said, "I sincerely hope you have thought this through as it's an extreme step to take and a person of your rank seldom succeeds with complaints about commissioned officers due to the fact that a fellow commissioned officer will investigate the allegation."

I told Bardwell that in my opinion a cover-up was in progress and unless I spoke up it would succeed and I would have been part of it. I said, "I have no choice."

He then told me he would have to advise the Commissioner of Police, such was the seriousness of the complaint. We agreed to a meeting in the District Commander's office at 9.30 a.m the next morning.

When I arrived at work the next morning I was approached by Paul Stevenson, who told me that I would have to put my complaint in writing in order for the Police Association to decide whether they would support me. In the interim, I was to speak with the local secretary, Constable Wally Nelson, to give him details of my complaint.

I agreed to do this.

Nelson was a man I had the utmost respect for but this was beyond him. He decided that he could not take the complaint from someone senior to him in rank so he suggested that I make a verbal complaint by phone to the secretary of the New Zealand Police Association, Dr Bob Moodie, a barrister and solicitor.

I outlined to Moodie details of my complaint against Dalziel while Constable Nelson listened on an extension phone. Moodie was emphatic that I should put my complaint in writing to him. He advised me to leave my complaint with Bardwell as it was, cancel the lawyer and advise Bardwell that full details of the complaint would be coming through the Police Association.

I immediately went to Bardwell's office and outlined to him details of my conversation with Moodie.

Superintendent Lance Bardwell seemed genuinely pleased and said, "I'm glad you are going through the Police Association but I have to advise you that the District Commander called in this morning and I had to advise him of your complaint. He said he will advise the Commissioner and no doubt Dalziel. Be prepared for trouble with your boss."

Bardwell then said he intended speaking to Dalziel later that morning and he was going to suggest to him that he might resolve the matter with an apology.

I was shocked to think that Bardwell could even consider such a serious complaint could be resolved with an apology. It illustrated to me the muddled thinking of commissioned officers.

My response was, "This is the most serious and damning allegation a police officer can make against a fellow police officer. I have not entered into it lightly and apologies were not relevant considering the seriousness of the allegation."

Bardwell seemed taken aback. I doubt whether he had ever encountered a similar situation in his police career. However, he agreed with me and I left his office.

Back in the CIB office, I noticed the District Commander, 'Bear' McLennan, in earnest conversation with Dalziel. So engrossed, in fact, they failed to notice me as I walked past them.

I returned to my office and began putting the children's sex inquiry file together with my recommendations.

The usual practice in the CIB is for the senior officer to 'minute' the file to another officer outlining, in writing, what inquiries he required to be done and any instructions he may have regarding the nature of the inquiries.

Dalziel had not given any written instructions on the file nor did he in subsequent months. Every instruction was given to me verbally, for obvious reasons, without any witnesses present. This was, of course, contrary to police general instructions and completely at odds with Dalziel's normal procedures. These departures from standard practice convinced me that he was up to no good.

One would have thought with the file now the subject of a serious criminal complaint against him, Dalziel would have been keen to show, by way of written instructions, that he was not hindering the inquiry by specifying just what he wanted done with the file. His failure to do so was not even commented upon let alone questioned by the police inquiry and the so-called independent examiner.

However worse was to follow in the next two years as the New Zealand Police Department did everything in its power to stop any inquiry into the Dunedin sex ring scandal, as it became known.

After I had filed my formal complaint with the Police Association through Moodie, I had almost daily visits from Dalziel requesting that I withdraw my complaint so we could then resolve the matter amicably. I rejected all his offers just as I rejected the attempts Rigor Mortis Scott made to play the peacemaker.

Scott told me that I was putting him in a difficult position because while he knew Dalziel was in the wrong he had to be careful, for the sake of his own career, to back the right horse. He said, "Tom, I can't see you ever winning this one."

I also had repeated visits from the Welfare Officer, Ron Bridge. The theme was always the same in that Dalziel was instructing Bridge to tell me the door was still open, so we could bury the hatchet.

Eventually Dalziel gave me an ultimatum. He told me to go to the Bear and Bardwell and tell them I was prepared to discuss the matter with all concerned and he would accept some blame for what had occurred.

It was Friday, 31 August 1984, and he told me he would give me until 4.30 p.m. that day to meet him halfway. He said, "If you do not, Tom, the boot will go in."

Ron Bridge also reported to me that Dalziel had told him, "If Tom doesn't come to the party, I'll be covering my arse and putting the boot in."

Bridge told me the Bear had approached him to see how the reconciliation was progressing. Bridge had told him things were not good as I would not budge from my original position and Dalziel was issuing threats, which had exacerbated the situation.

The Bear told Bridge that Laurie Dalziel had told him he was confident that he could resolve the matter.

I was completely flabbergasted at, firstly, the response of Dalziel and, secondly, the response from the police hierarchy at what was a serious criminal complaint by an experienced detective sergeant against the head of the district CIB.

Eight weeks after the complaint had been lodged, they were still pretending it never happened and trying to sweep it under the carpet.

I am quite sure that if such a damning complaint had been made against me by a fellow police officer then I would have moved heaven and earth to have an urgent inquiry carried out to clear my name.

Nearly every police officer in a similar position would do the same. But we had a detective chief inspector almost begging a subordinate to withdraw the complaint against him while the district commander waited in the wings without even commencing the inquiry.

What of the Commissioner of Police? Bardwell had said he had been contacted. Why would he stand by and allow such a state of affairs to continue? Even months later, when the media were hounding him, his office denied any knowledge of a complaint of perverting the course of justice having been made in Dunedin against a senior police officer.

While all this was going on, little detective work was being done. The Dunedin CIB virtually closed down while these other dramas dominated centre stage.

And what of the Police Association? Nothing was happening on that front either. Inquiries from the local association revealed that Moodie had misplaced the complaint and it had subsequently been overlooked.

Approximately one month after I had submitted my report recommending Lewis and Audrey be arrested and charged, the file was finally forwarded to the legal section for an opinion. The file had lain in limbo on Dalziel's desk during which time he tried to influence me to withdraw my complaint and to report the matter favourably for John Lewis.

Eventually, I decided to force the issue. I obtained a search warrant from the District Court for Audrey's address. I took Constable Devlin and another police officer and we raided her address in mid-September 1984.

When I spoke to Audrey at the door, she said, "What's going on? I was told this had all been squared off and all charges dropped. I better not be taking the rap on my own. Are you doing a warrant on John again? If I've been set up to take the rap for this then I'll take him and his mates with me."

I asked her who had told her but before she could answer a male voice yelled from behind the door, "Don't tell them anything."

I walked into the house and saw John Mann, known as 'Mad Mann', sitting in a chair stroking a young alsatian dog. I then remembered that surveillance had photographed Mad Mann loitering around the Little Hut coffee bar when Constable Devlin had met Audrey.

I said to Mad Mann, "So you're Audrey's pimp then, John?"

He said, "You'll get nothing out of me and nothing out of her."

Because of his propensity for violence, I warned him that he was to stay sitting in the chair until we had completed our search and any future obstruction would result in his arrest. Although he did not answer, he did as he was told.

Constable Devlin then came into the room and said, "Hello. Remember me, Audrey?" Audrey replied, "I'm not going to say anything."

Constable Devlin then said, "You and I met at the Little Hut coffee lounge, Audrey, in early August and you offered me a job in a sex show. Do you deny meeting me?"

Audrey replied, "Yes, I do. I don't have to answer any questions."

A search was made of the house and a Marquis de Sade book, and a woman's leather suit with holes cut out to expose the breasts and genitals were found, along with leather thongs, a whip and other books on bondage and sexual perversion.

The phone number of the Parkside Hotel was written in a book beside the phone and samples of Audrey's handwriting were taken under warrant. The handwriting was clearly the same as that on the advertisements seeking young girls for sex shows seized from the *Otago Daily Times*.

Armed with additional evidence, I returned to the CIB office and accosted Rigor Mortis Scott. I told him Audrey had been identified by Constable Devlin and we now had additional evidence linking her to John Lewis and the recruitment of young girls for participation in sex shows. I handed him a report for the main file, including the handwriting samples for the document examiner in Wellington, plus the extra evidence seized.

He didn't look pleased, and obviously he was still unsure if he had backed the right horse.

Later that day, he called into my office to ask me to go with Dalziel and him for a drive so we could have a cup of coffee together and thrash the matter out. He acknowledged that Dalziel had sent him and I refused his offer.

A week later, I learned that the Dunedin children's sex file had been hastily sent to the police legal section in Wellington without the additional evidence. Still later, I learned that the file that was sent had been interfered with and much of the documentary evidence against Lewis removed before being sent.

In early October 1994, some two months after I had officially complained, I suffered a serious injury on duty and I was confined to bed for two weeks and off duty for nearly two months. Because I was heavily sedated during the first weeks following the accident, I did not give the Dunedin sex ring scandal a second thought. I had more pressing problems with major surgery looming as a very real possibility.

As I convalesced at home, I began to receive disturbing reports from a number of my workmates that reports were being organised by Dalziel, Chookfeeder and Rigor Mortis attempting to show that I had recently been suffering from stress and my behavioural patterns had changed.

It was alleged that I was prone to outbursts of anger and my performance at work had begun to decline. This flew in the face of written advice from Dalziel to Bear McLennan only a week before our altercation which read, "As you are aware, Detective Sergeant Lewis is doing an excellent job on indecency and vice files in the interim. Since he has taken charge of that area, arrests and clearances have been excellent."

I was also given photocopies of reports that were being circulated by Rigor Mortis. These were petty in the extreme. One NCO was trying to curry favour by reporting on another for allegedly arriving late at work. Time taken for meals and morning and afternoon tea and observations about my demeanour and attitude were also noted. One example was the diary notation, "Saw Tom this morning, did not speak."

Lying in my sickbed and reading such garbage did annoy me and I sent for the Welfare Officer, Ron Bridge. Bridge told me he was aware that Dalziel had concocted a file of his own and was relying on Chookfeeder and Rigor Mortis to bolster his allegation that I was suffering some form of mental breakdown.

Obviously the aim of the exercise was to ensure I was thoroughly discredited should any inquiry be made into my allegations.

Bear McLennan was the recipient of these reports, which were used by the police administration in an attempt to dissuade me from pursuing my complaint.

Bridge told me that Dalziel was still issuing threats that unless I withdrew my complaint the boot would go in. He also told me that K.O. Thompson, the Commissioner of Police, had been in Dunedin for the annual Christmas visit and had been briefed by McLennan about my complaint. McLennan allegedly told Thompson he was ignoring it because Dalziel had told him it was an internal matter and he would get the complaint withdrawn.

Dalziel had often bragged about the fact that he and Thompson were close friends and he attributed his appointment as head of a CIB office, without any formal detective training, as an example of what Thompson would do for him. He alleged that he and Thompson had become close friends while travelling to and from work together in Wellington.

It truly was an amazing scenario. Here was an allegation of perverting the course of justice, a most serious criminal offence, not being investigated because the very person against whom the allegation had been made was insisting he could get the complainant to withdraw the complaint. The hierarchy of the NZ Police sat on their hands and waited for him to do it.

Because of these irregularities and the petty but vindictive harassment being directed at me while I was off work injured, the local Police Association decided to engage a solicitor, J. Bruce Robertson, now Justice Robertson of the New Zealand High Court. At that time he was a member of the crown prosecutors panel and he regularly appeared for the police department as a crown prosecutor.

Robertson knew how the police department worked and he wrote to the department requesting a copy of the report Dalziel had prepared against me. He was not able to obtain the file despite correspondence between himself and McLennan. The police department refused to supply a copy of the file to my solicitor, insisting that I come to the CIB office in person to uplift it.

As I was bedridden at the time recovering from injury, that was impossible so effectively I was denied the right of even knowing exactly what I was being accused of.

Robertson tried, with his senior partner, Hugh Ross, to point out to McLennan that he should sort the matter out internally. In other words, acknowledge my complaint and accede to my request to have the complaint properly investigated. Amazingly, he chose to ignore their warning that to continue to ignore the complaint could have serious consequences.

I finally returned to the CIB office in mid-January 1985 and I was immediately accosted by Dalziel. He appeared very sure of himself and he advised me that I should go upstairs and see the Bear and withdraw my complaint.

As I went to walk away from him, he said, "It's futile to continue with it. K.O. [K.O. Thompson, Commissioner of Police] was here at Christmas. He knows all the facts and he agrees that I didn't attempt to pervert the course of justice."

I replied sarcastically, "Is that because you told him so?"

He replied, "No, he read the file."

It was then that I asked Dalziel just what had happened to the file in the three months I had been absent. He replied, "Nothing. I was waiting for you to come back."

His reply stung me because it meant that a serious complaint, involving children, had been put aside for over three months ensuring that the chance of charges being laid were virtually nil.

That was the last time I ever spoke to Dalziel about the Dunedin sex ring.

Over the next three months I was subjected to persistent harassment and victimisation in an attempt to break me. It would take too long to relate all the incidents but they included approaching junior staff who had worked under me and asking whether I was a tyrannical type of boss who abused and overworked them, whether they thought I was under stress, whether I had ever committed any offence in their presence such as assaulting prisoners, drinking on duty or being late for duty.

A number of staff actually complained to the Police Association about these matters.

Various accusations were made by Dalziel, Chookfeeder Kelly and Rigor Mortis Scott. These accusations were never put to me but were given to Bear McLennan as authentic. Such was his involvement by then, he never even confronted me with the allegations.

The most serious harassment, however, was the surveillance of my wife and, to a lesser extent, my teenage daughter. A detective sergeant delivered to me photocopies of pages from Rigor Mortis Scott's diary in which were noted my wife and daughter's movements while he watched our home.

There were also notes of my wife's movements as he followed her about the city. My wife had her own commercial stationery business and she called on clients in all parts of Dunedin. Scott's notings were consistent with her calls on those dates so we had definite proof that he was stalking her.

This was serious and for the first time I realised just how dirty the brotherhood intended to play. After discussion with J. Bruce Robertson, we decided my wife should write a letter of complaint directly to the Minister of Police, Ann Hercus.

My wife was quite definite that her complaint was a separate issue. She was her own person, she had nothing to do with the complaint I had made and yet she and her daughter were being stalked by a police officer known to the department to have been involved in a scandal with sexual connotations a few years earlier.

About this time I also became aware of the contents of the report Dalziel had submitted to Bear McLennan. It was an amazing document suggesting that since learning my father was suffering from cancer I had become withdrawn and stressed. As a result, I was allegedly prone to exaggeration. It also mentioned that I had recently experienced difficulty in getting on with my fellow NCOs and my performance at work had declined.

The last page concluded with the sentence, "Under no circumstances is Detective Sergeant Lewis to see this file." Quite obviously, Dalziel did not have the guts to stand by his convictions.

The various people who read the report after it came into my hands commented that it lacked any credibility. Page after page was given to slating me, and if I had been even half as bad as depicted I should not have even been in the police let alone allowed to stay.

Yet here I was, a detective sergeant in the CIB, an acknowledged elite branch of the police, working on internal investigations, the most sensitive of police inquiries, right up until the time I accused Dalziel of perverting the course of justice.

The last paragraph of Dalziel's report summed up the fiasco. He stated that all he now wanted was for me to get on with my work. That was it! No recommendation of any disciplinary action to be taken against me, a subordinate who had accused him of a criminal offence. No recommendation of any disciplinary action to be taken for all the allegations he has made in his report. Not even a recommendation that this NCO who he alleged could not get on with his peers should be transferred out of the CIB.

All we had was a report that concluded with his wish that I get back to work and the rider that I never be permitted to see the contents of the report.

Both McLennan and Thompson stand indicted in that they never questioned the report, knowing full well that in the three months before my altercation with Dalziel I had:
• just received a national award from a New Zealand newspaper based on a recommendation from the Commissioner's office at

Police Headquarters for my work as a police officer beyond the call of duty

- only a week or so before my allegation against Dalziel, I had received a commendation regarding my work in vice and sexual offending areas

- been used by Dalziel as his right-hand man in both major and, more importantly, sensitive staff offending inquiries during the past five years. Both McLennan and Thompson were aware of this.

This clumsy attempt at a cover-up illustrates the confidence this brotherhood of commissioned officers had in their ability to manipulate the system. They were obviously confident their actions would not be under scrutiny otherwise they surely would not have left as many loopholes.

During March 1985, Bruce Robertson, frustrated in trying to deal with Bear McLennan, wrote to Commissioner Ken Thompson reiterating my original complaint about Dalziel and demanding action. Thompson's response was to sit tight and ignore the correspondence from Robertson.

The Police Association, by this time annoyed and frustrated by Thompson's lack of response, advised the *Sunday Times* that a serious complaint had been made against a senior Dunedin detective and the complaint was with the Commissioner, K.O. Thompson.

On Sunday, 7 April 1985, Alistair Morrison of that paper wrote an article along these lines, including that when inquiries had been made earlier in the week the Commissioner's office denied the existence of any such complaint.

The reporter was referred to the head of Internal Investigations, Superintendent Faulkner, at Police Headquarters. He, too, denied the existence of a complaint.

Alistair Morrison persisted and it became obvious to Thompson that he was not going to go away. The old police brotherhood tactics of sitting tight and holding the line, adopting the 'this too shall pass' strategy, was just not working so Thompson instructed Faulkner to admit he had a file. He told the *Sunday Times* the next day that the report had just arrived on his desk.

The obvious question was, where had it arrived from? It could have only come from one place – Commissioner Thompson's office. The complaint had been sent to him some weeks earlier by J. Bruce Robertson, therefore it must have been in his possession when he was first questioned about it and denied its existence.

It was also known to the Police Association that Thompson and Dalziel had discussed Robertson's letter of complaint around 29 March in some detail. A case of the Commissioner of Police wilfully misleading the press?

There were to be many questions asked about the involvement of K.O. Thompson in this sorry saga over the next twelve months and although he ducked and dived and managed to avoid a royal commission his credibility was seriously questioned by press and public alike.

During this high drama, I was at my holiday house near Wanaka. I was warned by my fellow officers that something was about to happen as Dalziel, Chookfeeder Kelly and Rigor Mortis Scott had been locked behind closed doors since arriving at work on Monday 8 April. Obviously Morrison's article had set the alarm bells ringing. I was also told that the phone lines between Police Headquarters and Dunedin were running hot. Bear McLennan and K.O. Thompson were also busy planning their strategy.

My informants in the CIB office told me about the effect this was starting to have on Dalziel. The brash, confident bullyboy had apparently been reduced, in a matter of days, to a shadow of his former self. He was pale and drawn and spent most of his time locked in his office with his faithful lieutenants.

On Friday 12 April, it became apparent what the police strategy would be. It used the local newspaper, the *Otago Daily Times*, to peddle its party line, despite many letters to the paper condemning the police approach.

A month later the *Otago Daily Times* ran a story which was factually incorrect. It was along the lines of police carrying out an extensive inquiry into the Dunedin children's sex ring but being thwarted by a lack of evidence and a legal void in their attempts to bring the offenders they had identified to court.

But the punchline came at the end of the front-page article when reporter Bryan James stated that one detective on the original inquiry team had become so incensed at the anomaly in the law that he complained to the Commissioner.

This statement was misleading. When it later became aware of the facts, the *Otago Daily Times* never bothered to publish a retraction.

On the other hand, the *New Zealand Truth* immediately picked up on the story and, as well as a front-page headline, devoted their second page to the Dunedin children's sex ring and the professional people who had allegedly been attending shows.

Alistair Morrison, of the *Sunday Times* followed up his 7 April article with another on 14 April. He commented how nervous everyone was at Police Headquarters about the Dunedin children's sex ring inquiry and how K.O. Thompson was now making noises to the effect that he would send Internal Investigations head Superintendent Faulkner to Dunedin to look into the matter.

Morrison also interviewed the Police Association's Dr Bob Moodie.

Moodie, who has a doctorate of law from Victoria University, did not pull any punches in the interview. He was adamant that the evidence elicited from the original inquiry indicated a prosecution could be brought against two people, possibly more. He was at a loss to understand how there could be a legal void. Moodie also mentioned that this was one of the most serious allegations a police officer could make against another police officer and it required a full and independent investigation.

Various other newspapers were probing including the national Catholic paper, the *Tablet*, whose editor, John Kennedy (known as Pope John in media circles), was experienced in investigating police corruption and cover-ups after being based in Melbourne for a number of years.

TVNZ's top investigative programme, Closeup, also came to Dunedin and carried out an in-depth inquiry into the Dunedin children's sex ring. They interviewed the complainants, who were adamant that there had been a police cover-up. After the show went to air in mid-April 1985, it was clear to a number of people that if there had been a cover-up it led all the way to the Commissioner's office.

The response from Dalziel was immediate. He issued writs – later called the Dalziel 'silencing writs' – against all the media organisations which had run the story. Most were not pursued through the courts but they did have the effect of silencing the media while the writs were in place and the matter sub judice.

I was interested to note that the lawyer appearing for him was one whose law firm had been mixed up in Capone's Speakeasy Restaurant. This establishment was also operating an upstairs brothel and when I closed it down and charged the management and staff I was keen to pursue inquiries into the owners, based on information elicited from the staff.

It was Dalziel who put a stop to this by handing me another inquiry which he insisted required my urgent attention. By the time I had discovered that this was a red herring, the avenues of inquiry in the Capones matter had closed.

Dalziel also trumpeted through the Dunedin police station like an enraged bull warning that anyone who spoke out against him would be liable for a civil action. This behaviour continued unabated during the later inquiry.

Even although complaints were made regarding his behaviour during the inquiry those complaints were ignored.

By this time K.O. Thompson, due to mounting pressure, announced a high-profile police team under his deputy, Bryan Gibson, would be going to Dunedin to commence, at long last, an inquiry into the allegations I had made against Dalziel.

The media were not happy. They had seen enough of the Caesar investigating Caesar policies of the New Zealand Police not to recognise another whitewash when they saw one. They demanded an independent inquiry and the Police Association and I agreed. We wanted retired former Chief Magistrate Sir Desmond Sullivan or former Judge Peter Mahon, famous for his exposures during the Erebus inquiry some years earlier.

We were later advised that an independent examiner would be attached to the police inquiry team to ensure impartiality. This occurred only after the Police Association told their members not to co-operate with a police inquiry team. So K.O. Thompson was finally forced to comply with the police and public demand for an independent person to head the inquiry.

Unbeknown to us, the independent examiner, John Gibson, was a member of the Police Tribunal, a man in regular and close contact with the police hierarchy. Therefore he was not independent.

Secondly, his input into the inquiry was minimal and he certainly did not monitor the police investigation as one was lead to believe he would. He merely turned up at the end of their inquiry and interviewed a select group of people, all arranged and programmed by the police inquiry team.

He stands indicted in that he:

- Did not even interview the complainants. Cathy actually forced Gibson to see her by going to his hotel but he did not record her conversation as it was not helpful to writing the matter off, which was quite clearly the object of the exercise.
- Failed to examine documents showing that not only had I been harassed but also my wife and daughter.
- Failed to take any action against Dalziel for threatening prospective witnesses.
- Failed to order the police inquiry team to take signed statements rather than notes of interviews. It was clearly shown that the inquiry team were being very selective in what was being recorded. One witness added five pages to what they had recorded when he demanded to see their notes of interview. It was obvious that they were 'verballing' but nothing was done about it.

Those who asked to see what had been recorded were politely but firmly put off. Some requested a copy of what had been recorded but this too was declined.

In my opinion, if this inquiry had been properly conducted, statements would have been taken. At the completion of the interview those being interviewed would have been asked to read and sign their statement.

Gibson:

- Failed to take any action after complaints of bias by myself and the Police Association. The Association advised me a police officer made a statement that his interview started with Chief Superintendent Mairs asking, "Would you like to tell us all you know about that devious little bastard, Detective Sergeant Lewis?"
- Showed no interest in complaints of harassment against me even during the inquiry.
- Refused to pursue an allegation by a senior NCO that he overheard one of the police inquiry team state to Dalziel on arrival in Dunedin, "Don't worry, Laurie, we'll do the best we can for you."
- Displayed indifference to the fact that the police inquiry team had openly fraternised with the people they were supposed to be inquiring into. This included going to their homes for meals; being picked up by them from the airport; having morning and afternoon tea with them; drinking with them in the police club of an evening.

The effect of this on prospective witnesses was devastating. Probably the worst example occurred when Faulkner was interviewing me at the Leviathan hotel in J. Bruce Robertson's presence. The telephone rang and we heard the voice of McLennan ask what time Faulkner would be arriving for dinner. Faulkner, embarassed to be caught out, stammered, "It's difficult for me because I'm junior in rank to him."

Gibson:

- Met me for my initial interview while still hung over from a drinking binge the night before. Although it was mid-winter in Dunedin, he was sweating profusely throughout the interview. He excused himself on a number of occasions to go to the toilet, or to go out on the balcony for fresh air or to make black coffee. He finally admitted that he had had too much to drink the previous night.

Later in the week I spoke to a Dunedin lawyer who asked me how

John was the day of the interview. I queried his reason for asking and he said, "He damm near drank a bottle of gin and the last we saw of him big Ollie [Paul Oliver, lawyer and former junior All Black lock] was carrying him back to his hotel."

This was a crucial interview in the context of his role as an independent examiner and it turned out to be a sham.

During the early weeks of the inquiry other allegations of selective interviewing were aired. Some of those being interviewed complained of the slanted way the interviews were conducted.

As a result, J. Bruce Robertson and I met the inquiry team and 'fronted' them about some of the allegations, particularly their failure to obtain signed statements.

I also raised the matter of Mairs beginning an interview with the comment, "Tell me what you know about this devious little bastard, Detective Sergeant Lewis."

Amazingly he did not deny the allegation, which prompted Robertson to demand an end to this nonsense of attempted "muck-raking". He said, "If you want to go back and muck-rake then we can certainly do that in relation to the past histories of Dalziel, Scott, Kelly and co. However I have ordered my client to restrict himself to the matters at hand and I expect you to do the same."

Gibson said, "No, I can assure you we are only looking at the sex ring issue, although I concede one person – you can guess who – wants to muck-rake. He wants to go back years."

Robertson appeared to accept their assurances despite my misgivings.

I then raised the issue of Dalziel's threats to people about to be interviewed and his silencing writs which had resulted in police officers being frightened to speak the truth.

One example that had recently been reported to me and Robertson was the case of Staff Senior Sergeant Sam Jones-Sexton. Jones-Sexton, an honest man, had been in regular contact with Dalziel in his role of arranging uniform branch relieving and transfers. He had often expressed his concerns about Dalziel's management style and expressed these concerns to the inquiry team and also his views on the sex inquiry.

He was approached by Dalziel in the cafeteria a short time after his interview with the inquiry team. Dalziel put his face in front of Jones-Sexton and said, "I've been told by John Gibson that I have been cleared of attempting to pervert the course of justice so now I am going to fix those who chose the wrong camp. Those who spoke out and backed Tom Lewis will suffer."

He was, according to Jones-Sexton, very intimidating and clearly meant what he said. An affidavit was taken from Jones-Sexton but it was ignored by John Gibson. It was, however, too much for Jones-Sexton, who retired when he reached 50 instead of the normal 55.

The other problem was the blatant intimidation being exercised by Rigor Mortis and Chookfeeder in their claim that if this inquiry did not clear Dalziel then the press and public would demand a change in policy regarding police officers investigating their own. Outside agencies would be brought in and more police would be charged.

The three police officers, Gibson, Mairs and Faulkner, said nothing. I asked if they were going to take action to prevent future occurrences but they refused to commit themselves. At this point, I expected Bruce Robertson to deliver a stern warning but he said nothing and the meeting ended.

One detective approached me a few days later and said, "Tom, you probably think I'm gutless and I don't blame you if you say so but I have a wife and two kids and for their sakes I cannot say what I overheard between you and Dalziel on the 10th of August. I just can't see you winning this after all that's gone on so I can't put my career on the line". At least he had the guts to tell me.

The police inquiry team continued on its merry way, even inviting subordinates who I had investigated for misdemeanours to come forward and 'empty their bucket' on me,

Some of these people, including my friend the Womble, really excelled themselves.

Many years later, when I obtained copies of their statements through the Official Information Act, I marvelled at their vivid imaginations. These statements, although used against me, were never put to me. I only heard of them after I left the police, courtesy of a typist who had been present when they were made. She knew the allegations were untrue and some years later she told me about them.

Later, a petition containing thousands of signatures was sent to the Prime Minister, David Lange, alleging that the inquiry had been a farce because among other things the findings had been based on evidence allegedly obtained from people who were not prepared to be named or have their evidence made known or tested.

It elicited the following response, "The examiner's report had contained minor deletions, principally to protect the identities of witnesses who were entitled to anonymity. Many of these people who spoke to the police inquiry team gave evidence on the basis of total confidentiality. I seriously doubt that any of them would be prepared to stand up and give evidence in a public forum".

John Kennedy, editor of the *Tablet*, said Lange's reply was the most astounding statement on human rights ever uttered by any New Zealand politician – that the people these anonymous people spoke against were not allowed to confront them, to test the statements or to even have access to what was said. Such evidence should not have been accepted by such an inquiry because it is worthless as those receiving it can be fed "scuttlebutt and falsehoods".

His front-page article in the *Tablet* of 19 March 1986, read, "In New Zealand today, a person no longer has the right to hear evidence against him, or to test the truth of that evidence."

When I applied for copies under the Official Information Act, the New Zealand police did everything in their power to prevent them being handed over. Even when I did receive them, most of the content had been deleted on the grounds that in some areas confidentiality had to be maintained.

Another important issue that was swept under the carpet was a letter which arrived addressed to me and signed by a woman who alleged John Lewis had exploited her sexually in similar ways to those reported and that she was prepared to talk to the police about it.

I went to Bruce Robertson with the letter and suggested we

arrange to have her interviewed. I was flabbergasted when he instructed me to hand the letter over to the police inquiry team. His argument was that an inquiry was in progress and therefore any such information had to go to the inquiry team.

Reluctantly, I delivered the letter to Peter Faulkner and I knew from his reaction that this avenue of inquiry would go nowhere. He said, "Is this the only copy?" When I replied it was, he was noticeably relieved.

I had, of course, kept a copy.

I asked the so-called independent examiner, John Gibson, when he first spoke to me in May 1995 what the result of that inquiry was. He seemed genuine when he said he was not aware of the woman's letter, assuring me that he would check it out with the inquiry team and let me know.

Despite regular reminders, he failed to deliver on this and a number of other requests.

It was obvious from Dalziel's comments about John Gibson clearing him of any major wrong doing in the early days of the inquiry that it was going to be a farce. Here we had the independent examiner supposedly telling the person under inquiry he was in the clear some four months before the Commissioner announced the result of the inquiry.

At that stage, he had not even seen many of the principal witnesses and, in fact, he steadfastly refused to interview witnesses who could have been crucial. Cathy, for example, was not interviewed by Gibson or the inquiry team even though she was clearly crucial as the inquiry started with her and she was involved throughout.

Gibson got around this problem by saying he and the police inquiry team were already aware of what she could tell them despite the fact that, in desperation to have her story heard, Cathy had approached Gibson at his hotel. He still refused to hear her out.

Then there was the amazing admission that they had not interviewed Audrey. It was absolutely crucial she be interviewed at length, particularly in the light of her remarks in front of Constable Devlin and Detective Constable Baines when they executed a search warrant on her address some weeks after my altercation with Dalziel.

Audrey implied that she had been told the matter had been 'fixed up' and she made the point that if John Lewis and his mates thought she would take the rap on her own then she would take them down with her. She also asked if another search warrant was being done on John's place.

Why wasn't she interviewed? How could Gibson and his inquiry team exonerate Dalziel when they had not even done the basic inquiry work?

During the next four months, the public and media awaited the result of the inquiry. Both the Police Association and Bruce Robertson told me the delay in announcing the outcome was unacceptable.

During this period, the harassment of my wife and daughter continued until we were forced to make a formal complaint to the Minister of Police, Ann Hercus.

In early September 1985, five months after the inquiry began, I heard through the Police Association that Thompson planned to announce the result of the so-called independent examiner's report and immediately go overseas.

I contacted a prominent member of the Police Association and he told me many weeks of soul searching and scheming had taken place in the Commissioner's office so that the expected furore following the announcement could be minimised.

He told me that Thompson was going overseas immediately the result of the inquiry had been made. This confirmed, in my mind, what I had feared from the time I learned of John Gibson's close association with the Commissioner – a cover-up was imminent. And so it proved.

When I finally read the report of John Gibson on 11 September, I was ready for the worst. Gibson's report was a bombshell. Of the nine findings he made, all were incorrect in fact.

The first finding relating to Dalziel perverting the course of justice read, "I find there was no attempt by Detective Chief Inspector Dalziel to pervert the course of justice; nor did anyone else. Detective Sergeant Lewis was not stopped in his investigation into the alleged illicit sex ring." This statement was made without qualification.

It was, of course, expected that a negative finding would be made because the police hierarchy had delayed investigation into the complaint for nine months. As every experienced investigator knows, if an inquiry into serious allegations is not begun within a reasonable time then chances of success are minimal. Allied to this was a police investigation team hellbent on protecting their commissioner. However to make such a finding without commenting on the delays in commencing the inquiry and the effect that had was an indictment of Gibson's credibility.

The rest of Gibson's findings were just as negative. He did make a finding of harassment occurring against me but he was quick to qualify this by stating that the harassment appeared to be of a minor nature.

The Gibson report was widely criticised. The head of the Police Association, Keith Morrow, said it raised more questions than it answered. Bruce Robertson, now a High Court Judge, said it was factually incorrect. Mike Guest, later a District Court Judge, and John Lewis's solicitor, told TVNZ's George Burck that he would have advised his client to plead guilty had he been charged with the offences I recommended.

Guest later repeated this to the police inquiry team in an interview with them on 1 May 1985 after being told by Chief Superintendent Mairs that the police inquiry team had no intention of reopening the inquiry into the sex ring as they had an opinion from the legal section that no offence in relation to this particular incident had been committed.

Guest's reply is most interesting: "I must say I am most surprised about your legal opinion. You must have some rumpty lawyers in your legal section."

The report was also at odds with Commissioner K.O. Thompson's statement on TVNZ's *Closeup* when he told reporter Brett Dumbleton that charges should have been laid.

The media, the Police Association and I requested access to the police inquiry file on which John Gibson alleged he based his findings. Our requests were denied by the police commissioner.

Little wonder the public clamour for investigation by a royal commission.

As Thompson flew out of New Zealand for a three-week sojourn overseas, he announced that both Dalziel and I were to be transferred from Dunedin in the interests of the police service. We were both effectively being demoted because we were both transferred to uniform branch duties.

The questions on everybody's lips were that if Dalziel had been cleared of perverting the course of justice, why was he being punished?

Why was he being dealt the same punishment as the person who made the allegation against him? Why wasn't I being disciplined for insubordination?

Commissioner Thompson was to be put through an inquisition over the next six months as he battled to avoid a royal commission into the Dunedin sex ring scandal.

In an interview with the *Dominion* on 22 October 1985, the president of the Police Association, Keith Morrow, explained the dilemma his association was facing. Thompson was accusing the Police Association, the media, and my legal advisers of not being specific in our criticism of John Gibson's report yet he was refusing access to the information in the report and inquiry file that would allow all three bodies to be specific.

Requests under the Official Information Act were denied. Reporter Mike Steel, of the *Sunday Times*, went to the Ombudsman to complain that police were deliberately obstructing his newspaper's attempts to get access to the inquiry file. He believed the inquiry team suppressed evidence of Thompson's involvement in the attempts to prevent an inquiry into the allegation against Dalziel.

The police successfully stalled the Ombudsman's office, which resulted in a stinging criticism of their obstructive behaviour by that department. The Ombudsman's office was, in fact, a toothless tiger throughout. The New Zealand police have always treated them with contempt and this was another example.

TVNZ's *Closeup* came to Dunedin and reopened debate on what was now generally regarded as a cover-up. They were obviously disappointed I did not attack the Gibson report but I was still a serving police officer and I was under orders that I was not to comment.

My solicitor, Bruce Robertson, stated he would go public over what he knew to be serious factual mistakes and omissions in the Gibson report. He later declined because he was of the opinion that any such criticism would adversely affect the appeal I had submitted.

When Thompson returned from his overseas trip he knew he was in trouble. Bryan Gibson, who had headed the police inquiry team, had been allegedly struck down by some mysterious illness. John Gibson, the so-called independent examiner, was starting to feel the pressure, stating that he would never again be involved in a police inquiry, and the public were clamouring for a royal commission.

Truth reporter Jock Anderson was back in Dunedin. Scenting a major scandal involving the Commissioner, he was unfortunately stopped in his tracks because Dalziel's solicitor warned of further writs and insinuated *Truth* would be acting in contempt by pursuing a story already the subject of a 'silencing' writ.

A Radio New Zealand talkback show on Dunedin's 4ZB was stopped as it went to air by another silencing writ from Dalziel.

Alistair Morrison of the *Sunday Times*, assisted by a tenacious young journalist, Mike Steel, was also causing stress levels to rise among the police hierarchy but undoubtedly the biggest threat to an exposure came from *Tablet* editor John Kennedy. He not only wrote the *Tablet's* editorials but was employed by a number of other newspapers throughout New Zealand to write feature articles.

The police inquiry team head, Bryan Gibson, was clearly a worried man.

He had returned to work and he contacted Kennedy offering him an all-expenses-paid trip to Wellington to discuss the Dunedin sex inquiry.

Quite properly, Kennedy refused the police offer of a taxpayer-funded trip but he did go to Wellington to meet Commissioner Thompson and Bryan Gibson.

They tried to present the police side of the story but when Kennedy asked for proof by being allowed to examine the internal police inquiry file and John Gibson's unabridged report, his request was firmly declined.

Kennedy was not impressed and he took the step of requesting that former Detective Senior Sergeant Selwyn Byers examine the way the inquiry had been carried out. Byers was a highly respected retired police officer and a friend of Bryan Gibson.

His involvement clearly worried Police Headquarters and a high-ranking police officer visited him at his home urging him not to accept Kennedy's request. Byers ignored him and a month later produced a comprehensive 57-page report.

His summary read:

I doubt whether I have ever seen a worse police inquiry file in my career. The complete absence of any professionalism, the complete departure of tried and true, normally accepted police investigational and interviewing practice, coupled with unique orders emanating from the very highest of levels that were counter-productive towards bringing the complaint to a satisfactory conclusion is the most shocking and disturbing thing I have encountered in the police.

Very high-ranking police officers completely abandoned their responsibilities over a period of time in a consistent pattern that brings the word 'collusion' to the fore.

The only logical conclusion for such irresponsibility must centre on Detective Sergeant Lewis and his allegations.

The departmental response was a 'closing of ranks' to weather out the storm, and this file is therefore only a part of the whole, the major inquiry, and it is the whole file that must be subject to the closest scrutiny.

With apologies to that eminent jurist Mr Justice Mahon, and his perspicacious observation in the Erebus Royal Commission 'an orchestrated litany of lies', the police inquiry here is nothing less than 'an orchestrated litany of deceit'.

SUMMARY:

The file was:

(a) Not planned in the normally accepted way synonymous with good police practice.

(b Not even properly executed to achieve an aim apparently chosen by the police administration.

(c) Not pursued with any degree of diligence or commonsense, and without any vestige of the professionalism normally associated with the New Zealand police.

(d) Neither controlled nor supervised to achieve a proper result.

(e) Completely and utterly deficient and devoid of basic interview and investigative techniques.

(f) Completely lacking in the attention to detail so necessary to achieve a satisfactory result for either the police administration or the complainant.

(g) Such as to bring into serious consideration the fitness of Commissioner K.O. Thompson, Deputy Commissioner B.W. Gibson, Chief Superintendent R.J. McLennan and others to hold office in the New Zealand police and . . .

(h) Such as to raise the spectre of collusion (with even more serious legal implications if properly investigated) among those named officers and others.

(i) Such as to raise doubts as to the competence and impartiality of the independent examiner, J.A.L. (John) Gibson.

Byers' 22,000-word report arrived on the desk of Prime Minister David Lange in November 1985 together with over 5000 signatures (obtained during a lunch-hour meeting in downtown Dunedin) demanding a royal commission of inquiry into the Dunedin sex ring scandal.

That, and the many letters to the editors of newspapers demanding a royal commission, caused Police Headquarters once again to try damage control.

Meanwhile, John Kennedy was becoming more and more vocal. He told reporter Mike Steel in an interview in late October that a royal commission into the New Zealand police was a matter of urgency. He said the original allegation could never have been substantiated after the police effectively blocked an inquiry into it for nine months.

He pointed out to Steel that the last such inquiry into police was also into a police commissioner, Mr E. Compton, and, "It was a much less serious allegation than the one we have here."

After weeks of hiding in his bunker, Commissioner Thompson finally emerged to make a press release to the effect that he was travelling to Dunedin in an attempt to finally put the Dunedin sex ring scandal to bed! An unfortunate turn of phrase – or was it an ill-advised remark from a man trying to appear flippant about an issue that was causing thousands of New Zealanders deep concern?

About this time I received an unexpected letter from my solicitor, Bruce Robertson. I was surprised that he had written to me when he could have discussed his feelings with me during one of our numerous meetings. In essence, he told me I had done all I could, and it would be best to stop pursuing the matter, and instead to think about myself and my family. Not the public, the police or the Police Association.

That afternoon, Thompson arrived in Dunedin to address a police staff meeting at the Dunedin Public Library. His object was to convince disgruntled Dunedin staff to drop the matter and get back to policing.

The police administration in Dunedin had been very busy trying to assist, copying the so-called independent examiner's report and handing copies to staff. To do this they used selected NCOs, usually those awaiting promotion and who had decided the die was cast in favour of McLennan and the police administration.

Some commissioned officers and NCOs who were most anxious for their own reasons not to see the matter reopened were advising staff that a royal commission would go back in time to examine other complaints about police misbehaviour and it would probably signal an end to police investigating police, which would result in more police officers being called to account for offences such as assault, wrongful arrest and so on.

Another matter which caused concern was the move by a couple of local Labour members of Parliament to arrange delivery of copies of the so-called independent examiner's report to all secondary schools and various organisations such as Lions and Round Table in the greater Dunedin area.

After the revelations at the NSW Royal Commission into paedophilia over the involvement of MPs and councillors, plus the remarks from Dunedin sex ring organiser John Lewis that MPs and other prominent people participated, the actions of the local MPs left many people feeling a little uneasy.

Commissioner Thompson received more than he bargained for when he arrived in Dunedin. Despite it being a cold, wet, spring day, hundreds of demonstrators hounded his every movement. So much so that we had the unprecedented sight of the Police Commissioner of New Zealand and the District Commander of Otago and Southland having to sneak into the Dunedin Public Library by a side entrance for their scheduled meeting with staff.

The meeting, and Thompson's embarrassing entrance, was widely reported on the electronic media as well as in most newspapers throughout the country. The *Otago Daily Times*, however, decided that the demonstrations, the petition signings and Cathy's lone vigil outside the Town Hall were not for its readers.

The carefully orchestrated staff meeting did not achieve what Thompson had hoped. Many police who attended later told me they could never recollect seeing Commissioner Thompson so paranoid. His theme was that there has been an inquiry, that inquiry had cleared a senior officer of an allegation of perverting the course of justice, and that was the end of the story!

What he refused to answer was, amongst other things, the fact that if that officer, Dalziel, had been cleared why was he being punished by being transferred back to the uniform branch in another city?

The Commissioner had stated that neither Dalziel nor I was being punished. We were being transferred for the sake of the service with no financial loss to either man. The assembled police knew this was an untruth. They knew that a CIB rank entitled the officer concerned to a tax-free amount of around $100 per week.

Many police officers were baffled at the lengths the department was going to in an attempt to thwart the setting-up of a royal commission. They believed that if the Commissioner, his inquiry team and Dalziel, John Lewis and members of Parliament had nothing to hide then let the media and the public have a royal commission into the Dunedin sex ring.

Deep down, most police officers knew there had been a major cover-up.

Many came to me personally and said, "Look, I don't know what the nuts and bolts of this are but since you are pushing for a royal commission that indicates to me you have nothing to hide – unlike the Commissioner, parliamentarians, and Dalziel and his mates, who are moving heaven and earth to avoid it."

The public were, of course, asking the same sort of questions.

It was about this time that I was approached by Mike Steel of the *Sunday Times* asking for a response to an interview he had with Police Association President Keith Morrow. Morrow had allegedly told Steel that the long-awaited pay rise for the police was at a delicate stage and that the early retirement scheme was also being negotiated.

He told Steel that the Minister of Police, Ann Hercus, was urging the Police Association to stop pushing for a royal commission into the sex inquiry and in return the pay increase and early retirement plan could be implemented without delay.

I made my own inquiries and I learnt that Steel was correct. For some time, rumours had been circulating about the reasons behind Hercus's reluctance to order a royal commission. David Lange, the New Zealand Prime Minister, had certainly played 'pass the parcel' in relation to the pressure that had been placed on him to order one. He had merely 'handballed' the petition and the controversial Byers' report on to Hercus.

Rumour had it that Hercus had problems of her own. She had been found in a rather embarrassing situation with a TVNZ employee while visiting the Chatham Islands. Commissioner

Thompson and the police hierarchy were well aware of her indiscretion.

Some years later she once again embarrassed her parliamentary colleagues while in the Chathams.

In 1985, Hercus obviously saw a way to end the impasse between the Police Association and the Commissioner's office – the pay rise and the early retirement package were it.

Coincidentally, I received a visit by a police inspector from Police Headquarters in Wellington. He told me that if I went to Wellington I would be working directly under a man who had been on the police inquiry team, Chief Superintendent Peter Mairs. He said, "You will also be working close to K.O. [Commissioner Thompson] and Bryan Gibson who have all had many sleepless nights over this. You can imagine the shit they will give you."

I was offered a generous disengagement package if I resigned from the police. It was certainly not as generous as those handed out today under the Perf scheme but I was to receive all the money I had paid into superannuation plus the government contribution.

In light of Robertson's comments in his letter to me suggesting that for my own sake and that of my family I cease battling the police department, and also the fact that the Police Association had been made an offer to drop their support for me, an offer I knew would eventually be too good for them to refuse, I went home to my wife to ponder our future.

I was still keen to carry on believing that one day the truth would out. Rather naively, in retrospect, I still considered that people would realise that behind all the lies, deceit, and posturing the simple fact was I was just a copper who had been given a job to do and I was determined to do it properly. The law applied equally to everyone in my eyes and I was not interested in the political repercussions of my probe.

My wife quite rightly pointed out all that had been lost in the smokescreen the Commissioner and his cohorts had created. She was tired of it and convinced that the whole thing had become so political that the real issue was buried in a morass of claims and counter-claims.

She believed that the Labour government of the time were involved and were only paying lip service in their assurances to the public that they would reopen the inquiry if the evidence warranted it.

We decided that night that we had done all we could and that it was time to get on with our own lives and start afresh. The next day I made the first move to resign from the New Zealand police by intimating I was interested in the offer.

Events over the next few weeks vindicated my decision. The victimisation directed at me was extended to my youngest son and daughter. My youngest son had joined his elder brother in the Otago representative sevens rugby team and they had travelled out of Dunedin to play. On their return, both went to the hotel that their club, University, patronised. While there, an altercation involving a policewoman occurred and my son was arrested for assaulting her.

Even when solicitor Michael Guest provided the police with evidence that this was a case of mistaken identity they refused to withdraw the charges. He was later discharged without conviction in the Dunedin District Court.

About the same time, my daughter was involved in a car accident and it was alleged the other car was travelling at excessive speed. Despite this, she received a summons charging her with careless driving.

Her lawyer contacted the police to obtain the particulars of the other driver only to learn he had been charged with drunken driving. This fact was withheld from us and, of course, once we became aware of it the police were forced to withdraw the charge against my daughter.

In my opinion, these charges would never have been laid under normal circumstances.

John Kennedy said to me, "They don't have the guts to harass you but they don't really need to. They will get at you through your wife and children."

He agreed with my decision to go, saying, "It's a terrible indictment when you have to go because you were honest enough to speak up."

He told me that when I went it would be difficult to get to the truth as I was a key figure in the fight to get a royal commission.

In March 1986, some 19 months after making my complaint, I left the New Zealand police after nearly 20 years' service.

16

The Aftermath

In late March 1986, I moved to Australia temporarily. I returned to New Zealand later in the year to sell my house and business and my children accompanied me back to Australia and we lived in Perth.

While I was back in New Zealand, I spoke to John Kennedy, who told me what had been happening during my absence, including a scandal at the Dunedin Central Station which had resulted in McLennan being hastily transferred to Christchurch while his wife and family continued to live in Dunedin.

Kennedy advised me to speak with *Sunday Times* reporter Mike Steel, who had been investigating the scandal. It concerned an allegation of the theft of a few tyres from the Dunedin police garage but what started as a minor inquiry quickly became a major one.

On 26 March 1986, Assistant Commissioner McEwan and Detective Inspector Lines arrived in Dunedin and were briefed on the inquiry by Detective Chief Inspector Fitzharris. What would have caused Police Headquarters in Wellington to send an assistant commissioner to Dunedin to investigate a staff inquiry involving a few tyres? After all, the inquiry had been assigned to the head of the Dunedin CIB, the person usually assigned to such investigations.

There was only one answer: Fitzharris' inquiries had revealed the involvement of some person senior to himself in Dunedin. That left only two officers, District Commander Bear McLennan and his deputy, Superintendent Bert (also known as Betty) Hill.

Steel, under the Official Information Act, obtained a copy of the 'file', if one could call it that after the huge deletions made to it. The eight pages of inquiries carried out by McEwen and Lines are deleted with the exception of twelve lines which refer to the theft of tyres from the Dunedin police garage.

The 'file' was written off on 17 April 1986. The part describing how the Assistant Commissioner reached his conclusion (he found no evidence in his inquiry of tyres being dishonestly misused) is blanked out.

The report was then forwarded to Police Headquarters in Wellington.

On 6 May 1986, a memo was sent to the complainant (name blanked out). The memo, in the name of Assistant Commissioner Rusbatch, stated that while the investigation had not disclosed any criminal activity, it had become apparent procedures adopted in the police garage in Dunedin and the administrative control required attention.

The *Sunday Times* decided that this was another cover-up and they attempted to expose it. Their suspicions were fuelled when an announcement was made in the good, old faithful *Otago Daily Times* that Police Chief McLennan was transferring to Christchurch at his own request!

Dunedin police only learned of their boss's transfer via the media. He did not have a farewell function; he slipped out of Dunedin quietly and alone. They asked the obvious question – why would a district commander opt to transfer away from his wife and children to live in the single quarters of an army barracks? Not only that, but he was effectively demoting himself.

The Dunedin staff had no doubt. I was told McLennan was moved, quick smart. K.O. Thompson just could not afford another major inquiry in Dunedin in the wake of the Dunedin sex ring scandal so it had to be another cover-up, and it was, according to my sources.

McLennan took early retirement a few months later and now lives back in Dunedin.

What of K.O. Thompson? This man had been under such pressure attempting to keep the lid on the various scandals occurring during his tenure as Commissioner that something had to give, and it did. Thompson suffered a heart attack and he retired shortly after.

It is interesting to note here that the Muldoon government had serious misgivings about Thompson just as he was about to become Commissioner. In a strange move which was never satisfactorily explained, they requested the retiring Commissioner to stay on for an extra two years, in other words delay his retirement.

Commissioner Bob Walton obliged and many police officers were grateful that he did because the 1981 Springbok tour took place during that time. The mind boggles at the thought of Thompson trying to lead the police department through what was an extremely difficult period.

Some amusing stories are told about the nifty footwork displayed by a number of senior commissioned officers when Bob Walton agreed to an extension of service. Many of these individuals had deserted Walton as the time of his retirement approached as they were intent on paying homage to the man they believed would be replacing him.

Imagine the consternation when it was announced that Bob Walton was remaining for another two years. Old Bob, a crafty old fox, had a lot of fun over the next two years as those who had treated him as yesterday's man desperately struggled to get back into his camp.

As well as the Dunedin sex ring, K.O. Thompson was involved in other cover-ups, including the unlawful taking of a police Land Rover by a close friend, a Chief Superintendent.

The Land Rover was taken outside normal working hours by the Chief Superintendent who drove it to his son's farm where it was used to pull out tree stumps. This caused extensive damage to the vehicle, costing thousands of dollars, which was finally dumped back in the police yard at Wellington.

A police inquiry later revealed the offender to be a Chief Superintendent, closely connected to Thompson. The inquiry was immediately stopped and the matter filed.

Disgruntled staff leaked the information to the media and a hunt was begun by Thompson to try and find the source of the leak.

Meanwhile, Police Headquarters and Thompson sat tight, held the line and adopted the famous police strategy of, "This too shall pass." And it did!

About this time, there was also a high-ranking officer exposed for indecently assaulting a number of females at an RSA club in a central North Island town. After the allegations were substantiated, the offender was summoned to national Police Headquarters. He left Wellington later that day as a retired police officer, on a full pension courtesy of a heart attack that had mysteriously occurred on his flight to Wellington. Until the time of his exposure, this man had been a prominent marathon runner and surprise, surprise he continued to run long after his retirement.

There was no court appearance for these serious crimes for either man. Little wonder police morale was at its lowest ebb during the time K.O. Thompson was Commissioner of Police.

17

Getting the Police that the Public Deserve?

On 13 March 1997, Justice James Wood ended the NSW police royal commission. After 451 days, 640 witnesses and 37,542 pages of evidence, it was all over apart from a separate report on paedophilia to be released later.

Justice Wood painted a picture of a NSW police department where cynicism, personal degradation, chronic alcohol abuse, low morale and a complete lack of commitment to the job prevailed. He stated that the police culture thrived because of its group loyalty, the tradition of mateship, peer group pressure and standover merchants.

In places like Kings Cross, Commissioner Wood found that police became involved in criminal acivities including drug addicts' "shooting galleries", open sale of narcotics in the streets, shootings and violence between competing drug lords, abuse of sex workers, assault, robbery and pornographic videos.

His report found "tacit assistance" by police allowing drug dealing to evolve from one-man operations into large enterprises in a well-established "partnership" between police, drug dealers, managers and owners of brothels, clubs and strip shows.

The commission was not convinced whether the failure by senior police to act was due to their incompetence or because of a deliberate policy to suppress the disclosure of matters harmful to the police service.

Now, after millions of dollars have been spent investigating one of the most corrupt police departments in Western society, perhaps the public need to examine their part in this widespread corruption of their state police. This was a corruption that went from the grass roots to the highest echelons, not only in the police but in Parliament, the judiciary, the education sector, business and the community.

For it to flourish, it required the public of NSW to turn a blind eye to what was going on. Any visitor could tell you that after walking through Kings Cross in Sydney, crime, drugs and prostitution were there for everyone to see. Under those circumstances, there had to be police corruption. Yet why has it taken decades to expose it?

Politicians resisted, right up until the end, the repeated requests for a royal commission. Why? Did they enjoy being the butt of jibes like, "NSW has the best police money can buy"? Or were they on the take as well? There is no doubt that some of them were, including at least one former premier of that state.

Take a walk through Kings Cross now, some months after the royal commission has finished. You will find nothing has changed. You can still buy all types of illicit drugs on the street. Prostitution is rife. Stolen property can still be bought without any worry of police intervention.

Go out to Cambramatta, where you will see the same scenario but only worse. You can even hire a killer there for a few thousand dollars.

Closer to Sydney in the suburb of Auburn, stolen property is bought and sold at the local hotel as though it were market day.

It is clear that the reforms recommended by the commission of inquiry will take time to implement although the NSW public have already seen some changes to policing their state with more to follow. They are also now better educated about the need to stamp out the vast corruption that existed and still exists among police.

So what did the NSW royal commission really achieve? Apart from its finding that serious corruption did exist through all levels of the NSW police, the royal commission also recommended:

• The formation of a new and powerful body, the Police

Corruption Commission, to hunt and prosecute corrupt police. The command structure of this commission has to be commended.

- A system for classifying conduct with four main categories: serious misconduct and corruption; misconduct; customer service matters; internal management matters.
- Stronger police regional Internal Affairs (IA) units with the central unit confined to a supervisory and intelligence role.
- Reviews into the keeping of criminal records, drug use by police and the structure of the Police Board.

The staffing of the commission has obviously been well thought through and I commend the use of former Supreme Court or High Court judges as Inspectors of the PCC and as Commissioners.

The PCC will be even more powerful than the Wood royal commission in that it will have the ability to intercept and monitor telephone conversations. "Its head, a full-time commissioner, must be a person of the highest reputation, integrity and commitment," said Commissioner Wood.

The PCC's 'watchdog' will be the Inspector of the PCC, a serving or former High Court judge. Where an agency is heavily committed to covert operations, relies on informants, and possesses powers of a type which could involve substantial infringements of rights of privacy, there is an obvious need for an Inspector of PCC in case investigators overstep the mark.

The banning of serving or former NSW police was to be expected. Justice Wood was also instrumental in the state cabinet appointing Peter Ryan as the new Commissioner of Police for NSW.

Ryan, a man of proven ability and impeccable character, is faced with a daunting task. He took over when morale was at an all-time low, with the public perception of the NSW police as inefficient, lazy and corrupt.

Unfortunately, the public have tended to brand all police as unworthy of trust or respect. While this is understandable bearing in mind the daily revelations coming out of the royal commission, the fact is there are some men and women who have not been corrupted and these officers must be disillusioned and dispirited at the image the community has of them.

Peter Ryan has made a start. He has moved against some of the officers who have brought disgrace to the police service. In doing this, he has had to face the full might of the NSW police, who brazenly staged a public demonstration against some of his changes.

These same individuals have spread gossip regarding the state of the Commissioner's marriage. When his wife recently returned to England to complete her university examinations, the 'police culture club' went for the jugular.

The press were advised that Mrs Ryan had separated from him and returned to England and she was forced to issue a strongly worded retraction from England in order to discredit the "police clobbering machine".

The front page of *Sydney's Daily Telegraph* of 18 February 1997 said it all:

Peter Ryan : His wife's message of support

"Sweetheart, I love you. Don't let the bastards get you down."

She told the *Daily Telegraph's* London reporter, John Ferguson, that she was incensed by "innuendo" about a marriage split, pointing out that it had come from officers her husband had been forced to sack or demote since taking over as Commissioner with the brief to overhaul the NSW police service.

She reiterated that she was in London for university examinations that would complete her degree in politics and international relations and she would be returning to Australia at Easter. To illustrate just how ridiculous the allegations were regarding her marriage she pointed out that her parents were in Sydney caring for her husband and children while she was completing her degree.

Having been on the end of similar treatment, I know just how low these individuals can stoop. When my own wife was 'stalked' and when the police administration, in trying to show that I was under stress, spread the scurrilous rumour that it was due in part to my wife losing a baby then it did hurt. But then the police do not always play by the Marquess of Queensberry rules as any person who has been set up can testify.

It is obvious that the Wood royal commission has been the catalyst for the reform of the NSW police and without it the corruption that spread like a cancer through the highest echelons of the police service, the bureaucracy, the judiciary, the education and welfare departments and in the wider society would never have been exposed.

This leads us to the obvious question: what of the New Zealand police with their 'holier than thou' attitude?

They have monumental problems ranging from corruption to incompetence with lots in between. They have, over the years, shown great dexterity in avoiding royal commissions or commissions of inquiry. This has not been good for the service and the image of police is on a downward spiral. Morale is at rock bottom and many of the more experienced police have elected to desert ship via the 'Perf' (Police Early Retirement Fund) scheme.

This extremely generous scheme, which is not available to other public servants, allows police to effectively opt out when the going gets tough. The official line is that it is a fund designed for police officers unable to cope either psychologically or physically with the demands of their work. That has turned out to be an absolute joke, albeit a costly one, for the New Zealand taxpayer! With a payout of more than $10,000 for every year of service for a constable, it really is a golden handshake.

It was a similar tale in the corrupt NSW police service. Police superannuation advisory scheme chairman Peter Cox told the royal commission that in 1993 about 53 per cent of retirements were on invalidity grounds. He said that this was to be expected because the benefits are very generous and they relate to the fact that the test for invalidity might be regarded as being a soft one. He went on to say there were many cases where psychiatric conditions were brought on by police work and went away when "police stopped being police".

Perhaps this tends to illustrate that the police culture is the same when it comes to 'rorting the system', be it in NSW, New Zealand or wherever.

New Zealand's Perf scheme was part of a very good deal brokered by the Police Association in 1985 when the Minister of Police, Ann Hercus, was seeking an end to the association's push for a royal commission into the Dunedin sex ring scandal.

In hindsight, it has been a disaster, not least for the taxpayer. The police service has suffered as well, due to the mass exodus of many experienced and competent members.

In all facets of police work, there is no substitute for experience and the Police Association and Police Headquarters threw years of experience out the door when they embraced this 'Perf' concept.

Police Headquarters also stand indicted for using Perf in a manner that was never intended. They have abused the scheme and, for the sake of the police service and the hard-done-by taxpayer, it should be abolished.

In an article in the *Daily Telegraph Mirror* on 1 February 1995, Cindy Wockner reported from the NSW police royal commission that Assistant Commissioner Jeff Jarrett had told the royal commission that those facing allegations of misconduct could fake sickness to avoid charges being brought against them. He admitted that police knew that illnesses could also be faked for pension retirement purposes.

It was admitted that counsel for the police service had recommended proceedings be brought against Assistant Commissioner Col Cole, who was medically discharged on full superannuation benefits after being suspended for his role in the Frenchs Forest affair, in which police covered up drug thefts at the station.

Under the New Zealand Perf scheme, there is a perception that the same scenario has been enacted many times. I know of at least one in recent years and I am sure a commission of inquiry would reveal millions of dollars have been 'rorted' from the public purse since the advent of the Perf scheme.

In June 1997, we had the case of the cross-dressing Constable Paul Jones. After his conviction for shoplifting (stealing a dress from a Palmerston North second-hand shop), he told the media that the theft had occurred a year earlier and he was not charged for six months. The case was drawn out as senior officers tried to get him to quit to avoid a scandal in the police.

Six months' delay in justice being carried out while the police 'culture club' tried to protect the image of the service and, of course, one of their members. Spare a thought for the victim, the shopkeeper trying to make an honest dollar. The New Zealand police certainly did not. They were too busy covering up.

The cross-dressing constable had obviously been well briefed by his superiors on just how to go about 'perfing'. When interviewed by the media, he had all the standard police lines such as, "This is not a sexual habit. Some people drink, others beat their wife. It's a mechanism of disengaging myself from the stress of the job."

In the New Zealand police, you only have to mention the word stress and you are guaranteed your golden handshake!

This type of rort, ripoff, call it what you like, was in vogue even before the Perf scheme was introduced. Remember the senior District Commander, the marathon runner, who indecently assaulted a number of women at his local RSA club and whose heart condition concided with his visit to Commissioner Ken Thompson's office to face criminal allegations?

There were signs that all was not well with the New Zealand police as far back as the Arthur Allan Thomas inquiry. Some police officers who should have been taken to task over that miscarriage of justice escaped due to the unfortunate death of a colleague from cancer. He became the scapegoat and in his absence much of the blame was laid on him. In a despicable display of opportunism, his former workmates blamed him for the controversial planting of the shell case on Thomas's property.

The result was that the inquiry never identified the real villains. This police cover-up was aided and abetted by acquiescence at several levels.

The family of the deceased detective cried foul and the New Zealand public were suspicious. The press talked about it but they did nothing and the police carried on.

During the late seventies and early eighties, while I was involved in investigating allegations of police misconduct, I witnessed a number of cover-ups. These were the days before the Perf scheme and had it been available I have no doubt that some of those investigated would have been given the golden handshake.

In a number of cases, criminal charges should have been laid; in others, the officers concerned should have been dismissed. The offences ranged from theft to indecent assaults as well as breaches of the Privacy Act. On occasions the offending police officer was told, "I have a file on you in my office with enough to put you before the courts. I'm not going to but remember you owe me!"

I doubt whether this type of behaviour was widespread although I was advised, when I protested, that I was wasting my time because some senior officers believed it was a useful method of ensuring future loyalty, particularly if the case against the member was not strong.

This was not the case in at least one of the inquiries I carried out as we had members of another government department available as independent witnesses and the offending police officer should have faced criminal charges.

This form of blackmail would be abhorrent to most police and I have always been of the opinion that it was not rife in the New Zealand police.

How can the 'culture' of the New Zealand police be changed other than by a royal commission?

It cannot while the belief exists that the comradeship embodied in their much-vaunted 'culture' extends to turning a blind eye to criminals among their own.

It will not while police continue to believe that police misbehaviour can be tolerated and accepted as part of the rites of the tribe.

Through the seventies and early eighties, there were signs that the New Zealand police service had allowed their standards to fall and under Police Commissioner K.O. Thompson that trend accelerated.

During the next ten years, the New Zealand police lacked leadership.

These people seemed to bow to one of the pressures of leadership which is NOT to do things. What the New Zealand police service needed then and definitely needs now is a strong leader who will say, "I know it's going to be painful, but it's got to happen and it will be done."

18

Leadership

As far as leadership is concerned in Australasia, Peter Ryan stands out like a beacon. In simple terms, Ryan impresses as a scrapper, a tough man with very strong principles who was 'imported' from the United Kingdom to right all that was wrong in the NSW police service.

He started by making it quite clear to the politicians just who was in charge. When Ryan attended his first meeting with the NSW police board late last year, he watched it put its finishing touches to its submission to government on the Wood royal commission into police corruption in NSW.

One of the recommendations was that the commissioner "shall implement decisions of the board". Ryan made it quite clear to the politicians that he was not going to be told how to do his job. Within a month or so, the board was gone!

Can you imagine any of our police commissioners following suit?

What about this refreshing quote when Ryan was interviewed shortly after taking over as commissioner: "I am not just a commissioner of police. I am a professional CEO. I do have a particular professional skill at the police service but I am a CEO of a $1.2 billion organisation of 18,000 people. I have to run it like a business because it is the taxpayers' money and I have to ensure we get the best value for them."

We have had commissioners of police in recent years who would not even get a job in middle management in the real world. They aspired to the rank of commissioner either through long service, which usually meant sitting on their hands and doing nothing because that way one cannot make a mistake, or being a political appointee. Deficient leadership is why we have police services debilitated by incompetence, misconduct and inefficiency.

Of course, Ryan has not stopped at sorting out political interference. He has also caused a few earthquakes at the top of the NSW police hierarchy. Some were found to be tainted by the royal commission and others were not but I suspect many would have fought change and obviously Ryan believed the 'stable needed some new brooms'.

About the same time as Peter Ryan took office, the New Zealand police service appointed a new commissioner, Peter Doone. During the mid-eighties, Doone worked in Dunedin temporarily and I met him socially.

I respect his intelligence but at the time of his appointment I did express my doubts about his mental toughness and his ability to deal with the politicians.

He has now been in the top job for some twelve months, long enough for others to look at and judge his performance. In the weekly *Sunday News* on 29 June 1997, a headline read:

He's Doone but not out, top cop stays upbeat despite tough year in the hot seat

The article, by Joseph Lose, reviewed Doone's year as Commissioner and he acknowledged that he had experienced a tough year. With a record number of officers, including senior staff, leaving disillusioned and allegedly stressed out (what a wonderful way to 'cop out'), Doone has obviously failed to lift police morale from the lows of the Dick (Teflon) McDonald era.

How has he rated in standing up to the politicians? Very poorly by all accounts. The Treasury razor gang went through the New Zealand police service like a cyclone, according to the report, and that newspaper article foiled Treasury mandarins' proposal to cut the service's spending to the bone.

The $100 million super-computer, which it is alleged will cut crime, is still soaking up loads of cash and months away from going on line.

The new centralised emergency dispatch system is riddled with problems and is causing even more delays to people in need. The crime rate is still escalating.

So how should one rate Doone? First we should read what the man had to say to Joseph Lose. Doone states that through all the change he has kept his vision, which is for a more streamlined, lean, efficient force. (He cannot even get that right as the word 'force' was dropped over twenty years ago.)

He stated that morale, which had plummeted, was now on the rise. However, the facts do not bear that out. If morale is on the rise, why is the New Zealand police service losing staff at a rate which is cause for major concern among politicians, the media and the public?

He then alludes to members having to pull together and focus on teamwork rather than the fractured lines. "The enemy is outside the police force, not inside," he states. That doesn't exactly equate to a police service with high morale.

Doone then goes on to say that he wants to see front-line constables making more decisions and taking initiatives. Then he talks about police at present relying on a top-down command to generate results, something he is hoping to reverse.

Well, Mr Doone, many of us believe you and your mates at headquarters have effectively driven out of the police service the people who had initiative and who were self-motivated.

His other statements also indicate he has lost the plot when he talks about decision making. It is not the constables that have to be given more power to make decisions but their immediate superiors, the sergeants and senior sergeants. These NCOs must have a proven police record to be promoted and not just the ability to pass police examinations as in the past. Most importantly, they must be mature, well-adjusted people who have proven leadership qualities.

A final thought on Commissioner Doone. As one wag said to me after looking at the photo of Doone in the *Sunday News*, "He can't even put his hat on properly. He looks more like a London bus conductor than a cop."

Compare his appearance with that of Commissioner Ryan who

looks and acts like the consummate professional police commissioner.

With scandals rocking the New Zealand police almost daily, what is needed is strong leadership. While in New Zealand, I spoke to former police officers who were disgusted at the damage being done to the police image.

Policewomen – apparently with the approval of the police hierarchy – pose for girlie calendars showing heaving cleavage and glistened lips; the cross-dressing shop-lifter instead of being immediately charged was offered a golden handshake if he would go quietly; the Wanganui District Commander, Superintendent Alec Waugh, was charged with 20 fraud charges.

We have also had one of New Zealand's top QCs, Peter Williams, blasting the police over their handling of the Garner case in which a detective faked an attack on himself alleging that Satan-worshippers had been responsible and had also burned his house down.

Williams correctly pointed out that the media bombardment by the police in the early stages of the investigation should have left them most embarrassed. They made emotive pleas and released a detailed description of the alleged attacker of Garner and a compusketch, stating that the attacker might have chosen Garner as a human sacrifice.

Williams pointed out that Garner's guilty pleas to eight charges should show people that they should always be wary of police statements and the police should keep an open mind when carrying out inquiries. "Police went along with an assumption which was later to be proved wrong. Much of the early statements made by police on national television and radio were propaganda."

Williams was pointing out that distributing so much propaganda could prevent an accused person getting a fair trial. In this case, it only caused embarrassment when their own man, Garner, was charged with arson, false pretences, wasting police time, making a false complaint and four charges of forgery.

The Tania Furlan murder investigation was another case of the police tying themselves into a particular line of inquiry to the exclusion of all other avenues. The only reason an arrest was made was because the offender, Christopher Lewis 'mouthed off'. Had he not done so, the police would still be chasing their tails. They had centred all their inquiries around the mistaken belief that the offender was a female!

We also have the Peter Ellis fiasco as another badly handled inquiry that will come back to haunt the New Zealand police in the near future.

The Bain murder inquiry also falls into this category. The police were reluctantly forced to order an inquiry into the manner in which the initial murder investigation was carried out. They managed to have the inquiry made by one of their own and the results were, sadly, predictable.

I predicted that even their own man, Brian Duncan, would have to find fault with the original inquiry, but I also predicted that there would not be any blame directly attributed to any members nor any accountability accepted.

An excellent example of the way police react to offences committed by fellow officers occurred after a senior Hutt Valley police officer tested positive to two breath sniffer tests at a drink-driving check point on 21 December 1996. Despite this, he was allowed to leave the checkpoint without going through an evidential breath screening test. His wife was permitted to drive the car from the checkpoint.

What was the police reaction to this? It was reported that the constable who allowed the officer to leave the checkpoint would receive an adverse report while the checkpoint supervisor would receive counselling! I can think of a number of serious disciplinary and criminal charges that they should have been facing.

But what of the senior officer? The Upper Hutt District Commander, Rob Robinson, said that he, the senior officer, the man who managed with the help of his police mates to evade conviction, would now have the chance to admit or deny the charge. He then put in a plea of mitigation for his mate by stating, "The incident was an error of judgment on the senior officer's part."

What rubbish! It was a deliberate attempt to evade a conviction.

Then we have the embarrassing situation that occurred in Christchurch where the police department had to pay $20,000 in compensation and $5000 in costs to a police constable who tried to blow the whistle on possible police corruption and copped the usual response of harassment and transfer.

Not only did the Employment Tribunal impose the monetary penalty, the Adjudicator, Jeff Goldstein, criticised the evidence of police officers including that of the head of the Christchurch CIB, Detective Chief Inspector Bob McMeeking, and other senior officers.

He said his view was that the Police Department's focus was not on finding out the truth but on ensuring that the constable's allegations were seen to be unfounded.

In this case, despite criticism of senior police by Jeff Goldstein, no action was taken against those officers. The Southern Regional Commander, Paul Fitzharris, said that despite the tribunal's ruling, police believed they had made the right decision. If that was the case, why did the police not appeal the decision?

When it comes to homicides, the public expect a professional dedicated approach from the police but the Bain and Furlan cases have not been the only botched murder inquiries in recent months.

One of the worst examples was the case of the young Samoan girl, Agnes Alli-Ia-Va, who was murdered in Auckland in 1992 but who police insisted had committed suicide. This was police incompetence of the worst possible kind because while they pursued the wrong line of inquiry the offender(s) were escaping justice.

Later, in an apology to the family, a senior Auckland police officer attempted to absolve himself and the department from blame by stating that the Detective Inspector responsible for this debacle had taken early retirement. Another instance of a golden handshake for a monumental botch-up.

Right up there with the worst examples of gross incompetence is the Janine Law homicide inquiry. After a two-month investigation, police concluded she died from an asthma attack. Fortunately one detective was unconvinced. He approached his superiors and after much procrastinating a new investigation began in 1994, six years after the muder file had been written off! In 1995, 34-year-old James Tamata pleaded guilty to raping and murdering Law.

And what of the 'whistleblower', the man who was unconvinced? You have guessed it. He is no longer a police officer. Like former Invercargill police constable Mike Cairns, who exposed a cover-up over a double fatal road accident, the pressure from the 'police brotherhood' was too much to bear.

I have highlighted only a few of the instances where inquiries have been inefficient operations with incompetence of an unacceptable magnitude. After all, I no longer live in New Zealand and these examples are only those which have been brought to my attention by serving and retired police officers. I have no doubt they represent only the tip of the iceberg.

Perhaps the last word should go to Deputy Assistant Commissioner Barry Mathews, who recently described a third of the district commanders throughout the country as incompetent. He also criticised other senior staff and NCOs, stating many were not up to the required standard.

I was amazed. Here was a senior police officer prepared to speak up against 'the brotherhood,' to tell the truth.

Under pressure from the Police Association and Commissioner Doone, Mathews did backtrack and he later apologised for his remarks but for the public and the media it was none the less a clear indication of the state of the New Zealand police.

With headlines such as, "Time to get tough on gangs," "Crims go free, prosecutions ditched as crime wave overwhelms police," "Gangs recruiting eight-year-olds to commit serious crimes," now common in New Zealand newspapers, the police response was to conduct a nationwide survey to gauge the level of public confidence in their work!

Police national headquarters planning and policy guru Gavin McFadyen said officers would use the results of the survey to develop a "trust index" measuring the level of public confidence in a range of areas of police work.

What bureaucratic nonsense! Another great example of how police at national Police Headquarters are being endlessly inventive in their capacity to find new ways to deflect the public's concern from the department's inability to do the job they are paid well to do – controlling crime and violence – on to some hair-brained survey.

I acknowledge that it is easy to criticise without offering solutions to the problems that confront police. However, the basic problem in both New Zealand and Australia is the lack of a police presence on the streets.

How many years is it since anybody saw a uniformed police officer walking his beat in the suburbs? Twenty, more like thirty. Forget your community constables. More often than not they are police officers being put out to pasture. They are either awaiting retirement or regarded as useless front-line officers and community policing has been the place to hide them.

I am talking about taking the fight back to the streets. Building police houses in the suburbs with a small police station attached and making the local cop responsible for his 'patch'. Within a very short time, they will know who lives and moves in their patch.

The constable who works on his own in a station in the suburbs soon learns how to become a good police officer. If you do not, you will not survive. You learn people skills. The type of skills our young constables today do not acquire because they are faceless people to the public at large. They are just people who turn up in uniforms to record details of a crime; people the complainant will probably never see again.

Contrast this with the role of the suburban police officer. He lives in the area. His children probably go to school there. His wife shops there and may also work there. He has a vested interest in that suburb and he will under normal circumstances do his utmost to ensure that the lid is kept on crime.

Today, with modern communications, he can have back-up within minutes. Not that a good police officer will require assistance very often. When I was on the beat in the suburbs, shopkeepers and residents provided any back-up that was required.

Let's forget about building police stations or patrol bases in the suburbs, let's go back to putting good, solid police officers in charge of individual suburbs. A small room for an office attached to a police house is all that is required.

The main goal, however, should be to ensure that the officer concerned is freed from unnecessary paperwork in order that he can carry out his main role of being a pro-active police officer, and that entails walking the streets of the suburb under his control for at least five hours of his shift.

Apart from the crime prevention element, the local cop was always a virtual bank of information. As a young aspiring detective, I soon learned where to get my information from – the local cop in the suburbs. He told me what went on in his area, he told me who had been in his area and if there had been a crime on his patch, he could, more often than not, name the offender!

The mere fact that he is moving among the community, among the shopkeepers, businesspeople, residents and the youth of the area, should ensure that if any serious crime occurs he can tap into his sources to ensure that investigating police get a head start in their inquiry.

For too long now detectives have been behind the eight ball when investigating serious crime because they do not have the trust of the public. They are strangers coming into an area to investigate a crime. When they have finished, they disappear once more. Why should the public trust them?

Not so the local cop. He will be there tomorrow if they need him and the day after. If he asks them to co-operate, they will. They can talk to him in confidence because he is one of them. It removes the 'them and us' mentality between police and the public.

I will make a prediction that criminal offending would decline if such a strategy was implemented. Just have a look at how much reported crime comes from youthful offending and opportunist offending. It has been proven that a police presence is a deterrent to crime.

How can I be so sure about all this? I have worked both systems.

It is time to learn from past mistakes. Let's not only put police back on the beat in the metropolitan areas but in the suburbs as well.

Let me also add that the attributes I recommend for a sole-charge suburban police officer are those of our country police officers. The sole-charge constable in the country and bush has always had my utmost respect. As a young police officer, I relieved at country stations and the country cop and his wife and family were the unsung heroes of the police service.

It disappoints me to have to point out the dismal performance of the New Zealand police in recent years because until 1990, despite many cockups, cover-ups and the odd bit of corruption, the New Zealand police would have ranked in the top three police services in the world.

Their decline during this decade has been due to a lack of leadership.

They seem to be staggering from crisis to crisis and with the subsequent lack of public confidence they now rate on a par with their Australian counterparts.

19

The Final Curtain

On Tuesday, 23 September 1997, at approximately 2.30 p.m., I received a call from a New Zealand journalist. He told me that Christopher John Lewis had electrocuted himself in an ingenious manner in his cell at Mt Eden prison by ripping the wires from his cell television set and placing the live ends against his temple. Before this, he had wrapped a wet towel around his head, wet his feet and sat in a metal chair.

He was awaiting trial for the brutal murder of expatriate Australian Tania Furlan so perhaps he decided it was appropriate to die in an 'electric chair'.

The New Zealand media had been eagerly awaiting Lewis's trial because once again they would have the opportunity to revisit the events of 1981, the year Lewis was first arrested for serious crimes, the year he tried to shoot the Queen.

Many journalists believed that if Lewis were convicted of the Furlan murder the police would be forced to explain once again their bizarre behaviour in relation to him over many years. Some rather naively believed that Lewis would confirm that a deal was struck with police in 1981 and one journalist was even naive enough to visit him in prison before his trial in the forlorn hope that he would tell all.

That was not the Christopher Lewis style. He only admitted what the police or media knew and could prove. He volunteered nothing.

The feeding frenzy of the media did result, however, in the public being left in no doubt that Lewis did fire a shot at the Queen and did intend to kill her.

The *Otago Daily Times* finally declared that it was not a cover-up but a playing-down of the incident.

After Lewis's suicide, various media organisations attempted to contact me in order to sensationalise Lewis's activities once again. Although I was happy enough to co-operate with them in acknowledging the truth of the facts they already had, I refused to give any interviews because I had agreed to talk exclusively to one particular television station and one weekly magazine.

This was extended on the advice of a prospective publisher to include a national radio programme in New Zealand. That particular radio programme went a long way towards finally getting to the truth in the assassination attempt because they decided to test my assertion that Lewis's lawyer of 1981 would confirm that there had been a coverup by doing the obvious – checking with him.

It never ceases to amaze me that so many journalists, both in the past and on this occasion, ignored the most obvious avenue of inquiry. I was often left wondering whether they were actually seeking the truth or just wanting to do a beat-up.

A journalist friend summed it up in 1987: "Anywhere else in the world, journalists would be fighting like a pack of hungry wolves to get at this story and wring the truth out. Here they sensationalise it and forget it or, as in the case of one newspaper, try to back the police claim that it's not true without even interviewing the other side."

The interview with J. Murray Hanan, a respected Dunedin lawyer, completely vindicated my claims of a police cover-up in relation to the attempt on the Queen's life.

I have never spoken to Murray Hanan since leaving Dunedin in 1986 yet his version of the events of that time are virtually identical to mine. Murray Hanan knew when Lewis first appeared in court, the day after his arrest, that the charge he was facing of armed robbery was only the 'holding charge'. He was made aware that Lewis would be facing very serious charges which could include treason and attempted treason. He was aware of much of the evidence we had as well as what Lewis himself told him. Obviously, considerable weight has to be given to his version of events.

Hanan, interviewed on Television New Zealand's *20/20* by Richard Langston, said, "I would have expected them to level a charge of treason. That is what I expected to have to defend. My problem was that Lewis would have probably pleaded guilty to it. However, it could have been laid and it wasn't."

He later added that Lewis had the intent, and the fact that after the first attempt was thwarted he followed the Queen and later fired a shot suggests that within the meaning of the act the charge of treason could have been laid. "And it should have been," he said. "They did have a good case."

When asked why the police didn't lay the more serious charges, Hanan said, "Political embarrassment. It's not the done thing to have someone shoot at the Queen, and the security aspect would have put the New Zealand police force's competence in question."

It was left to Deputy Commissioner Ian Holyoake to reply on behalf of the New Zealand police. This man's main claim to fame is that he is the nephew of former Prime Minister Kiwi Keith Holyoake. He has even acquired Sir Keith's nickname, being known among his contemporaries as 'Kiwi'.

This is the same Ian 'Kiwi' Holyoake who appeared on *60 Minutes* earlier this year over the Ross Appelgren affair. Australian newspapers had exposed the New Zealand police for assisting Appelgren to settle in Australia even though he was prohibited from entering the country due to his criminal convictions.

Holyoake denied all knowledge of the matter until the interviewer handed him a document which clearly illustrated he had full knowledge.

Hardly the most credible person to have fronting for the New Zealand police?

Holyoake's response was predictable: "There was never ever an attempt by Lewis to shoot at the Queen in 1981," he said, although he did not say how he came to this conclusion.

He later made an even more amazing statement: "Lewis fantasised, made some plans but when the time came he never got into position. He got sick of waiting for her to arrive so he fired a shot in frustration." This he said he read from Lewis's own statement.

The question is - which statement? Obviously not the one made to Detective Harrod on the night he was apprehended but the later statement taken with the express purpose of covering up the attempt on the Queen's life, during the time I was on leave.

He then attacked me, insinuating my motive in speaking out was for publicity: "He's only going on about this because he's writing a book."

In 1987, when I was contacted by concerned media and police about the way in which police were playing down Lewis's potential danger to the public, when he was armed and on the run, firstly near Christchurch and later in the Buller Gorge, I was not writing a book. I spoke out because I could see that the New Zealand police were endangering the lives of innocent citizens and all because they feared any publicity about Lewis would ignite further speculation about the suspected cover-up during the royal tour of 1981.

I had absolutely nothing to gain personally by speaking out. I knew the police response would be to attack the messenger, in order to deflect media and public attention from the issues raised.

I was gratified to learn during a Radio Pacific talkback programme in 1995 that my decision to speak up probably had saved the lives of four people. Warren, who phoned from near Christchurch, thanked me for speaking up in 1987. He said, "We lived in a remote area and Lewis was hiding out there although at the time we were unaware of the danger we were in due to the police not publicising his potential danger. After he had been arrested in Auckland, we were visited by police who advised us that Lewis had been intending to kill us all.

"They told us how he had been in our home while we were sleeping and how he had taken beer and food from our fridge. They found a plan on him of the interior of our house, who slept in what bedroom etc, and he had admitted he had intended returning the next night to kill the family and set fire to the house after taking food and supplies in the family car.

"The only reason he didn't carry out his plan was because his photo was in every newspaper and on the television screens after the publicity given by former Detective Sergeant Lewis. Fortunately for us, he decamped from the area."

When I heard of Kiwi Holyoake's comment that I was only speaking out because I was writing a book, I thought of Warren. A man and his family who would have, in all probability, been wiped out by Lewis. I also thought of Tania Furlan's husband and young family.

Perhaps if people like Holyoake had come clean about Christopher Lewis and treated him like the criminal and psychopath he undoubtedly was, Tania Furlan might be alive today.

Kiwi Holyoake also told the interviewer that the case had been reviewed several times. This raises the question, by whom and when?

The only person I can recollect even speaking about the case was another senior police officer, Stuart McEwan. In 1987, he spoke as an authority on the matter only to have to admit later, after he found himself at odds with the version of former Commissioner Bob Walton, that he had not even read the file before speaking.

This was the same Stuart McEwan who caused the Prime Minister, David Lange, to distance himself from McEwan's statements until he, McEwan, obtained the file from Dunedin and read it!

In the light of J. Murray Hanan's statements, one would have expected a more professional police response.

The press then pursued Holyoake over the taxpayer-funded holiday Christopher Lewis and his girlfriend enjoyed in November 1995 when CHOGM was held in Auckland. The line of questioning was, "If Lewis did not really represent a serious danger and never attempted to shoot the Queen in 1981 – merely fantasised as you have said – why was it necessary to move him offshore at the time of CHOGM?"

Holyoake replied, "It was the people in charge of the operation that negotiated with him to go to Great Barrier Island . . . I think at our expense . . . it was minimal. We talked to local people and tour operators to make sure he didn't leave the island. He only stayed a few days."

Bryan Rowe, who was allegedly in charge of the security, also stated that Lewis was left on the island without any additional police security to keep him there. He acknowledged that the lone local police officer was aware of Lewis's presence and the local airline and tour boat operators were requested not to give him passage from the island.

Unbelievable? Not where the New Zealand police are involved! Here was a man, arguably one of the most dangerous psychopaths New Zealand has produced, considered too dangerous to be left in Auckland, a city teeming with thousands of extra police and security, shipped unescorted and unguarded to an island one hour away where he could choose from hundreds of watercraft moored around the island to return to Auckland city. What a shocking admission of gross incompetence!

The question that should have followed from all this was: if we are to believe that over the years Christopher Lewis's activities and dangerousness have been not played down, how do you explain his taxpayer-funded holiday to get him out of the way when dissidents in the past have been put in custody if they were perceived to represent a danger during a royal tour?

It should also be noted that Christopher Lewis's charge after firing at the Queen in 1981 was only one of recklessly discharging a firearm, and it was mentioned, almost as an afterthought, that the Queen was in North Dunedin at the time. The facts were brief and were treated as such by the sentencing judge (who later stated he was never told the true facts).

Accordingly, Lewis was sentenced to three months' imprisonment to be served concurrently with the three years he received for armed robbery. In effect, he did not receive any extra term for that particular offence thanks to the way the police kindly presented it. Compare this with the fate of two young women who each threw an egg at the Queen in 1986. Each was sentenced to six months' imprisonment!

What of Commissioner Doone? He is obviously acting in accordance with the time-honoured police traditions of sitting tight, let's hold the line and hopefully this too will pass. To hell with the damage being done to the police image.

What of Police Minister Jack Elder? If his performance in relation to the Ross Appelgren scandal is anything to go by, don't hold your breath!

A point that has been made to me many times in the past is that if governments are fair dinkum about law and order issues why is it that the lowest-ranked and often least-competent minister is assigned the important post of Minister of Police? It occurs in Australia as well as New Zealand.

Last but not least is the reaction of the other individual the police put forward to present their 'party line' to the media, Detective Sergeant Galland. Galland was a junior detective in 1981 when he was part of my 'suspects squad'. He interviewed only Geoff.

Geoff was the easiest of the three to interview. He came from a good home and he had fallen under Lewis's evil influence to such an extent that it appeared that it was a huge relief to him when they were apprehended.

Detective Sergeant Galland said: "Lewis was easy enough to deal with and had these grandiose ideas. There were things he's done and there were other things . . . that were different"!

It is interesting to compare Galland's opinion of Christopher Lewis with what other people involved with Lewis either before or immediately after his arrest in 1981 had to say.

Firstly, his co-offender Paul: "I suppose I can say I've met a psychopath. Chris really was something else. When I knew him he would pull the heads off mice or birds just for the hang of it and he tried to strangle a neighbour's daughter with a leather whip he made.

"He tried to kill a man and his son by firing at them at Tomahawk Beach and he once threatened to kill our co-offender in the armed robbery because he thought he might talk.

"[He] Fired a shot at the Queen, and blasted a shot from the shotgun when we committed the armed robbery."

Paul also remembered having a loaded shotgun put in his face by Lewis who then said he was joking. When they were fifteen, Lewis pointed a loaded shotgun at an old lady and demanded a ride to the shops.

"He was like no one else I've met before or since, but then you probably only meet one true psychopath in your life," said Paul.

His lawyer, J. Murray Hanan, also witnessed Lewis's penchant for plucking the heads off pets. Of Lewis's killing of his pet mice, Hanan had this to say, "It just looked like he was plucking feathers off a chicken."

He also said, "I always considered him a very grave danger and risk. He was a person who needed to be locked away for permanent treatment for a very long time. He played mind games, even with me."

A teller at the Andersons Bay Post Office Savings Bank, who does not wish to be named, remembers the day Lewis and his accomplices robbed the savings bank. She remembers three hooded figures, one wearing an ammunition belt across his chest and carrying a single-barrelled sawn-off shotgun, one holding a pistol in each hand and the other a double-barrelled sawn-off shotgun. Lewis fired a shot from the shotgun and he later admitted to police that he wanted to kill one of the staff who had not moved quickly enough.

His co-offenders said they had to talk him out of killing either the staff or customers. "He was out of control," said one of them.

The teller described the incident as a nightmare. "The shot missed me by an inch and a half. It was right there and I've had nightmares for years. It just whistled past me [and] if I had been two inches to my right or someone else had been in front of me there would have been a body."

She recalls telling police after the robbery, "They were all masked, all I could see were the eyes. There was something about Chris Lewis's eyes that were quite terrifying.

"I said they scared me . . . he was horrible." I said, "That boy is going to kill somebody."

After Lewis killed himself, she said, "My ghost has been laid to rest. May he rot in hell."

Is it little wonder many people still regard police as 'Plods' with masters of understatement like Holyoake and Galland?

Of course, they are not the ones at the 'coalface' each day. They are not the officers who bear the brunt of public ridicule and distrust as they walk through hotels or along the streets.

Unfortunately, it is the front-line police officers, the majority of whom are genuinely attempting to do their best in a difficult job, who end up bearing the brunt of cover-ups. Little wonder then that morale is at an all-time low, that front-line police have little respect for their leaders at Police Headquarters, that staff shortgages have reached unacceptable levels after mass resignations over the past few years, and that recruitment is at its lowest level.

These are all symptoms of a department that has been mismanaged and is now out of control.

20

Shades of
Misleading Cases

As someone who has been unfortunate enough to have been involved in two major police coverups, I have, over the years, thought long and hard about the motive behind them. I have come up with a number of theories but they have all fallen short when it came to fitting the pieces into 'the jigsaw'. As an investigator, the failure to be able to piece it together has been a constant source of frustration to me.

In early October 1997, I was phoned by a New Zealand journalist who relayed the questions he put to, and the answers he received from Kiwi Holyoake regarding the attempt on the Queen's life in 1981.

Holyoake fed him the same party line as he had fed the journalists before him, "I will read from Lewis's statement." Which he then did.

Unlike all of the journalists before him, this particular chap had obviously been doing his homework. He asked Holyoake if he could name the police officer who had taken the statement that he, Holyoake, was quoting from? Holyoake replied, "Detective Murray Lewis."

The significance was not lost on the journalist concerned because he was aware that Christopher Lewis had made a full confession to the late Detective Tony Harrod on the night he was arrested. He now had an admission that the police were quoting from a statement taken while I was absent on leave, which was undoubtedly the 'watered-down' statement designed to fit a less serious charge. The statement, in fact, used to replace the very incriminating statement Harrod had taken from Christopher Lewis on the night of his arrest.

When this was relayed to me all the pieces of my 'jigsaw puzzle', which included the assassination attempt on the Queen in 1981 and the Dunedin children's sex ring inquiry of 1984, fell into place. It is at this point parallels with A. P. Herbert's Misleading Cases can be drawn because of the confusing surname 'Lewis'!

My officers and I had believed that the 'watered-down' statement made by Christopher John Lewis had been taken by John Chookfeeder Kelly who, with Dalziel, had been responsible for the preparation of the security orders for the duration of the Queen's time in Dunedin.

This was based on the fact that Dalziel had told me Kelly would be taking over the arrest file. However, in the light of what has now been revealed, it makes sense that Kelly, who along with Dalziel had his own reasons for not wanting an inquiry into the substandard security arrangements that existed, would have delegated the taking of the 'watered-down' statement to a subordinate like Murray Lewis.

Murray Lewis, like Dalziel and Kelly, was a product of the now-abandoned police cadet system.

It was Murray Lewis's father, John David Lewis, who in 1984 was the person identified as being behind the recruitment of young schoolgirls for unlawful sexual activities and sex shows. Lewis senior used his prostitute, Audrey, to recruit these young girls for these shows where it was alleged doctors, lawyers, politicians and prominent citizens paid large sums of money so they could be spectators and later participants.

It is now history that in 1984 Dalziel was alleged to have stopped inquiries into Lewis senior's activities and, although in a later inquiry he was cleared of perverting the course of justice, he was removed from his position as head of the Dunedin CIB and transferred to the uniform branch in Christchurch.

The inquiry was hamstrung by police delaying tactics and cover-up allegations after it was established that the 'independent examiner' appointed to review the inquiry had connections at Police Headquarters.

The general dissatisfaction by the public, which included signed petitions requesting a royal commission of inquiry and demonstrations in the streets, resulted in the formation of the Police Complaints Authority to review future alleged police cover-ups.

One of the reasons for the finding that Dalziel had not perverted the course of justice was the lack of a motive. Why would a Detective Chief Inspector, the regional head of a CIB, risk his career and imprisonment to assist in covering up the paedophile activities of the father of one of his junior staff?

However, if Murray Lewis did take the 'watered-down' statement from Christopher John Lewis in 1981, then he had both Dalziel and Kelly in his debt.

Dalziel, with the backing of Kelly, had been singing the praises of Murray Lewis for some years before 1984. He had, in fact, tried to influence me to report on Murray Lewis in a favourable manner to assist his promotion over more senior staff.

Then in 1984 when I apprehended Murray Lewis' father for a series of serious offences which involved paedophilia, Dalziel made it clear to me that "we don't need to charge John Lewis."

The result was John Lewis and the others concerned were never brought to justice. The Dunedin children's sex ring inquiry was effectively stopped in its tracks.

Also of interest are the actions of Murray Lewis in 1995 when I was about to speak on talkback radio in New Zealand at the time of CHOGM. Before going on air, one of the announcers, Jenny Anderson, told me the station had been amazed at the reaction of (the then) Detective Inspector Murray Lewis, CIB chief at Tauranga. He had been telephoning the station ever since the programme had been advertised threatening all kinds of repercussions if the show went to air.

She actually asked me when we were on air whether I could explain just why this man would be so upset. I was confused myself because to the best of my knowledge Murray Lewis had never been involved in the arrest and subsequent inquiries into Christopher

John Lewis and the incident involving the Queen.

After giving the matter some thought I said, "I was in charge of the team of detectives and Murray Lewis was not part of that team. He was a junior detective at the time. There are other matters where I have been involved with him but they do not relate to the matter we are discussing today."

How wrong I was! It now appears from Kiwi Holyoake's statement in October 1997 that Murray Lewis took the 'watered down' statement from Christopher Lewis. It was that statement that justified a less serious charge against Christoper Lewis and assisted Dalziel and Kelly in the cover-up over the attempted assassination of the Queen. Dalziel and Kelly would no doubt have felt indebted to the officer who took the statement.

This leads me to the view that the cover-ups in relation to the attempted assassination on the Queen and the Dunedin children's sex ring inquiry may have been related.

I now question whether there was ever any political interference.

The only way to establish the truth into these matters is by way of a Commission of Inquiry. All those appearing before such an inquiry would be required to give evidence under oath. They would be warned before giving evidence that anyone attempting to mislead the inquiry could be charged with perjury.

I therefore call upon the government of New Zealand to instigate such an inquiry as soon as practical, not only in these matters but a wide-ranging inquiry in the NZ Police. It is long overdue!

> Standing up for your rights is never easy,
> It may risk losing your job or being threatened,
> It can cause family turmoil,
> Almost always it results in emotional upset.

> However anyone who has felt stuck or trapped in
> a corrupt system and who has dared to challenge
> that system knows the sweet rewards of exercising
> PERSONAL POWER.